ON
OPS

**LESSONS AND CHALLENGES FOR THE
AUSTRALIAN ARMY SINCE EAST TIMOR**

PROFESSOR TOM FRAME is the Director of the Australian Centre for the Study of Armed Conflict and Society (ACSACS) at UNSW Canberra. He served as a naval officer for 15 years and completed postgraduate studies in history, theology and sociology before being ordained to the Anglican ministry. He has been Bishop to the Australian Defence Force, patron of the Armed Forces Federation of Australia, a member of the Council of the Australian War Memorial, and judged the inaugural Prime Minister's Prize for Australian History. Professor Frame is the author or editor of more than 30 books, including *The Shores of Gallipoli*; *Living by the Sword? The Ethics of Armed Intervention*; *Moral Injury: Unseen Wounds in an Age of Barbarism*; and *Anzac Day: Then & Now*.

DOCTOR ALBERT PALAZZO is the Director of Research for the Australian Army and has written extensively on Australian military history. His major works include *The Australian Army: A History of its Organisation, 1901–2001*; *Moltke to bin Laden: The Relevance of Doctrine in Contemporary Military Environment* and *The Future of War Debate in Australia*. His recent research has focussed on the effects of resource limits and climate change on the future character of war.

ON
OPS

LESSONS AND CHALLENGES FOR THE AUSTRALIAN ARMY SINCE EAST TIMOR

EDITED BY
TOM FRAME & ALBERT PALAZZO

UNSW PRESS

A UNSW Press book

Published by
NewSouth Publishing
University of New South Wales Press Ltd
University of New South Wales
Sydney NSW 2052
AUSTRALIA
newsouthpublishing.com

National Library of Australia
Title: On Ops: lessons and challenges for the Australian army since East
Timor / edited by Tom Frame and Albert Palazzo.
Cataloguing-in-Publication entry
ISBN: 9781742235097 (paperback)
          9781742242453 (ebook)
          9781742247847 (ePDF)
Series: ACSACS series; 3.
Notes: Includes bibliographical references.
Subjects: Australia. Army – Operational readiness.
          Military art and science – Australia – Forecasting.
          Operational readiness (Military science)
          Australia – Military policy.
          Other Creators/Contributors:
Frame, T.R. (Thomas Robert), 1962 – and Palazzo, A.P. (Albert Pellegrino),
1957 – editors.
Dewey Number: 355.00994

Design Josephine Pajor-Markus
Cover image 'Australian Army in Tangi Valley, Afghanistan' ABIS
Jo Dilorenzo, © Commonwealth of Australia

Canberra

CONTENTS

ACSACS SERIES

This book is part of a series produced by the Australian Centre for the Study of Armed Conflict and Society (ACSACS) – a UNSW Canberra Research Centre at the Australian Defence Force Academy (ADFA). ACSACS seeks to become the pre-eminent Australian venue for assessing the past, present and likely future impact of armed conflict on institutions and individuals in order to enhance public policy and raise community awareness through multi-disciplinary scholarship of the kind this series of books embody.

Established in 2012, ACSACS utilises the strength of academic research conducted at UNSW Canberra and draws on the university's close and continuing relationship with Defence that began in 1967. In bringing together acknowledged experts in diverse fields of study, the centre hopes to produce creative solutions to a variety of problems, whether questions of history or challenges in policy.

ACSACS also serves as a significant focal point for academic activity prompted by the Centenary of the Great War (2014–18), the 75th anniversary of the Second World War (2014–20), the 50th anniversary of Australia's involvement in the Vietnam Conflict (2015–22) and the 25th anniversary of the first Gulf War (1990–91). ACSACS is well placed to interpret these stories of valour for the thousands of local commemorations being planned across the nation. With its hugely significant database of 1st AIF personnel and computer-assisted analysis of Australian Taskforce-Vietnam operations,[1] the centre's resources are indispensable tools for those researching Australia's war effort.

The titles published within the ACSACS series will engage both specialist and general audiences with the expectation that individual titles will become standard reference works or textbooks for undergraduate and graduate teaching at UNSW. The subjects reflect the centre's principal areas of interest: the Australian experience of military operations and armed conflict with a particular focus on history, ethics and economics.

The centre's website is: <www.acsacs.unsw.adfa.edu.au> and its staff can be contacted at <acsacs@adfa.edu.au>.

Previous Titles

Anzac Day: Then & Now, 2016

Moral Injury: Unseen Wounds in an Age of Barbarism, 2015

CONTRIBUTORS

Lieutenant Colonel Ben Alward is an Intelligence Officer in the Australian Army who graduated from the Royal Military College (RMC), Duntroon in 1999. Since then he has held a range of operational, planning, and instructional appointments in Australia, the United Kingdom and the Middle East. He is a graduate of the Australian Command and Staff College and holds a Bachelor of Commerce from the University of Southern Queensland, as well as a Master of Defence and Military Studies from the Australian National University (ANU). He is presently employed as the Staff Officer Grade 1 – Intelligence Development, within Army Headquarters.

Lieutenant Colonel David Beaumont is a serving member of the Australian Army, with operational experience in Army and Joint logistic roles on Operation Warden (East Timor) in 1999, and Operations Bastille, Falconer, Catalyst and Slipper in the Middle East from 2002. In his current appointment as Staff Officer Grade One – Logistic Plans at Headquarters Forces Command, he is primarily engaged in developing support arrangements for Army's transformational change under 'Plan Beersheba', and in operational concept development. He is currently researching the Australian Defence Force (ADF) approach to strategic logistics as a PhD candidate at ANU.

Dr John Blaxland is a Senior Fellow at the Strategic and Defence Studies Centre (SDSC) at ANU. He holds a PhD in War Studies from the RMC of Canada, an MA in History from ANU, a BA (Hons) from UNSW and is a graduate of the Royal Thai Army Command and Staff College. He is a former Chief Intelligence Staff Officer (J2) at Headquarters Joint Operations Command and Defence Attaché to Thailand and Burma. His publications include *The Australian Army from Whitlam to Howard, Strategic Cousins, Revisiting Counterinsurgency, Information-era Manoeuvre, Signals, Organising an Army* and 'Australia, Indonesia and Southeast Asia' in *Australia's Defence: Towards a New Era*. He is the author of volume two of the official history of the Australian Security Intelligence Organisation (*The Protest Years*) and co-author of volume three, due to be published in 2016. He is a Minerva Research Initiative grant recipient for a study on 'Thailand's Military, the United States and China', and editor of *East Timor Intervention: A Retrospective on INTERFET*.

Major Reuben Bowd was educated at Waverley College and Saint Ignatius' College in Sydney, and is a graduate of the Australian Defence Force Academy (ADFA) and RMC Duntroon. He held a variety of appointments in the Regular Army and saw service with the Peace Monitoring Group in Bougainville (2003) and the Regional Assistance Mission to the Solomon Islands (2003–04). He graduated BA with Honours from UNSW Canberra and shared the LCF Turner prize for 'outstanding performance in history'. Before transferring to the Army Reserve, he graduated LLB with Honours from UNSW. As a solicitor, Reuben has practised as a Senior Associate at Clayton Utz and is currently a Legal Counsel in Transport for NSW. Reuben is author of *A Basis for Victory: The Allied Geographical Section 1942–1946, Doves Over the Pacific: In Pursuit of Peace and*

Stability in Bougainville, and *Simple Solutions to Complex Matters: Identifying fundamental principles of Alternative Dispute Resolution in the multinational effort to broker a resolution to the Bougainville 'Crisis'*, and has contributions in the second edition of the *Oxford Companion to Australian Military History*.

Major Anthony Chambers was commissioned into the Australian Army Reserve as a medical officer in 1995. He has deployed on operations to Bougainville, East Timor, the disaster relief operation to Banda Aceh (Indonesia), Iraq, Afghanistan and the Ukraine. He is currently posted to the 3rd Health Support Battalion as a general and trauma surgeon. In a civilian capacity he is a consultant surgeon specialising in cancer treatment at St Vincent's Hospital (Sydney) and a Senior Lecturer at UNSW.

Associate Professor Stephen Coleman co-ordinates Ethics and Leadership in the School of Humanities and Social Sciences, and is Program Director of Military Ethics at the Australian Centre for the Study of Armed Conflict and Society (ACSACS), UNSW Canberra. He has published on a diverse range of topics in applied ethics, including military ethics, police ethics, medical ethics, and the practical applications of human rights. His most recent book, *Military Ethics: An Introduction with Case Studies*, was published by Oxford University Press.

Professor Tom Frame joined the RAN College in 1979 and served in the Navy for fifteen years. He was appointed Director of ACSACS at UNSW Canberra in 2014 and is the author or editor of 30 books, including *Living by the Sword: The Ethics of Armed Intervention* and *Moral Injury: Unseen Wounds in an Age of Barbarism*.

Colonel Scott Gills trained at ADFA and RMC Duntroon between 1991 and 1994, before being commissioned into the Royal Australian Armoured Corps. Following his selection for service in the Australian Intelligence Corps, he completed a wide range of command, training and staff appointments spanning the tactical, operational and strategic levels. His operational deployments have been to multiple theatres, and include deployments at battalion, division and corps-level, such as Special Forces, inter-agency and combined/joint experience. Following his posting to the J2 Branch of the Joint Chiefs of Staff in the Pentagon, he was appointed the inaugural Director of Intelligence Surveillance and Reconnaissance – Army in 2014.

Dr Leanne Glenny is the Program Director for post-graduate communication studies at the University of South Australia, with research interests in government communication, ethics and social media. She is presently in the early stages of research examining the discourses used in traditional and new media when discussing post-traumatic stress disorder (PTSD) and the Australian military. Prior to her first academic appointment at the University of Canberra, she served for 17 years in the Royal Australian Corps of Signals, completing Staff College in 1996, with her final military appointment in Defence Public Affairs and Corporate Communication in 1999–2000. She has completed a PhD, a Masters in Marketing Communication, graduate diplomas in management, and a Bachelor of Arts in Journalism. She is also a Fellow of the Public Relations Institute of Australia.

Lieutenant Colonel Michael Harris joined the Australian Army as a Specialist Service Officer in 1997. He has been deployed on a wide range of domestic and international operations, including Papua New Guinea, Timor Leste, Iraq and the

Middle East. He has received a Chief of Defence Force (CDF) Commendation for his contribution to the 1st Joint Public Affairs Unit, an Australian Army commendation for his support to the Al Muthanna Task Group, an ADF Silver Commendation for his contribution to 'Operation Slipper', and a Commander Australian Theatre Commendation for his efforts with Joint Task Force 112. He is currently studying for a Masters of Philosophy (Research) in Public Policy.

EMERITUS PROFESSOR DAVID HORNER AM was Professor of Australian Defence History at SDSC within ANU for 15 years. A graduate of RMC Duntroon, he saw active service as an infantry platoon commander in South Vietnam. As a Reserve colonel he was the first Head of the Army's Land Warfare Studies Centre. He is the Official Historian of Australian Peacekeeping, Humanitarian and Post-Cold War Operations. Among his 32 books, he is the author or joint author of two volumes of the six-volume official history series. He is also the official historian for the Australian Security Intelligence Organisation.

THE HONOURABLE JOHN HOWARD OM AC was the 25th Prime Minister of Australia, leading the nation from March 1996 to August 2007. He served in the House of Representatives (as the Member for Bennelong) from 1974 to 2007 and filled several ministerial and shadow ministerial posts prior to 1996. Re-elected in 1998, 2001 and 2004, his government authorised Australian military operations in Bougainville, East Timor, the Solomon Islands and the Middle East. He was made a Companion of the Order of Australia (AC) in 2008 and a Member of the Order of Merit (OM) in 2012. He is the second longest-serving prime minister of Australia.

Professor Peter Leahy AC joined the Australian Army in 1971 and served in the Royal Australian Infantry Corps with postings around Australia and overseas. He concluded his career in the Army in 2008 as Chief of the Army with the rank of Lieutenant General. He served in this appointment for six years. His period of command was marked by the continuous global deployment of Australian soldiers on high tempo, complex and demanding combat operations. He was also responsible for the rapid expansion and development of the Army to meet the changing demands of modern conflict. Since leaving the Army, General Leahy has joined the University of Canberra as a Professor and become the foundation Director of the National Security Institute. He has been appointed to the boards of Codan Limited, Electro Optic Systems Holdings Limited and Citadel Group Limited. Additionally, he is a member of the Defence South Australia Advisory Board, Chairman of the Salvation Army Red Shield Appeal Committee in the ACT, Chairman of the charity 'Soldier On' and a Trustee of The Prince's Charities Australia. Recently he served as a member of the First Principles Review panel.

Mr Brendan Nicholson was raised and educated in New Zealand and then spent 12 years working as a journalist in Africa. During that time he developed a strong interest in defence and foreign affairs and broad strategic and national security issues, which he has maintained during nearly 30 years in the Australian media. He is currently defence editor of *The Australian* newspaper and is based in the press gallery at Parliament House in Canberra. He has made regular trips to Afghanistan and Iraq and has covered a wide range of defence issues, from complex and sometimes controversial equipment purchases and efforts to change outdated attitudes, to the performance of the men and women of the ADF on operations.

Dr Albert Palazzo is the Director of Research in Strategic Plans Army, a part of the Australian Army Headquarters. He completed his doctorate at Ohio State University and his thesis was published as *Seeking Victory on The Western Front: The British Army and Chemical Warfare in World War I*. He has published widely on the history of the Australian Army and the contemporary character of war. His major works include *The Australian Army: A History of its Organisation, 1901–2001, Moltke to bin Laden: The Relevance of Doctrine in Contemporary Military Environment* and *The Future of War Debate in Australia*, and a primer on how to forge land power is in production. His current research is focused on the effect of resource limits and climate change on the future character of war.

Lieutenant Colonel Tim Rutherford is a cavalry officer in the Australian Army who graduated from RMC Duntroon in 1999. Since then, he has held a range of command, planning and instructional appointments in Australia, Europe, the Middle East and Africa. He is a graduate of the Australian Command and Staff College and holds a Bachelor of Professional Studies (Peace Studies) from the University of New England, as well as a Master of Military Studies and a Master of International Law from the Australian National University. He is currently employed as the Staff Officer 1 – Surveillance and Reconnaissance within Army Headquarters.

Professor Amin Saikal AM FASSA is Distinguished Professor of Political Science, Public Policy Fellow, and Director of the Centre for Arab and Islamic Studies (Middle East and Central Asia) at ANU. He has been a Rockefeller Foundation Fellow in International Relations, and Visiting Fellow to Princeton University, Cambridge University and Institute of Development Studies, University Sussex. He was awarded the Order of Australia (AM) 'for service to the international community and education through the development of the Centre for Arab and Islamic Studies, and as an author and adviser' in January 2006, and is an elected Fellow the Academy of Social Sciences in Australia. His latest books include: *Iran at the Crossroads?*; *Zone of Crisis: Afghanistan, Pakistan, Iran and Iraq*; *Modern Afghanistan: A History of Struggle and Survival*; *The Rise and Fall of the Shah: Iran from Autocracy to Religious Rule*; *Islam and the West: Conflict or Cooperation?*; *American Democracy Promotion in the Changing Middle East: From Bush to Obama*; *Democracy* and *Reform in the Middle East and Asia: Social Protest and Authoritarian Rule after the Arab Spring*.

PROFESSOR CRAIG STOCKINGS is the Official Historian of Australia's involvement in East Timor, Afghanistan and Iraq and is based at the Australian War Memorial. He was formerly Associate Professor of History at UNSW Canberra and Deputy Head of the School of Humanities and Social Sciences. He graduated from UNSW Canberra with a BA (Hons) in History and Politics in 1995 and from RMC Duntroon as an infantry officer the following year. He was posted to 3 RAR and served in a range of regimental appointments. Following an operational deployment to East Timor and an appointment as the Aide-de-Camp to the Governor General, he embarked upon an academic career. He holds a Graduate Diploma in Education, a MEd, an MA (International Relations), and a PhD in History. Some of his more recent publications as author/editor include *Bardia: Myth, Reality and the Heirs of Anzac*, *Zombie Myths of Australian Military History*, *Anzac's Dirty Dozen: 12 Myths of Australian Military History*, *Swastika over the Acropolis: Re-interpreting the Nazi Invasion of Greece in World War II*, *Before the Anzac Dawn: A Military History of Australia to 1915* and *Britannia's Shield: Lieutenant-General Sir Edward Hutton and Late-Victorian Imperial Defence*.

DISCLAIMER

Each chapter represents the views of the individual contributor. The views expressed by contributors are their own opinions and do not necessarily represent the position of the Commonwealth of Australia, the Australian Defence Force, the University of New South Wales or any organisation with which they were or are now associated. The publication of their chapter in this book does not imply any official agreement or formal concurrence with any opinion, criticism, conclusion or recommendation attributed to them.

ACRONYMS

ABCA	American, British, Canadian, Australian and New Zealand Armies' Program
ACSACS	Australian Centre for the Study of Armed Conflict and Society
ADFA	Australian Defence Force Academy
AFP	Australian Federal Police
ANAO	Australian National Audit Office
ANU	Australian National University
AO	area of operations
APC	Armed Personnel Carrier
ASEAN	Association of South-East Asian Nations
ASIO	Australian Security Intelligence Organisation
AST	Australian Strategic Theatre
BASB	Brigade Administrative Support Battalion
BRA	Bougainville Revolutionary Army
CAL	Centre for Army Lessons
CNRT	National Council of East Timorese Resistance
DOA	Defence of Australia
FPDA	Five Power Defence Arrangements
FSB	Force Support Battalion
FSG	Force Support Group
INTERFET	International Force for East Timor
ISAF	International Security Assistance Force
ISIS	Islamic State of Iraq and Syria
ISR	Intelligence, Surveillance and Reconnaissance

JCSS	Joint Command Support System
JLU	Joint Logistics Unit
JSU	Joint Support Unit
JTF	Joint Task Force
MFO	Multinational Force & Observers
MIF	Maritime Interception Force
MPA	Military Public Affairs
NATO	North Atlantic Treaty Organisation
NCO	non-commissioned officer
NORCOM	Northern Command
ONA	Office of National Assessments
PMG	Peace Monitoring Group
PTSD	post-traumatic stress disorder
RAAF	Royal Australian Air Force
RAMSI	Regional Assistance Mission to Solomon Islands
RAN	Royal Australian Navy
RAR	Royal Australian Regiment
RMC	Royal Military College, Duntroon
SAS	Special Air Service
SASR	Special Air Service Regiment
SDSC	Strategic and Defence Studies Centre
SEATO	Southeast Asia Treaty Organisation
TMG	Truce Monitoring Group
TNI	Indonesian Army
UNAMET	United Nations Mission to East Timor
UNSCOM	United Nations Special Commission on Iraq
UNTAET	United Nations Transitional Authority in East Timor
WMD	weapons of mass destruction

LESSONS AND LEARNING

TOM FRAME

When the Cold War ended in 1990, no one could (or did) predict that over the next 25 years Australian Army personnel would be deployed to Rwanda, Cambodia, Somalia, Bougainville, East Timor (officially known now as Timor Leste), Afghanistan, Iraq or the Solomon Islands. Although I was then serving in the Navy, I do not recall anyone even suggesting that these were places where Australians would be sent in the foreseeable future. In the wake of the Soviet Union's sudden and unexpected collapse, the immediate question for uniformed people was: 'What do we do now?' For the previous four decades, planning had been primarily focused on containing the spread of communism and countering Russian influence around the globe. The post-Cold War world was an unknown place and the contribution that the Army would make to Australian defence and regional security was unclear. In this sense, Australia was not alone as most governments and armed forces faced similar questions and grappled with similar challenges. How did the Australian Army answer these questions and what was its response to the challenges? Was it willing to learn from the past and reshape itself for the future?

Like all large and sprawling decentralised organisations, parts of the Army have opted for self-preservation and lost sight of holistic concerns. Similarly, senior officers have opposed change because it threatened their position or weakened their power while non-commissioned officers (NCOs) have been as guilty as anyone else of preferring form over substance, and hankering after halcyon days of tighter discipline and meek compliance. Observers of the Australian Army will, of course, have their own opinions about its intellectual mood but here it is argued that for the greatest part the Army is not only committed to 'lessons learned' but that its leaders are also dedicated to cultural change if such is required for the Army to meet the challenges arising from a highly fluid strategic environment and a rapidly changing operational climate. There is a demonstrable readiness to think long and hard about deep and divisive issues that will determine the Army's capacity to serve the national interest and to defend the Australian people and their property. Plainly, there is no tolerating for complacency and no excusing incompetence.

The Howard Government, which exercised national leadership from March 1996 until August 2007, did not come to government with a blueprint for reshaping the Department of Defence nor did it have fixed or even firm views on Australia's defence and security needs. Other than quarantining Defence from a series of funding cuts across all areas of Commonwealth activity, the Howard Government was open to advice on reforming the Department of Defence and renewing the Australian Defence Force (ADF). It came as a surprise to the then Prime Minister and his government that the end of President Suharto's rule would lead quickly to Indonesia offering self-determination to its 27th province, the former Portuguese colony of East Timor. The world was quickly changing and Australia's place within it was being redefined.

In the process, the Army invested heavily in the development of a rigorous intellectual culture in which difficult questions are asked and demanding answered offered. Other than a very small number of personnel who participated in international peace-keeping and peace-monitoring missions, by the early 1990s a generation of Army officers and soldiers had not seen any form of operational service. Their entire experience was of a peacetime army that was committed to training for conflicts that were difficult to predict and even more difficult to describe. Would the Army be sent to a friendly country in which superpower rivalry was being played out by local surrogates? Would the Army be required to stand between hostile factions in a civil war? Would the Army need to defend the Australian continent and the off-shore islands against unknown adversaries? The Army would continue to train diligently but uncertainty remained about where and when the Army would be deployed while few public officials were prepared to say against whom.

Norman Dixon's contention in his controversial work, *On the Psychology of Military Incompetence*, that military establishments attract and retain people with little interest in creativity and minimal reserves of initiative, cannot be said of the Australian Army today. It provides a number of forums where candid assessments of its performance are offered and critical appraisals of its short-comings aired. Notwithstanding a residual anxiety that negative commentary might be resisted by senior officers, resented by political leaders and result in impaired promotion prospects for the would-be critic, there is an openness to self-critique within the Australian Army that the parliament ought to welcome and the public aught to commend. This book, for example, is a joint initiative of the Australian Centre for the Study of Armed Conflict and Society (ACSACS) at UNSW Canberra and the Army's Modernisation and Strategic Planning Branch.

Each of the following chapters began as presentations to a conference held at UNSW Canberra in June 2015. The contributors were assisted in the preparation of their chapter by comments and suggestions from those who attended the conference, where discussion and debate was positive and constructive. Each contributor was given a specific topic and asked to focus on the lessons to be learned and the challenges to be faced from Australian Army operations since the international intervention in East Timor in September 1999, the largest and the most demanding deployment for the Army since the withdrawal of its personnel from South Vietnam in 1972.

The chapters that follow are divided into five parts. The first part is devoted to the 'big picture' with three overviews of Australian defence and security spanning the past forty years. The second part contains two divergent views 'from the other side of the hill'. In essence, what did the Australian presence look like among those who either welcomed or resented the arrival of the Australian Army. Part three is devoted to specific operational issues, including command and control, intelligence gathering and assessment, and logistic support. The four chapters in this section are intended to be complementary as they tackle similar issues but from different standpoints. The fourth part of this book concerns public information and the role of the media, and the difficulty of balancing what the Australian public can and should be told about deployments and restrictions on the flow of information associated with operational security. Part five focuses on ethical concerns, principally the involvement of uniformed personnel in operations that do not relate directly to the defence of Australia, and the growing incidence of unseen injuries, principally moral injury, among those who are deployed overseas. The book closes with a general assessment of the Army's performance and a summary of the lessons learned since 1999 and an inventory of the challenges the Army is yet to negotiate.

In his chapter, Mr Howard recognises that both the nation and its military were unprepared for what followed. In the wake of the international intervention in East Timor, the government realised it had to invest more heavily in Defence and close a number of serious capability gaps that had become apparent after 1999. Mr Howard notes that the intervention was a turning point in the nation's attitude to military power and a catalyst for its effective use in other places. But he concedes that the Army was indeed stretched to the limit of its capacity in the period 2003 to 2006 with so many simultaneous deployments. Although each was conducted with professionalism, the Army had accepted substantial burdens that could not continue indefinitely.

In chapter 2, Professor David Horner, who saw active service in South Vietnam with an infantry battalion, outlines the strategic and political environment that led to the rapidly increasing operational tempo that marked military service after 2001. He describes the 'long peace' the nation enjoyed between the early 1970s and the late 1980s, the emergence of the United Nations as an international constabulary in the 1990s and the strategic and diplomatic factors that led to the intervention in East Timor in 1999. Professor Horner then charts the origins of Australian involvement in the 'global war on terror' as part of a fundamental shift in Australia's view of the world and its place within it, concluding that 'the challenge for contemporary policy-makers is to craft a new defence policy that draws on the vast experience gained from these 15 years of operations but not to be confined by it.'

Professor Peter Leahy, drawing on his own military career and tenure as Chief of Army, begins chapter 3 by noting the marked change of mood within the Army before and after 1999. For decades the Army had been preparing for what now seems a very unlikely war and was confronted with challenges on a very broad front when the government committed Australian forces to East Timor following the violence that erupted after the independence plebiscite was held on 30 August 1999. Professor Leahy identifies some of the lessons that emerged from the intervention and the challenges associated with maintaining the Army at a much higher level of operational readiness for a much longer period.

In chapter 4, Professor Amin Saikal draws our attention to the enduring consequences of the US-led coalition invasions of Afghanistan and Iraq and the continuing presence of Western military personnel in both countries. He explains that optimism followed an end to oppressive regimes in Kabul and Baghdad but quickly subsided and that 'Afghanistan and Iraq are in the grip of long-term structural violence and instability that threatens their very survival, and the war on terror has failed to stamp out the scourge of violent Muslim extremism in the region and beyond.' He says that the 'best way to deal with violent extremism in the Middle East and beyond is to change the conditions that give rise to such extremism.' Haunted by decades of authoritarianism, social and economic disparities and injustices, he believes the region has suffered from Western policies that have demonised and disempowered for what he asserts are 'domestic political gains and regional geopolitical ends.' The Australian government needs to realise that 'military actions on their own cannot bring stability and security to the Middle East.'

Major Reuben Bowd surveys the view 'on the other side of the hill' in Bougainville and the Solomon Islands in chapter 5. He notes that both missions were not only successful but that they have become international models for handling civil unrest and social instability. Drawing attention to the dynamics of inter-agency co-operation, Major Bowd emphasises the need for cultural sensitivity and the importance of securing local goodwill and support for a mission where success is measured in political and social terms, rather than according to a military calculus. He concludes that both operations highlighted the importance of identifying 'the right personnel, with the right skillsets, to perform vital "forward-facing" roles at the right time.' This provision included linguists and those with negotiating skills, abilities that the Army does not always esteem or maintain.

In chapter 6, Professor Craig Stockings explains why the Australian Army often encounters difficulties in learning lessons from deployments and outlines the contribution that can be made by those beyond the Army to a candid and critical appraisal of its performance. Concentrating on just the first week of the international intervention in East Timor, he identifies a raft of problems and shortcomings, frailties and failings that could have imperiled the success of the entire mission. He goes on to argue that many of the issues raised by the International Force for East Timor (INTERFET) deployment have still not been adequately addressed, possibly because the mission was so successful and the Army has been preoccupied with demanding operations in Afghanistan and Iraq. While Professor Stockings does not doubt the Army's corporate willingness to learn, he has concerns about its approach and the persistence of forces that militate against reform and renewal.

In chapter 7, three intelligence specialists, Colonel Scott Gills and Lieutenant Colonels Ben Alward and Tim Rutherford, look at the Army's Intelligence, Surveillance and Reconnaissance (ISR) capabilities and contend that neither the Australian Army nor its coalition partners were ready to go to war in 2001 and have spent the intervening period adapting (while fighting) to previously unimagined conditions. They suggest that the Army's intelligence gathering capability has far outstripped its analytical capacity and that much that is, or could be, helpful to operational commanders is not made available because of an analytical lag. They note the technological advantages enjoyed by adversaries who have unfettered access to civilian software and hardware, and the need for organisational change within the ADF to optimise the benefits that enhanced ISR can bring to Australian operations abroad.

Lieutenant Colonel Dave Beaumont and Dr Allison Sonneveld both deal with logistics in chapters 8 and 9. They outline the supply and support problems the Army has sought to overcome since the intervention in East Timor and the need for major changes in both the Army's internal organisation and its attitude to technological solutions. It is surprising the extent to which the Army has struggled to resource its own people when serving abroad and the depth of its reliance on the goodwill and generosity of Australia's friends and allies as well as contractors. Lieutenant Colonel Beaumont observes that the problems he identifies have been the subject of numerous Australian reviews and reports over the last decade, and 'until the Army overcomes these impediments and real change is implemented, it will continue to gamble with its own preparedness.' Dr Sonneveld warns that if the circumstances of warfare continue to change the Army 'might not be able to buy its way out of a logistical problem'. In noting that failure to address logistic issues has plagued military commanders since Alexander the Great, she says 'there is no excuse for a poorly supplied and badly equipped army'. Furthermore, inadequate logistic support can have consequences as dire as poor training.

Chapter 10 draws attention to the role of healthcare

professionals in recent Army operations. Major Anthony Chambers, a specialist surgeon in civilian life, points out that in addition to dealing with operational casualties, Australian uniformed medical personnel have been involved in humanitarian aid and disaster relief missions in which treating non-military people has been the principal objective. He notes the Army's substantial reliance on part-time and Reserve personnel and the attention that has been given to the integration of Army medical care with both ADF joint procedures and with protocols developed by Australia's major operating partners. Major Chambers draws the reader's attention to the difficulties associated with providing adequate training for uniformed personnel who do not often see violent trauma injuries in the civilian hospitals where they usually gain clinical and surgical experience. In sum, the Army struggles to find sufficient numbers of suitably trained people to deal with the demands produced by the full range of operations in which its personnel are engaged. While the military healthcare system has managed to cope since 1999, its limitations need to be recognised and respected.

There is a common theme linking chapters 11, 12 and 13. Media organisations want more information than Defence is usually prepared to give them and the tussle continues to find the right balance between the public's entitlement to be kept informed of the conduct and progress of military operations and the need for military operations to be afforded the necessary level of security. Mr Brendan Nicholson writes from first-hand experience as a senior journalist with *The Australian* newspaper. He believes that the Army is paranoid about security to an extent that is counterproductive: stories highlighting the skill and professionalism of Australian officers and soldiers do not appear in the print or electronic media. This leads some Army personnel to conclude that no one is interested in their work or that no one cares whether they succeed or fail. Dr Leanne Glenny explains what is at stake for the Army in achieving a balance between public information and operational requirements, and points out where and how the Army can improve its performance in protecting and, indeed, enhancing its corporate reputation. Lieutenant Colonel Mike Harris concedes that the entire ADF has struggled with growing demands for information and expectations that the reporting of military operations will be more transparent. He counsels proactivity rather than reactivity and is generally positive about what the information revolution can bring to reporting of the Army's activities, which are overwhelming positive and constructive, and this will generate goodwill towards uniformed personnel.

The final two chapters concern the ethical dimensions of military service and the emergence of many new issues since the end of the Cold War. Associate Professor Stephen Coleman contrasts operations in previous decades and those since 1999 and observes a fundamental shift: Australians are increasingly being placed in harm's way not in the direct defence of the nation's territory or people but as part of humanitarian missions whose objective is usually the prevention or cessation of crimes of atrocity. He contends that the nation's political leaders must have very good reasons for sending young Australians to dangerous places and notes that those reasons are not always explained clearly or argued compellingly. The relationship between the state and the soldier has changed and not only because the Australian Army is an all-volunteer force. Uniformed personnel are now being used to give expression to Australia's foreign policy objectives in addition to providing for the physical defence of the continent and the offshore islands. This is an ethical issue that has not attracted the attention it deserves. In my chapter on moral injury, I argue that many of the unseen wounds sustained by deployed military personnel are better termed moral injuries than instances of post-traumatic stress disorder. Because military personnel are sent to places where there has been a collapse of civil order and whole populations have been engulfed by barbarism, it is not surprising that the moral compass orientating the ethical bearings of young men and women serving in the Army has been damaged by an experience of living in a place and among a people whose sense of right and wrong bears no relationship to what deployed personnel have experienced and relied upon at home. I outline several areas of future research, including a plea for a closer focus on the Australian experience of armed conflict and deployed service. The American experience is very different and should not determine the way in which moral injury sustained by Australians is addressed.

The final chapter by Dr John Blaxland, a former intelligence officer with considerable diplomatic experience, contrasts the Army of 1995 with the Army of 2015. In sum, the Army of twenty years ago was informed by very different strategic advice and preparing for a very different set of probable contingencies. He believes the Army has done a good job over the past 15 years. It has met the expectations of successive governments and served the national interest at home and abroad. As a large and burgeoning organisation that is not in control of its own destiny, the Army has managed to balance the desire for reform with resource uncertainty and strategic unpredictability. The pace of change has probably been too slow and many lessons have either not been learned or the insights dissipated by the two- to three-year posting cycle and the arrival or promotion of people in key positions who are not motivated by the same set of impulses and imperatives. Dr Blaxland closes with the suggestion that the Army needs to better educate the nation's leaders about what it can and can't do in an operational sense, and ranks a better informed political class among the most pressing priorities. After all, it is the parliament that decides how much money the Army will receive from the public purse and it is Cabinet, made up entirely of civilians, who will decide where and when Australian military power will be used. Clearly, the Australian Army has come a very long way since 1999.

***

In surveying the past fifteen years, this book might appear to be an accidental work of history. In one sense it is, because the participants are looking back on the past at things that have happened in order that they might better prepare for what could occur in the future. But is this an effective approach to learning lessons and discerning challenges? Are the conclusions reliable? If so, what makes them compelling? After all, the future is unlikely to be identical to the past. But if operational effectiveness is inherently logical and battlefield success is ultimately predictable, there is no excuse for not assessing the recent past as a reliable guide to the nearer future. What worked in one place might also work in another; what created problems in one setting is probably going to be problematic in a range of others. This is not to suggest that the stresses associated with peacekeeping in Somalia were overcome in East Timor; that the Army's success in the Solomons was predicated on its performance in Bougainville; or, that the principles of insurgency warfare refined in Afghanistan could be applied without modification in Iraq. But there were elements of the Army's experience in Somalia, Bougainville, and Afghanistan that could be translated to East Timor, the Solomons and Iraq. Other insights only become apparent when the observer is further away from the event being observed. This is especially the case when it comes to intelligence analysis and logistic support.

Five to ten years later the comprehensive character of some problems become visible.

In the case of cultural deficiencies, the causes and consequences of an organisational mindset might not be apparent for decades. For instance, the can-do attitude that characterises the contemporary Army might increase the government's policy options in the short-term but create the impression long-term that armies can be maintained 'on the cheap'. The can-do attitude among uniformed personnel can readily translate into a make-do attitude among elected leaders drawn more to political capital than military spending. If the Army can do a good job with minimal resources, why increase outlays and risk the possibility of waste? The Army's task is to balance depictions of what it can do with predictions of what it can't, should investment remain weak.

This book is, in a sense, the 'second draft' of the Army's history since 1999. The first draft was provided by the journalists who covered the operations described in detail in the chapters that follow. But ultimately, this collection of insights should not be judged as a work of history for two reasons. First, most of the contributors are not historians and have not applied historical method. Second, the events being described are recent – almost current – and the usual separation of time that historians seek between an event and its assessment simply does not exist. The 'dust has not settled' sufficiently for there to be clarity of vision although events in East Timor are quickly becoming more conducive to historical analysis. But the contributors have looked back and discerned pertinent lessons from the recent past. This is why their work is essentially a second draft. Their task was less to uncover what happened and more to explain why it happened to provide a better insight into the lessons the Army is trying to learn and the challenges it is attempting to face. More broadly, as editors we hope this book will prompt discussion and provoke debate about what the Army can glean from its recent experience and how that learning should be absorbed and reflected in the way the Army goes about its business both now and into the future.

The one problem that many of the contributors identify is the amorphous nature of the whole notion of 'military effectiveness'. It remains a concept with an ill-defined nature despite the existence of several quantitative and qualitative approaches to its measurement. But merely measuring military effectiveness is far from the end of the matter. In *The Effectiveness of Military Organizations* Allan Millett has suggested that it poses new and equally important questions for both leaders and commanders:

> What kinds of military effectiveness are most important and in what conditions? For example, to what extent can tactical or operational effectiveness offset strategic ineffectiveness? … Similarly, within the strategic, operational and tactical categories, what types of effectiveness are most important and in what conditions? For example, what contributes most to overall tactical effectiveness-technological sophistication or unit cohesion? Obviously both are crucial, but which counts for more and under what circumstances.[1]

This series of questions is a reminder that often the most important lesson and the most pressing challenge is posing and then pondering the right question. We hope that this book will encourage thinking not only about the answers but whether the right questions are really being asked.

PART 1: THE BIGGER PICTURE

INSERT HERE

1

THE ARMY AND NATIONAL INTEREST

JOHN HOWARD

There was an enormous increase in the military operations in which Australia was involved during the time that I was Prime Minister from March 1996 until August 2007. I have to say at the outset that it was not entirely what I expected. Politics is a combination of the widely anticipated (often, in reality) and the totally unexpected. When I was elected Prime Minister I had no idea of what lay ahead for this country and I dare say very few of our foreign policy, strategic or military advisers had any idea either. Nobody could have envisaged the intervention in East Timor. I certainly do not believe that anybody would have foreseen the coming of terrorism in the form of attacks on Washington and New York in the September of 2001. There was an entirely different attitude in official circles on both sides of politics about active interventions in Pacific Island countries, such as the Solomons, and we were still living in the long shadow of the Vietnam conflict's aftermath, although that war had ended more than twenty years before my government was elected. Nonetheless, it was a period of time in which there was, in my judgement, a subdued level of public consciousness about potential military involvement in a range of situations abroad as the conflict in

Vietnam had evoked enormous controversy in the community. There remained intense feelings about it – not about the quality of the military contribution by Australian forces, but about the strategic wisdom of the involvement and the continuing consequences of that involvement – and this influenced public attitudes towards the use of Australia's military capabilities in any context.

When the Coalition parties came to government one important decision we took was to ring-fence Defence from any expenditure cuts in our first budget. It is fair to say that was an attitude that was substantially maintained during our time in office and, of course, in addition there were significant increases in many areas of Defence expenditure. We ordered a review – there are always reviews when governments come to power, whether it is in Defence or anywhere else – into the financing and management of the forces. The first Defence Minister in my government, Ian McLachlan, announced that an inquiry led by Vice Admiral Chris Barrie (who later became the Chief of Defence Force) would seek to use the language of the trade, to shift resources away from 'the back office to the sharp end'. I will leave others to decide whether or not that was successful. But our initial commitment to exempt Defence from expenditure cuts was the basis of the Coalition's commitment to national security. There would be no defence on the cheap; it needed to be properly funded.

The turning point for me and the whole government in relation to defence was the International Force for East Timor (INTERFET) operation. It required careful decision-making that was conscious of both the long- and short-term political and diplomatic consequences of Australian action, and it demanded substantial additional investment in supplies and equipment. This was not the first occasion on which the Coalition Government had deployed Australians abroad – and this is often overlooked.

In response to the continued refusal of the Iraqi regime led by Saddam Hussein to comply fully with the United Nations resolution on weapons inspections, we had sent a Special Forces contingent to the Middle East in 1998. They were deployed with strong bipartisan support. Together with Opposition Leader Kim Beazley, I met the contingent in Western Australia before they departed. Their mission was to co-operate with other allied forces in helping to enforce the air space and flying restrictions associated with implementing the resolution. A deal was subsequently brokered by the Secretary-General of the United Nations with the Iraqi regime, and the Australian personnel came home. But there was a fundamental change of mood in the political arena of our own region in 1999.

The origin of this mood change was the very unexpected decision of the President of Indonesia, Dr BJ Habibie, to contemplate significant change with respect to Indonesia's policy on the continuing occupation of East Timor. I wrote to Dr Habibie, who came to office following the resignation of General Suharto early in March 1998. My letter urged him to hold a plebiscite on the future status of East Timor within Indonesia. He certainly surprised us when he agreed to hold such a plebiscite without delay, and to include the option of complete separation from Indonesia. This went beyond our government's expectations.

This proved to be a deeply unpopular decision in some sectors of Indonesia, especially within their armed forces. In the months before the vote there was widespread violence committed by rogue elements of the Indonesian military in East Timor. The situation deteriorated to such a degree that by the early months of 1999 it was obvious to many of us in the government that military intervention was a very real possibility. Should force be required to reinstate order and to restrain local militias, the government was aware that Australia would be expected to play a substantial role in any intervention. After all, we were the largest and most prosperous nation in the region. I made it clear that if we were to play a major role in the intervention it would include overall leadership. I had come to the conclusion that this was the sort of operation in which Australia needed to be in a position where we could exercise maximum control and direct influence.

History records my intense disappointment with President Bill Clinton when he told me the United States was unable to provide any ground forces to be part of an intervention in East Timor. I genuinely thought at the time that a contingent of American ground forces would be needed and, in my naivety, I thought they would be provided, given the shared history of our two nations. Despite my personal dismay, and that of the entire government's feeling of being let down, Washington's response did have a positive dimension. The expressed American inability to provide ground forces did Australia an enormous favour in the long run, because it meant a more comprehensive commitment from us than might have been.

Australia provided the bulk of the forces with important contributions from many other countries, particularly New Zealand, Thailand and South Korea. It was very much a regional operation. But the greater assumption of responsibility by Australia meant we were able to identify many deficiencies in both our planning processes and operational procedures. From my perspective, the intervention revealed the serious deficiency we were facing when it came to any kind of sea and airlift capacity. Without much of the logistic support that was subsequently provided by the United States the whole operation would not have been as successful. As a footnote and in fairness to the Clinton Administration, once they were aware of the depth of our disappointment at their inability or unwillingness to provide ground forces they were certainly quick to provide other kinds of assistance, including considerable diplomatic support. On reflection and notwithstanding the mistakes and inadequacies the intervention revealed, Australia is entitled to look with a great deal of pride and satisfaction on the quality of its diplomatic and military effort in East Timor after 1999.

In sum, the East Timor intervention had two important consequences. The first was its transforming influence on the mindset of the Australian people about the contemporary role of the Australian Defence Force (ADF) in national life. There was an almost universal wave of support for both the government's decision to play a major role in East Timor and the widespread affirmation of the quality of the ADF's contribution. We were greatly assisted, of course, by the absence of significant battle casualties – always a vital issue when it comes to military involvement. The transition of East Timor from Indonesian sovereignty to the protection of the United Nations and then to independence and self-government had attracted international commendation and domestic approval. The only critics were from among what I would loosely call the Jakarta-centric sections of the foreign affairs commentator community, who operated on the principle that you never even think about offending Jakarta.

The overall reaction of the Australian community to our involvement in East Timor was one of pride. The intervention rekindled the defence community's continuing but perhaps subdued belief in the capacity and the commitment of our uniformed men and women. In the broader community, it generated pride in the capacity of ADF personnel to represent the country in an effective and generous way. In addition to their warfighting ability, Australians could see that uniformed personnel were also intricately involved in humanitarian and peacekeeping work as part of their duties. East Timor provided us with a very significant example of that dual capacity.

After the post-Vietnam hiatus in which the ADF retreated into the background of national life, once again their activities were front and centre in popular consciousness. This was, in my judgement, an overwhelmingly positive development, but it meant there would be continuing focus on expenditure within the Defence portfolio. There would be renewed debate about the extent of Commonwealth outlays and where the money would be spent. While the East Timor intervention had almost overwhelming political support, subsequent military operations were not to attract that same level of support, and I will come to them in a moment.

Never having served as Defence Minister and certainly claiming no special experience as a defence expert, I didn't pretend to have a detailed knowledge of all the deficiencies that came to light in 1999, and in the years that followed. We learned some very salutary lessons because we were forced to assume the ultimate responsibility in the absence of American involvement. It was the first time that we had been involved in any kind of contested military operation for decades without some kind of operational involvement from United States forces. Therefore, we were obliged to look very closely at our own capability gaps.

The deficiencies in our airlift abilities later led to acquisition of Boeing C-17 Globemaster III large transport aircraft, which have proved so valuable in a range of contingencies, most recently during the operation that followed the shooting down of Malaysian Airlines MH-17 over the Ukraine. It's good to remember, too, that the standout vessel of the Timor operation was the wave-piercing catamaran HMAS *Jervis Bay*. It had been a commercially constructed vessel known as *Incat 045*, built by an outstanding Australian company for civilian use. *Jervis Bay* is now a metaphor for what East Timor taught us about our capabilities, and we should be very grateful for these lessons. The government learned a lot from that experience, and we invested heavily over a period of years in equipment of this kind.

The other lesson that East Timor taught me, and which impressed itself on other members of the government, was that Australia would need to play the sort of role we were obliged to play in East Timor whenever that sort of eventuality arose in our region. The success of the East Timor intervention meant that the rest of the world in a sense breathed a sigh of relief. International bodies noted that Australia had the ability and the willingness to play a major role in operations of this kind in our part of the world.

Several years later Australia was asked to play a significant role, albeit in different circumstances, in the Solomon Islands, as the lead nation in a Pacific Forum force that sought to restore law and order in the former British colony. The Regional Assistance Mission to Solomon Islands (RAMSI) also involved the Australian Federal Police (AFP). As in East Timor, Australian was able to demonstrate our capacity to take a lead role in the region but we were also reminding the rest of the world that Australia could be relied upon to be a good international citizen.

By this time I realised that ADF operations were at the high and low ends of military capability. At the high end we were partnering coalition allies in operations such as Iraq and Afghanistan, and at the lower end we were taking the lead in our own region. It was partly because of these varied demands that we decided towards the end of our term in office to establish two new battalions. The need for flexibility also influenced the decision to enhance the Army's tank capacity and on other equipment acquisition of a lesser magnitude.

As I look back on that period of my prime ministership, I can see it was marked by a high level of operational tempo for the ADF. But it was also a period in which I believe we learned from our mistakes and took stock of our deficiencies. Although we (and I use that work collectively here, to include everyone involved at a political and a military level) have emerged to a situation where public regard for the ADF is as high as I have known it in my lifetime, it is important that we try to understand just what lessons were to be learned and what deficiencies revealed. As I look back at what I can remember of the attitude of the Australian people in the mid 1990s, it was not so much of indifference but that the Army's place was far from the forefront of public consciousness. Twenty years later that is certainly no longer the case.

Let me make some specific observations of the Army based on the particular vantage point that I enjoyed both as Prime Minister and more particularly as the Chairman of the National Security Committee of Cabinet. During my time in office the National Security Committee of Cabinet became a very active part of the Executive Government. It had the authority (as it still does) of the full Cabinet, particularly from the time of the East Timor intervention. Its membership included the Prime Minister, the Deputy Prime Minister, the Treasurer, the Foreign Minister, the Defence Minister and the Attorney-General, with other ministers co-opted when necessary. Also included, except on very rare occasions, was the Chief of the Defence Force, the Secretary of the Department of Defence, the Secretary of Foreign Affairs, the Secretary of the Prime Minister's Department, the Director-General of the Australian Security Intelligence Organisation (ASIO) and the Director-General of the Office of National Assessments (ONA), which is the chief distillation point, if I can put it that way, of intelligence that comes to government. At other times, officers such as the Commissioner of the AFP contributed to the deliberations.

It was far and away the most effective Cabinet committee during my time in government and I can best measure that effectiveness by the constant requests I received from ministers outside the National Security Committee to join. They were regularly calling on me or my Chief-of-Staff Arthur Sinodinos with well-documented arguments as to why their contribution to the National Security Committee of Cabinet could enhance its output. I steadfastly rejected all of those requests because I thought the group brought together precisely the people who could make the right decisions.

From the view of operational decision-making I cannot emphasise too much how valuable it was to have present at all of those meetings (other than on rare occasions when raw party politics was being discussed) the continued presence of these senior advisors and our capacity to argue, among other things, the merits of detailed acquisition decisions. There were many energetic discussion about the acquisition of particular pieces of military equipment and, of course, vigorous debates between the Treasurer and the Defence Minister about the escalating costs of all this.

One of the realities that emerged from my experience of these discussions and debates, and I suspect it is the experience of all governments, is the extraordinary difficulty of precisely estimating the ultimate cost of large equipment acquisitions for the Army, the Navy and the Air Force. This has been a challenge for lots of countries, including those with large indigenous defence industries. Bringing together the political, economic and operational aspects of national security in the context of a Cabinet committee discussion was, I thought, an effective approach, and one that was preserved by subsequent governments. Previous governments had their own foreign affairs and defence committees but they never quite operated with the same consistency and in the same pattern as the Cabinet committee in my time as Prime Minister.

In considering Australian involvement in actions in Iraq and Afghanistan, I am naturally aware that they were clothed with a lot more controversy than the operations in East Timor and the Solomon Islands. That operations in the Middle East were controversial did not alter in any way the professional commitment of our uniformed men and women. Afghanistan has become Australia's longest military involvement. Its protracted nature has made me acutely aware of the reality that no matter how strong the public commitment to a military operation at the outset may be, any deployment in which Australia is involved, short of total war, will inevitably struggle to preserve public support the longer the commitment remains.

Initial support for Australia being involved in Afghanistan was overwhelming. In 2001, opinion polls measured between 70 and 80 per cent public support for Australian involvement. This was helped by strong bipartisan support. The Labor Opposition supported the operation and maintained that support when in government. But over time public support invariably declines and, as casualties mount, the support tends to decline even further and even faster. Declining support is an ever-present reality for those involved in prosecuting the war on the ground. It is something that those who take decisions politically must always bear in mind. The level of public support for continuing operations in Afghanistan is mirrored in Britain and the United States. Australia is not alone is seeing support for prolonged campaigns slowly ebb away.

In contrast to the decision to invade Afghanistan after the 11 September 2001 terrorist attacks in the United States, the decision to invade Iraq after Saddam Hussein's regime obstructed the efforts of United Nation's inspectors to confirm that Iraq had divested itself of all weapons of mass destruction (WMD) was deeply divisive and politically controversial. I am conscious of continuing debate about the 2003 invasion and the inability of the coalition consisting of the United States, Great Britain and Australia to locate any WMD during its occupation of the Iraq. But I also sense a realisation among the population that the more recent Australian involvement in Iraq is a very different mission, dealing with the latest manifestation of political and religious instability and potential threat of that instability in the Middle East.

It is a measure of Australia's political maturity that everyone accepts that the ADF is the servant of government and an implement of our national security policy. People of all political persuasions endorse the traditional relationship between the elected political arm of government and our non-politically aligned armed forces. The diarchy arrangement, where Defence is led by uniformed personnel and administered by civilian personnel, has worked well throughout the history of our Commonwealth and requires no reform or even fine-tuning. In fact, I cannot imagine an alternative to the present arrangements that would not result in the downgrading of the roles or the responsibilities of uniform personnel within our Defence establishment. I would not support any diminution of the place of uniformed leaders in the development of policy, the acquisition of equipment or the conduct of operations. Having uniformed people being part of these activities was never going to alter the fundamental authority of the elected government. Therefore, I saw no need to assert greater civilian control. But there will always be debate about the relationship between the uniform and the civilian branches of Defence.

I do not think there is a perfect structure or final answers to many of the questions that are often asked about where the role of one ends and the other begins. There will be more inquiries but that is not to say that all inquiries are bad. Some inquiries are worse than others because of their limited application and because they consume resources. But inquiries are like stock-takes and are an inevitable part of life in a democratic society that legitimately demands that government be accountable for the money it spends. Despite its special place in our national life, Defence must be seen to act responsibly just as it needs to be as accountable and as transparent as any other section of government. The idea that some sections of government are entitled to escape scrutiny is, of course, a false notion. While it is easy to attack the Department of Finance and the Treasury, they have a very legitimate role across the whole government and that is to hold everybody to account.

As I look forward to the next ten to 20 years, bearing in mind the unpredictability of the previous two decades, I think the East Timor–Solomon Islands-type role is likely to continue in our part of the world. There is sufficient instability to expect that operations of this kind could well be necessary. The biggest single strategic issue within our territory is, of course, the continuing relationship between the United States and China. The manner in which these often-fraught interactions are managed will heavily shape the course of events in our region and across the entire world. It is the most important bilateral relationship in the world by most measures. I belong to the school of thought that does not accept that some kind of conflict between China and the United States is inevitable. Commentators are misreading the situation if they propagate the view that a war is unavoidable. The role of countries like Australia is to do everything possible to diminish the tendencies in either of those countries to accept that a conflict is inevitable.

My own judgement is that China does not really want anything to divert her attention from dealing with a complex array of extraordinary internal problems. China has many more internal problems than most people realise. For instance, China faces a huge problem of demography. This is a view I share with many other observers. Trying to turn around the aging of the Chinese population will take decades. It is a country that, to use a cliché, will grow old before it grows rich. It is in aggregate terms a huge economy but in per capita gross domestic product it lags a long way behind many countries, not only in Western Europe and countries such as Australia, but even among its regional neighbours. Like all nations that have emerged economically and have become powerful financially, China will continue to assert diplomatic will and test her capacity and her influence in the region. This is, in part, what we observe with the Spratly Islands. But we need to understand in responding to all of these pressures the undesirability from the Chinese point of view to have too much attention and too many resources diverted away from maintaining the still quite delicate internal balance between the newly enriched hundreds of millions of middle class and those who are still living in, relatively speaking, abject poverty. More people have been lifted out of poverty in China in the last 20 years than perhaps at any other stage in human history since the Industrial Revolution. This is a remarkable humanitarian achievement. But it also carries significant risks of political instability into the future.

I am persuaded that people born into middle-class affluence tend to take their good fortune for granted and then look around for greater political freedom. People who transition from poverty to middle-class affluence in their lifetime are perhaps willing to accept political instruction and political authoritarianism. As more and more people in China fall into the first category, the greater the tendency to demand greater freedom. Managing those demands will require remarkable skill and creative leadership. Engaging in a conflict with the United States is a distraction the Chinese political elite neither wants nor needs.

Conversely, when looking at the role of the United States in our region it is important to understand the overwhelming desire of most nations to have greater American involvement in their national life and not less. I remain puzzled at the often-used word of 'pivot' to describe American policy in our region. I was under the impression that the United States had never left and can see no evidence for the assertion that it had. The idea that it represents some very significant change in American policy to have the sort of things that were epitomised in President Obama's 'pivot speech' to our own joint session of parliament (a speech with which I fully agreed in substance) is surprising. To my way of thinking, the idea that the United States had even contemplated reducing her influence in this region was never on the horizon. But the important point to note is that nations such as Thailand, Japan, the Philippines, Malaysia, Singapore and even Vietnam are highly anxious that the United States remains heavily involved in the Asia–Pacific region and one of the reasons is apprehension about Chinese intentions. The most important but the most difficult bilateral relationship in the region remains that between Japan and China. The difficulties are the product of decades of ill will with some issues related to the Second World War. The development of a better relationship is a matter for China and Japan. Other than urging discussion and dialogue, there is little that Australia can do.

There is much the Australian Army obviously can and plainly has learned from operations since 1999. Despite its esteem for traditions, customs and conventions, the Army has shown itself equally committed to creativity, initiative and innovation. It is to the credit of the Army's contemporary leadership that it is willing to concede that some mistakes have been made and some shortcomings have become apparent in its experience of operations since the intervention in East Timor, even as it performed in a manner that brought great credit to those who served and credibility to the nation they served. Any suggestion that the Army prefers to live in the past is dispelled by examining recent campaigns and can be justified in that the Army of the present is educated and enriched by its experiences. As someone who has exercised national leadership and used the Army to implement government policy, I could not have asked for a better approach to institutional renewal and cultural reform.

2

THE EMERGING STRATEGIC ENVIRONMENT

DAVID HORNER

For more than 15 years – from the International Force for East Timor (INTERFET) deployment to East Timor in September 1999 to the formal withdrawal from Afghanistan in December 2014[1] – the Australian Army was involved in almost continuous military operations, many involving considerable numbers of troops and at a relatively high tempo. For those soldiers serving in the Army, the operations during this 15-year period was 'business as normal'. Many of them would have known no other situation. But this period stands in stark contrast to the previous 27 years. This chapter outlines here the strategic and political environment that brought about this change and will provide context for the more detailed discussion of this period of operations that follow. The starting point is the INTERFET deployment in 1999, but what happened before that intervention is important because the events during this earlier period played a large part in setting the stage for the operations of the new millennium.

The long years of peace

When the last combat troops withdrew from South Vietnam in February 1972 it seemed that Australia had seen the end of overseas military operations. In addition to finalising the end of Australia's commitment to the Vietnam conflict, the Whitlam Government (elected in December 1972) began to wind down Australia's forces in Malaysia and Singapore and vowed that Australia would 'never again send troops to fight in Asian mainland wars'.[2] This did not mean that the government had completely foresworn the use of military forces in support of global multilateral institutions. Prime Minister Gough Whitlam was willing to provide troops for United Nations-authorised peacekeeping missions. But for various reasons few peacekeeping forces went overseas during the time of his government.

The Coalition Government led by Malcolm Fraser (elected in December 1975), built upon the ideas of the previous three years and spelt out its policy in its 1976 White Paper, 'Australian Defence'. The paper began by outlining the changes in Australia's strategic circumstances, noting that the former imperial powers had withdrawn from the region, the United States had disengaged militarily from mainland South-East Asia, the nations of the Association of South-East Asian Nations (ASEAN) – Indonesia, Malaysia, the Philippines, Singapore and Thailand – had made notable progress in 'nation building', Papua New Guinea had become independent, and while China was no longer seen as a major threat the Soviet Union had achieved nuclear strategic parity with the United States. The government argued that the area of Australia's prime strategic concern was the adjacent maritime area, the countries and territories of the south-west of the Pacific, Papua New Guinea, Indonesia and South-East Asia. Consequently, Australia's primary defence requirement was for increased self-reliance.[3]

In the event of a 'fundamental threat' to Australia's security it was expected that United States military support would be forthcoming, but short of this Australia should be able to handle the situation more independently. This did not mean a diminution of the United States alliance; indeed, Australia's independent capacity was enhanced by American support. Although the White Paper's fine print allowed for troops to be deployed on 'operations elsewhere if the requirement arose', it seemed that after the Vietnam experience successive Australian governments resolved never again to send sizeable land forces overseas. The White Paper also heralded the beginning of a new entity that we now all take for granted, namely the Australian Defence Force (ADF).

For two decades Australia's only overseas commitments were small numbers of personnel to several peacekeeping missions. But most soldiers who joined the Army in the early 1970s faced the prospect of never serving overseas in their entire career. For them, Defence policy translated into a series of major training exercises, often based on unlikely scenarios.

Return to overseas deployments

The attitude of eschewing overseas commitments began to change in March 1987 when the Hawke Labor Government released its Defence White Paper, 'The Defence of Australia 1987' (DOA87).[4] It reiterated the 1976 White Paper in stating that the policy was one of self-reliance within a framework of alliances and regional associations. DOA87 proposed an enhanced defence capability to defeat any challenge to Australian sovereignty and to respond effectively to attacks within Australia's 'area of direct military interest'. Although the priority for force development was to prepare to meet low-level contingencies in the north of Australia, the government recognised the need 'to be capable of reacting positively to calls for military support further afield from our allies and friends, should we judge that our interests require it'.[5]

No sooner had this policy been enunciated than events occurred that questioned whether the policy was in tune with changes taking place in the region. Within a few months there was a military coup in Fiji, and Australia deployed forces to facilitate the evacuation of Australian nationals, had that proved necessary. By 1988 a civil war had broken out in the Papua New Guinea island of Bougainville, with at least the possibility that Australia might become involved. It was the start of a long saga of regional peacemaking and peacekeeping that moved from mediation to peacekeeping in Bougainville, and a decade or so later to peace enforcement in East Timor and the Solomon Islands.

Events further afield were also affecting Australia. In December 1987 the government agreed to deploy a naval clearance diving team to the Persian Gulf to provide protection for neutral tankers and seaborne cargoes under threat during the Iran–Iraq War. Although the deployment did not go ahead, the decision was significant for several reasons. For the first time since the Vietnam War the government approved the deployment of military forces to a potential, although admittedly limited, combat situation. The pivotal importance of this decision is illustrated by *The Australian* newspaper's defence correspondent and former Army Major, Peter Young, who said that it 'will be seen by some as coming dangerously close to a replay of how Australia got involved in Vietnam'.[6] Although the United States had not formally requested Australian support, the government had responded to an American veiled request, indicating that the demands of the alliance were still alive. After DOA87 the United

States had expressed great concern that it signalled the end of future Australian military support. Having won the argument in the Labor Party, Prime Minister Bob Hawke and his Defence Minister, Kim Beazley, would be more confident when deciding to support the Americans following the Iraqi invasion of Kuwait in 1990.

Further, Australian peacekeepers were deployed well outside the area of Australia's direct military interest in 1988 and 1989. In 1988 a team, under United Nations auspices, helped monitor the ceasefire between Iran and Iraq, and in 1989 an engineer contingent went to Namibia as part of a United Nations force supervising the transition of the territory to independence. Also, in 1989 the army sent a nine-man mine-clearance training team to Pakistan; this commitment continued for five years.

These commitments were made possible by a major change in world affairs – namely the end of the Cold War and the beginning of what optimistic world leaders described as a New World Order. Peacekeeping missions could now be approved by the United Nations Security Council without one of the permanent members applying a veto. Thus, when the Iraqi forces of Saddam Hussein invaded Kuwait in August 1990 the Security Council authorised a Maritime Interception Force (MIF) to apply sanctions against Iraq. The Hawke Government was in the happy position of being able to respond to the United States, which wanted Australian involvement, but to do so under the United Nations' umbrella. The government committed three naval ships, but as a result found itself locked into supporting the American-led coalition when it began combat operations to eject Iraqi forces from Kuwait in January 1991.

After what proved to be a successful operation, the United Nations Security Council passed resolutions demanding that Iraq give up its weapons of mass destruction (WMD). These WMD included biological, chemical and possibly nuclear weapons as well as the means to deliver them, such as long-range rockets. Research centres where these weapons had been developed or were still being developed were to be dismantled. Sanctions would be applied by the MIF while United Nations inspectors entered Iraq, located the WMDs and ensured that they were destroyed. One thing often leads to another. Australia had played only a minor role in the 1991 Gulf War, but having advocated a strong role for the United Nations, Australia could not resist a request from Washington to provide a naval ship for further MIF operations on rotation, and to contribute to the teams of WMD inspectors. These commitments continued throughout the 1990s, and led eventually to Australia's involvement in the invasion of Iraq in March 2003.

Meanwhile, in the favourable strategic environment following the Gulf War, the United Nations authorised more peacekeeping missions. Australia played a major role in the peacekeeping mission in Cambodia between 1991 and 1993, providing the force commander and the Force Communications Unit. Australia also provided a much smaller communications units to the UN peacekeeping force in Western Sahara between 1991 and 1994. In 1993 the Keating Labor Government deployed an infantry battalion to Somalia as part of a United Nations-authorised peace-enforcement mission. Then the following year the government approved two successive six-month tours to Rwanda by a medical contingent (with infantry protection) in support of a United Nations peacekeeping force. The United Nations was unable to prevent mass slaughter in Rwanda. By the time this mission ended in 1995, the government had lost its enthusiasm for international peacekeeping. Somalia and the United Nations mission in Bosnia (in which Australia was barely involved) had also been failures.

The Howard Government

The election of the Howard Coalition Government in March 1996 did not change Australia's attitude to peacekeeping, which, as mentioned, had cooled considerably. The government had come to power with a policy of revitalising the United States alliance relationship, which it alleged had been weakened under the Keating Government. The main focus of the Australia–United States relationship was the Asia–Pacific region, although the 1997 Sandline Affair in Papua New Guinea – involving the controversial use of private military contractors to end the secessionist uprising in Bougainville – alerted the Australian Government to the possibility that it might need to deploy forces in the South Pacific.

The concern with the Asia–Pacific region was shown in a succession of government policy statements. The government's paper on foreign and trade policy, released in August 1997, declared that a 'key objective' was to 'strengthen further the relationship between Australia and the United States', but it was directed particularly at the Asia–Pacific region.[7] The government's defence policy, released four months later, reiterated that the 'highest priority' needed to be given to 'maximising interoperability with the United States', and talked of Australia's 'key strategic interests in the Asia–Pacific region'. The policy identified 'three basic tasks' for the ADF: 'defeating attacks on Australia'; 'defending Australia's regional interest' and 'supporting Australia's global interests'. The policy paper declared that as well as 'our strong focus on the Asia–Pacific region, Australia also has clear strategic interests at the global level'. The 'foremost' of these interests was support for the United Nations in its primary function of 'resisting aggression around the world'. In practice it would be most likely that any substantial effort by the United Nations would be led by the United States.[8]

The government's emphasis on the region was soon shown in December 1997 when it contributed personnel to a New Zealand-led Truce Monitoring Group in Bougainville, after New Zealand had brokered an end to fighting between the PNG Government and the Bougainville Revolutionary Army (BRA), which was formed in 1988 to secure the island's independence from Port Moresby. The following April Australia took over leadership of the renamed Peace Monitoring Group. This commitment, known as 'Operation Bel Isi II', was to continue for five years.

The government now made a decision that was of fundamental importance in the lead-up to the invasion of Iraq in 2003. Since 1991 Australia personnel had played a major role in the United Nations Special Commission on Iraq (UNSCOM), which was charged with finding and destroying Saddam Hussein's WMD, including providing the chairman of UNSCOM in May 1997. The Iraqi regime put innumerable stumbling blocks in the way of UNSCOM and in October 1987 banned US inspectors from the country. By the end of January 1998, US President Bill Clinton had decided that he might need to take military action. On 7 February, Washington asked Australia formally to contribute to a coalition force. The Australian Government, with bipartisan support, agreed and offered a Special Air Service (SAS) squadron and two RAAF Boeing 707 tanker aircraft. In agreeing to take part Australia set a precedent that was hard to overlook come 2003. These forces were duly deployed to Kuwait as part of Operation Pollard. But the United Nations Secretary-General struck a deal with Hussein and the strike on Iraq did not go ahead. An ADF liaison officer continued in Kuwait with the Coalition Joint Task Force, and provided Australia with forewarning of future American operations.

In view of Hussein's intransigence, the United States now asked Australia to deploy a frigate to the MIF. Australia had not deployed a frigate to the region for three years, but on 28 March 1999 the government announced the revival of Australia's role in the MIF – one that was to gain significance following the terrorist attacks on New York and Washington on 11 September 2001. In a desire to enhance alliance relations with the United States, Australia had been drawn back into the Middle East with a stake in seeing the Iraqi regime stripped of its WMD.

Meanwhile, events in East Timor were attracting the attention of the Commonwealth Government and, even more so, the general public in Australia. The story of the INTERFET operation is well known and is covered in more detail in Chapter 4 by Craig Stockings. The deployment of combat-ready troops to East Timor and the successful completion of the mission was the biggest test of the quarter-century development of the ADF. It was not just the challenge of deploying and sustaining 5500 personnel in the latter months of 1999 that made it important, but the additional challenge of maintaining a substantial force on the island over the next six years. More broadly, as James Cotton has described it, the East Timor commitment had 'a profound effect on many aspects of Australia's security and defence posture'.[9] Defence priorities were reordered and the Army bolstered two of its under-strength battalions and improved its logistic capability to enable the force in East Timor to be sustained.

Following the INTERFET deployment, and while troops were still serving in East Timor, the government released a new Defence White Paper in December 2000.[10] The strategic analyst, Hugh White, described the policy as 'committing the government to a new and more expansive conception of Australia's strategic interests and military objectives and to substantial and sustained increases in defence funding'.[11] The priority task for the ADF was the defence of Australia, followed by contributing to security in the immediate neighbourhood. The third priority was to support Australia's wider interests and objectives by being able to contribute effectively to international coalitions of forces to meet crises beyond Australia's immediate neighbourhood.

The terrorist attacks of 11 September 2001

This third priority took on increased importance when barely nine months later, on 11 September 2001, members of the Al Qaeda Islamist terrorist group attacked the World Trade Center in New York and the Pentagon in Washington DC. Following the attacks, President George W Bush declared a 'global war on terrorism'. On 20 September he demanded that the Taliban government in Afghanistan hand over the Al Qaeda leaders to the United States and close the terrorist training camps. When the Taliban refused, the Americans commenced airstrikes against targets in Afghanistan on 7 October. American Special Forces elements entered Afghanistan and joined a loose collection of anti-Taliban forces known as the 'Northern Alliance' in their fight against the Taliban. The Afghanistan capital of Kabul fell to the Northern Alliance on 12 November. The Taliban, and Al Qaeda, were then pushed back into the mountains along the border with Pakistan, where fighting continued.

Australian Prime Minister John Howard happened to be in Washington when the planes struck the World Trade Center and the Pentagon. He immediately pledged Australian support to the United States. In what was a largely symbolic gesture, Australia then invoked the ANZUS alliance by which the United States and Australia agreed to consult if either of them were attacked in the Pacific. The Australian Government believed that the terrorist threat applied to Western countries around the world, not just to the United States, and that the countries needed to stand together against the threat. Australia was not the only country to come to America's assistance. The North Atlantic Treaty Organisation (NATO) declared that the attacks of 11 September amounted to an attack on all NATO countries.

With bipartisan support, Australia undertook to provide military assistance to the United States in its war against terrorism, directed particularly at the terrorist base in Afghanistan. This support – known in Australia as Operation Slipper – consisted of about 1300 ADF personnel from the three services, although the most noteworthy operations were carried out by the SAS. By the time the Special Forces soldiers withdrew at the end of 2002 they had cemented their reputation for professionalism and ability among the other Coalition partners.

The 2003 invasion of Iraq

Even before the fall of Kabul, the United States Government was looking beyond Afghanistan. President Bush was concerned that Saddam Hussein had refused to allow United Nations inspectors to complete their internationally authorised task of ridding Iraq of WMD. There was no evidence that Saddam Hussein was co-operating with Al Qaeda or supporting it materially; however, Bush and his advisers saw Al Qaeda and Iraq's potential possession of WMD as a threat to the United States and more generally to world security.

For Australia, the war on terrorism assumed a personal dimension when in October 2002 Islamist terrorists exploded bombs on the Indonesia island of Bali. Of the 202 people killed, 88 were Australians. This made the Howard Government even more determined to support the United States in the global war on terror.

As Iraq continued to refuse to allow United Nations inspectors to complete their mission of identifying and destroying its WMD, the United States threatened to invade Iraq to complete the task. Intense diplomatic efforts were made to persuade Saddam Hussein to comply. But as American preparations for possible war continued, the Australian Government decided in January 2003 to deploy forces to the Middle East so they would be available for operations if the government decided to participate in an invasion, if it eventuated. All the forces had arrived by early March 2003.

With Iraq remaining defiant, the United States decided to proceed with the invasion, supported principally by Australia and Britain. The Howard Government maintained that because Iraq had failed to comply with United Nations Security Council resolutions concerning its WMD, the United States and its allies possessed the necessary authority to invade. Critics claimed that the United States should have waited for the outcome of inspections that Iraq had agreed to facilitate in late 2002, and that the invasion was not justified and probably illegal. Britain supported the United States with substantial forces; Australia sent 2000 ADF personnel.

The Howard Government's decision to join the 'coalition of the willing' to invade Iraq was controversial within Australia and was criticised by the Labor Opposition. The government claimed that it was intent on removing the threat of Iraq's WMD, but the most important factor remained a continuing commitment to support the United States. Australia's contribution was finely managed to ensure that casualties were kept to a minimum. Partly determined by the prevailing weather, the invasion of Iraq began in the evening of 19 March 2003, when coalition forces, including Australian SAS personnel, crossed into Iraq. Baghdad was captured on 9 April and President

Bush declared that combat operations were over on 1 May.

After months of searching, no WMD were found. Prime Minister Howard continued to argue that there was sufficient intelligence to hand that Iraq possessed, or would soon possess, WMD and this would justify the government's decision.[12] The Australian Army's Director of Research in Strategic Plans Albert Palazzo, who has written the Postscript to this volume, has previously and persuasively argued that the Howard Government never adopted the American plan, which was to change the regime in Iraq. While Howard believed there was a case for invasion based on Hussein's refusal to abandon possession of WMD, the government's prime policy goal was to use its commitment as a means of strengthening Australia's security relationship with the United States. The government achieved that aim with no fatal battle casualties and hence 'from the perspective of a national security cost-benefit analysis, Australia's decision to participate in the Coalition against Iraq was the correct one'.[13] In seeking to enhance its relationship with the United States, while contributing only a modest a force, Canberra's commitment to the Iraq War displayed similar motivations to Australian commitments to the Korean War, the Vietnam conflict and the 1990–91 Gulf War.

Continuing commitments

As the conflict in Iraq unfolded, a complete breakdown in law and order in the Solomon Islands occurred. In July 2003, at the request of the Solomon Islands' Prime Minister, and in what amounted to a major policy shift, Australia led a regional force known as the Regional Assistance Mission to Solomon Islands (RAMSI) to restore domestic order and to strengthen the political, legal and social authority of the Honiara government.

The Australian Government continued to give priority to operations in the near neighbourhood. While substantial forces still remained in the Middle East, Canberra actually had more troops in East Timor and to Solomon Islands than Afghanistan and Iraq in the initial deployments. The importance of the near neighbourhood was emphasised when Australia deployed a number of ADF elements to Indonesia in early 2005 to provide emergency assistance after the 2004 Boxing Day tsunami.

The American-led coalition in Iraq soon found itself fighting a savage insurgency in which Washington sent ever-increasing numbers of troops, supported by personnel from other countries. Australia could not avoid increasing its commitment and in mid 2005 deployed a task force to southern Iraq to provide security for a Japanese engineering team. When the Japanese withdrew the Australian contingent's task transitioned to an over-watch role for the regional government. The Australians served in one of the least dangerous areas in Iraq, rotated several times, had restricted rules of engagement and suffered no combat deaths. The Labor Government elected in November 2007 and led by Prime Minister Kevin Rudd had vowed in Opposition to withdraw Australian combat and training units from Iraq. The withdrawal began in June 2008. By the time the last soldiers departed in July 2009, about 20,000 ADF personnel had served in and around Iraq over a six-year period.

After Australia's initial commitment to the invasion of Afghanistan in 2001, a new government was elected in Kabul. But the security situation remained fragile and in time slowly deteriorated. An Australian Special Forces Task Group returned to Afghanistan in September 2005. Australia's commitment to Afghanistan was supported by both major political parties, which believed the Taliban were supporting terrorism and that the government in Kabul should not be allowed to fall. International support for the government led by Hamid Karzai was authorised by the United Nations and was provided by the International Security Assistance Force (ISAF).

In September 2006 an Australian Reconstruction Task Force, with a strong protection group, deployed to Afghanistan to undertake civil construction work and to train local tradesmen. Australian Special Forces personnel returned to Afghanistan in May 2007 to take the fight to the Taliban in Oruzgan province. The soldiers soon found themselves engaged in intense battles. The Australian force in Afghanistan continued to grow and in mid 2009 the Reconstruction Task Force expanded to the Mentoring and Reconstruction Task Force, which included a robust combat element, an engineering group, and a mentoring and liaison team to work with an Afghan infantry battalion. By this time more than 1500 troops were serving in Afghanistan.

Meanwhile, Australia had been busy in its near region. Australia sent substantial forces to the Solomon Islands and East Timor (now known as Timor Leste) in 2006 after rioting and other violence broke out in both countries. At one stage Australian combat troops were engaged in operations across four countries – Afghanistan, Iraq, the Solomon Islands and Timor Leste. Before the year was out, Australian troops had also been deployed to Tonga, where pro-democracy riots in the capital Nuku'alofa destroyed much of the country's small central business district.

Implications for Australian defence policy

These constant commitments posed considerable challenges for those who were trying to shape Australia defence policy. On one hand there were the demands of dealing with increasingly costly and contentious operations, especially as the war in Afghanistan dragged on and the Taliban remained active. On the other, there were increasingly complex and unsettling questions about Australian strategic objectives and defence priorities, especially with the continuing rise of China as an economic power – one that was gradually flexing its military muscles.

Prime Minister Howard continued to pursue the policies contained in the 2000 White Paper, with its focus on the defence of Australia and regional commitments. But not everyone agreed. There were two strands to the defence policy debate. Some analysts and policy-makers argued that conventional inter-state conflicts were less of a threat and the ADF should be shaped to deal with the sort of commitments that had become common in the first ten years of the new millennium – those requiring land force deployments. These commitments would require a larger Army. And, indeed, because Howard was known to have a 'soft spot' for the Army, there had been some developments in this area. Two infantry battalions were re-raised and more equipment purchased. The government committed itself to purchasing two large helicopter dock (LHD) ships that would enable the ADF to develop a substantial amphibious warfare capability, and enable them to better deploy and support troops around the region.

Conversely, other analysts argued that conventional conflicts remained a credible threat and stressed that Australia could not afford to fall behind in dealing with threats of this kind. This being so, greater investment in the RAN and RAAF was needed. In response, the Howard Government approved the purchase of three air warfare destroyers and 24 FA-18 Super Hornets to cover a capability gap that would not be filled until the delivery of the F-35 Joint Strike Fighter. Superimposed on these debates about defence policy was the question of how Australia should respond to the threat of terrorism at home and abroad. The commitments in Iraq and Afghanistan could be seen as a response to terrorism, but the government also introduced domestic measures that generally were undertaken by agencies other than the ADF.

As noted earlier, the Rudd Government withdrew Australian forces from Iraq but maintained the nation's commitment in Afghanistan. Rudd also persisted with the broad policy settings of the Howard Government when a new Defence White Paper was released in 2009.[14] This White Paper confirmed the focus on the region and conventional military threats. The rise of China was noted as an important feature of the new strategic environment. Without much explanation and few details, the government announced that the six Collins-class submarines should be replaced with 12 new submarines.

Despite the concerted efforts of NATO and the United States, the Afghanistan War dragged on. Australia's involvement was supported by Prime Minister Julia Gillard, who succeeded Kevin Rudd in mid 2010. Concern over the protracted nature of the war and the rise in Australian casualties led to parliamentary debate but the commitment continued after the election of the Coalition Government led by Tony Abbott in September 2013. The commitment formally ended in December 2014, although some forces remain. By then more than 25,000 Australian troops had served in Afghanistan and 41 had been killed. It had become Australia's longest war.

Fifteen years after INTERFET and the largest deployment of Australian personnel since the end of the Vietnam conflict in 1975, the ADF was on operations in areas near and far from Australia for a variety of reasons. They were supporting the US alliance, striking at international terrorism, restoring order in nearby countries, acting as peacekeepers and providing emergency relief after natural disasters. The challenge for contemporary policy-makers is to craft a new defence policy that draws on the vast experience gained from these 15 years of operations but not to be confined by it.

3

COMBAT READY?

PETER LEAHY

I entered the Royal Military College in 1971, just as the last of our troops were withdrawing from South Vietnam. After graduating from Duntroon in 1974 my career was predominantly one in an Army at peace, what some have called 'the long peace'. There was, of course, the occasional United Nations deployment but nothing serious happened unless we count football games against the 6th Battalion RAR. Towards the end of this long peace, deployments to Rwanda, Cambodia and Somalia were a foretaste of what was to come. A few Army thinkers were reading Robert Kaplan on *The Coming Anarchy* and Paul Kennedy on *The Troubled and Fractured Planet*. But not the 'Defence of Australia' White Paper adherents in the Federal Parliament, in the Department of Defence and in some parts of academia. They rejected forward defence or, to use the word that was at one time banned, 'expeditionary' operations. The Army was assigned the role of strategic goalkeeper against a mythical enemy that never turned up. Who can forget the Kamarians and the Musorians as the representatives of that mythical enemy? They were such obliging enemies. We used to be able to tow their homeland around Australia and position it wherever we wanted.

In the 'Army 21' review of the mid 1990s the Australian Army was thrown a bone and told that it needed to prepare to defeat an understrength enemy battalion somewhere in northern Australia. What was sad was that the Army was so desperate for a purpose that it accepted the challenge with glee and set about designing an Army to deal with low-level conflict and raids in the north of Australia. The conflict, the raids and the redesigned Army did not happen. Strategic guidance was off. I well recall a line from the 1994 White Paper that said the Australian Defence Force (ADF) would be structured for the defence of Australia other than at the margins. As a colonel contributing to the White Paper, I immediately asked how big was the margin. The reply was 15 per cent. This was nowhere near enough to ensure the Army was ready for what was to come.

After the change of government in 1997 this focus on continental defence began to change very subtly and strategic guidance began to shift to an offshore role for the Army. The change in guidance did not, however, permeate adequately through the system to result in meaningful and timely changes to the Army before East Timor appeared on the horizon. The task of managing combat readiness in an intense environment after 1999 was always going to be difficult. The Army was not in a fit shape to cope well with a new series of demands. Reflecting back on my career about the only thing that really happened in my first 25 years in the Army was that it got smaller. In 1974, after all training commitments under the *National Service Act 1964* were completed, the strength of the Army was around 30,000. In 1999 it was around 24,000. Currently the figure is around 30,000 with some modest increases expected in the nearer future.

The need for strategic guidance

Overall there was no strategic justification for the Army and, consequently, the Army struggled. As Michael O'Connor, the then Director of the Australian Defence Association remarked, 'An Army without a strategy and a strategy without an Army.' While the Army struggled during 'the long peace' it is interesting to look back and see that somehow the Army kept alive its focus and the ability to fight. I think it quite remarkable that an Army that had been at peace for so long was able to lead a coalition in 1999 and produce the results on the battlefield that it has achieved over the last decade and a half. We owe a lot to that generation of soldiers from the 1970s to the 1990s who kept the spirit of the Army alive. Their focus on training, the maintenance of standards and the Army ethos was selfless and generous. They were instrumental in maintaining the Army's sense of self-worth and competence so that a new generation of Australians could take the Army to war when asked, and make us proud.

Recently, when making comments on the performance of the Iraqi Army, I have had cause to consider again the constitute elements of combat power. Combat power is about training, equipment, doctrine, organisational structure and readiness. But the most important element of combat power is morale or the will to fight. Australians soldiers have shown a will to fight since 1999. No one has blinked and their performance has upheld the standards set by their predecessors. The Army may have languished operationally and pondered its strategic role but when called to serve the national interest it proved itself more than capable of discharging all of the demands placed upon it by government. But how ready and what were the risks?

Soldiers will, of course, do as they are directed. Governments need to note this principle and ensure that when they task the

Army they have provided the resources, the budget, the strategic guidance, the time and the support needed to complete the task. This was the problem of the principal period after 1999. What became a decade of frequently intense and competing global requirements presented the Army with a serious of difficult organisational challenges. The Army was asked to complete multiple, protracted global missions. Units and personnel were deployed to places that had not been the subject of detailed planning or forward preparation. On 10 September 2001, who would have imagined that the Australian Army might deploy to Afghanistan. Who had the maps? How would we get there? What language did they speak? Put simply: we weren't ready. Yet, just over a month later we had a Special Air Service Regiment (SASR) squadron on the battlefield.

Identifying and managing risk

An Army should expect that it will be directed to conduct combat operations. But it should also expect the right strategic guidance, equipment, training, joint support and sufficient personnel. The Australian Army was plainly ill prepared for the demands placed upon it after 1999. There was an inherent risk of failure. Inevitably, for an Army this means injury and death and, for a nation, defeat. What bothers me most is that the assessment of risk throughout this period fell fairly and squarely on the wellbeing of the troops we were sending into harm's way. Government was given options and could choose deployments. They were able to pursue Australia's national interests. But in large part the troops deployed on operations personally bore the brunt of the risk. This is the wrong place for risk. This is one of the most important lessons of our recent past. Both the ADF and the

Department of Defence need to find better ways of assessing and articulating strategic, operational and tactical risk, and handing those assessments fairly and squarely back to government. Army is perhaps the worst of the services in assessing and articulating risk. How else could we have not spoken out clearly and consistently about the difficulties in meeting the direction in successive White Papers that we deploy, sustain and rotate a brigade-sized force offshore and have a battalion ready for other operations?

Lessons from the East Timor intervention

The decision to deploy a large number of Australian personnel to East Timor involved some complex contingencies. If the Indonesians had decided to resist the arrival of an international force we would have been in real trouble. My own perspective on East Timor is that of the Chief of Staff at Headquarters, Australian Strategic Theatre (AST). What was probably the easiest thing we could have been asked to do theoretically, turned out to be most difficult practically. If we were going on an operation the Army couldn't have asked for a more straightforward task: proceed to East Timor, deal with a poorly organised militia and conduct a less-than-civil but not violently aggressive handover of the former Portuguese colony to international jurisdiction without provoking resistance from the resident, regular Indonesian military forces.

Geographically the mission couldn't have been closer to Australia. It was approved by the United Nations and there was solid international military and diplomatic support. Combat operations were limited and mercifully casualties were few. But our operations in East Timor showed up glaring deficiencies in both plans and provisions throughout the whole ADF. This was largely because strategic guidance had not placed proper emphasis on conducting an offshore operation. The principal strategic task upon which we were then focused was the defence of Australia not an expeditionary operation.

The list of deficiencies is long:

- headquarter structures were immature
- the three services were not well practised in working together
- logistics over-the-shore capabilities were limited
- strategic lift was seriously inadequate
- there wasn't enough protected mobility for the ground force
- we had extremely limited experience in managing and leading a coalition force
- the force was poorly equipped
- force preparedness and readiness were inadequate.

Plainly, there were many lessons to be learned and challenges to be met. East Timor was to provide an important agenda for reform and renewal over a number of years.

Combat readiness

The role of a Service Chief is to 'raise, train and sustain' their service as well as deliver combat ready forces to the Chief of the Defence Force. Combat readiness might be the ultimate aim and the end product of the military craft, and it was certainly the thing that has been most needed since 1999, but the routine business of the Army had to proceed as well.

Over the period that I served as a Service Chief (2002–08), the main organisational priorities included expansion of the

Special Forces, the implementation of the Hardened and Net-worked Army and, later, the introduction of the Enhanced Land Force program. All of these innovations took time and effort to implement. So, too, did the added recruiting and initial training effort required as the Army grew from a strength of 24,000 personnel in 2000 to its present size of around 30,000 personnel. Lots of things had to be managed and juggled. I challenge anyone to identify another organisation that could have coped better with an expansion of this size and nature while at the same time conduct global combat operations. But, of course, the overall focus of the Army was on major combat operations in Afghanistan and Iraq, and a few years later on Afghanistan and then Iraq. As well as commitments in the Middle East there were what we might now call 'routine operational events' underway elsewhere, including peacekeeping forces in Bougainville and the Solomon Islands, observing the military-led government in Fiji, participating in border protection duties, contributing to a broad range of humanitarian and disaster relief operations, handling evacuations from the Middle East, and being involved in the 'standard' range of United Nations deployments around the world and the Multinational Force of Observers (MFO) in the Sinai.

Readiness is all about having soldiers with the right equipment, the right individual and collective training, at the right place, at the right time. Achieving this state can be hellishly expensive and demanding for the organisation and the individual. An element of risk is unavoidable. The primary means of dealing with this risk is managing 'readiness notice'. Troops are held most ready for high-likelihood, high-consequence events. The degree of readiness can vary from as little as a few hours for the most likely and most dangerous threats, such as terrorist attacks, to many months or even years for forces less likely to be required for deployment. Holding forces at too high a readiness notice is a lazy method of management. It is wasteful on resources and wears troops out. Similarly troops kept at too low a readiness notice may conserve resources but asking them to expedite their readiness notice and deploy early places them at an unacceptable risk of mission failure.

As I reflect on the period from 1999 to 2015, most prominent is the duration and consistency of the demand for combat forces. The Army has just released an internet-based video program on Afghanistan called, 'The Longest War'. The longest war. That says something noteworthy when we consider the previous century and its protracted conflicts. Multiple deployments to multiple theatres take a toll on individuals and their families. So one significant aspect of managing combat readiness over the last 15 years is that there has been little respite. Much has been asked of our soldiers and their families. As Chief of Army I felt an enormous amount of pride and gratitude for their resolve, determination and commitment.

I need to emphasise one particular point regarding East Timor: the need for the INTERFET intervention developed quickly and, unlike many other United Nations deployments, positive international consensus and Security Council approval were rapidly forthcoming. This meant we had to move quickly to assemble an Australian force but also to develop a workable international coalition. It is simply remarkable that Lieutenant General Frank Hickling, as Chief of Army, was able to adjust the readiness notice for key Army units unilaterally in early 1999. But he did, and his decision was a key element in ensuring that the Army was able to deploy throughout August 1999 to conduct evacuation operations and then, in late September, deploy a main force after the Indonesian military was ordered to withdraw.

Readiness is a complicated notion. The first thing to recognise is that service chiefs neither hold nor operate all the levers.

Over the period under review, as the ADF became increasingly joint and whole of government in nature, many agencies were obliged to come together at the one time and place to deliver combat readiness. Thus, much of the work to achieving and managing readiness was at the strategic and budgetary level.

Designing the force

Decisions to commit forces to an operation are taken always at the political level. These decisions, while conscious of the need to deploy force, are not always attentive to the appropriateness and availability of the force. This was particularly so in the context of Australia's involvement in Afghanistan and Iraq.

Designing suitable forces took a lot of negotiation, manoeuvring and management with our main coalition partners. In the case of Afghanistan in 2001, there was really no choice other than to send the SASR. This was also the case in March 2003 with respect to a deployment to Iraq. They were our most ready and appropriate forces. Beyond these initial contributions there was an enormous amount of work required to determine the task to be undertaken and then to design a suitable force. To reiterate a previous point, change was not restricted to 1999. The force deployed to Al Mutannah in Iraq in 2005 was simply a reflection of the force that was available. It is no secret that the United States would have preferred that Australia was able to offer a more powerful, versatile, task-oriented and combat-focused force. The force that eventually deployed was the product of the available forces, their capability and our assessment of the risk. The Army was concerned about their lack of armoured-protected mobility and firepower to be involved in some of the more kinetic tasks that might have eventuated. This influenced both their tasking and the areas to which they were deployed. The fact that we created a combined arms group (drawn from 52 different Army units) rather than deploy an established unit is a telling comment on the anachronistic character of our regimental and corps structures.

Once the tasks were settled and the requirements determined, the Australian force had to be regrouped and specially prepared. In the early days we were not good at this. Things were often rushed and haphazard. In essence, forces were going 'ready or not'. It was only in later deployments that we developed a system that suitably prepared and assessed the force before it was formally handed over to Joint Operations Command. Lieutenant General Hickling deserves much praise for his foresight in developing the combat training system that was the foundation of mission rehearsal and assessment processes and determined whether a force was indeed ready for deployment. Also creditable was the work done by a number of Army commands to ensure that forces were ready and capable. Eventually little effort was spared in focusing the equipping and training pipelines on the needs of a deploying force.

Equipping the force

One of my big concerns as Chief of Army was equipping the force with the best and most modern equipment. It was a strange feeling after decades of constrained budgets to realise that money was no object. Prime Minister John Howard actually said to me one day, 'Peter, nothing but the best for my troops.' I took the Prime Minister at his word and made the most of his goodwill. In the early part of the new millennium the defence procurement system was unable to cope with the increasing demands of readiness. It was not sufficiently responsive in meeting the rapidly changing requirements and was too slow in delivering what was needed. In sum, peacetime procurement processes were totally inappropriate. It was only with the introduction of the rapid acquisition process that we began to equip deployed forces with the right equipment in a timely manner.

The first SAS forces deployed into Afghanistan during October 2001 reported the presence of armoured vehicles on the battlefield and requested modern, long-range anti-armour weapons. The Army asked the Defence Materiel Organisation to meet the need and was told there was a trial underway. The trial had been going on for many years, more than a decade by my reckoning, and it was designed to select a bunker-busting weapon. It is important to remember that the strategic guidance of the time did not comprehend the presence of armoured vehicles as part of the 'Defence of Australia' scenario. There would be small raids on the continent or an offshore island and little more. The Army did not need weapons to combat tanks.

After a considerable struggle, the Javelin anti-armour weapon was eventually acquired and deployed with the SASR element to Iraq in March 2003. Plainly, the provision of a vital battlefield asset was too slow. There were many other examples of this tardiness. They included the delivery of cold weather gear, body armour, communications equipment, armoured protected mobility, weapons, and so on. There were times when I wondered whether some elements in the Department of Defence actually realised we had soldiers in combat. How dare we interrupt their standard routines and normal processes?

At least there was a happy ending to the Javelin story. I visited the SAS in late April 2003 after they had captured Al Asad airbase in Western Iraq. It was there that I heard the story of how the Javelin system had been used in battle. The SAS member who briefed me spoke with great pride about how he had used the weapon to destroy an attacking enemy force. The brief concluded with two observations: first, the nature of the battlefield changed substantially that day; second, the enemy never returned to the area. This is the kind of combat impact you want: troops who are able to outmatch the enemy decisively. But the Army should not have to struggle against bureaucratic complexity and organisational inertia to get the right weapon onto the battlefield in a timely manner.

Plainly, some things did not go so well. During one of my visits to the Al Mutannah Task Group in 2005, the Commanding Officer, Roger Noble said something that still bothers me. He remarked that I was of 'little use to him'. I am sure that he meant officers operating at strategic level in Canberra or, at least, I hope he did. In essence, we were giving him inadequate guidance on the objectives to be achieved and insufficient advice on how he might achieve them. I think he was right.

In many ways, this deployment and others like it were 'set and forget' missions. The mere fact of deploying forces was the achievement of the political aim. What they did while deployed was not made the subject of enough thought. Commanders were left to cope with constant changes to the operational environment without the strategic guidance they all required and which some sought. The same criticism can be applied to operations following our return to Afghanistan. At least there we recognised the changing nature of the mission and adjusted both the nature of the name and its composition. They were thereafter referred to as the Reconstruction Task Force, Mentoring and Reconstruction Task Force, Mentoring and Liaison Units, and so on.

Doctrine

Another area where commanders were left isolated was in the development of doctrine. In Afghanistan things gradually morphed into a counter-insurgency campaign. Commanders on the ground saw the need to support the local population and set about doing so. But the available doctrine was old and stale. The Army's efforts to revitalise the doctrine were slow and inadequate. This did not help combat readiness.

Around about 2003 I found myself self-consciously telling those who would listen that the Army was at war. We were no longer a peacetime force waiting for something to happen; it was happening and we were deploying substantial combat forces. It was an important internal message that I hoped would alter the mood within the Army and start to change individual outlooks. With so many operations and missions underway we were on a war footing. Deployments and not training were driving the Army. We were taking casualties and our soldiers were experiencing multiple deployments. They needed to be in a state of mind that prepared them for this reality. The 'I'm an Australian Soldier Campaign' made a significant and lasting contribution to steeling our soldiers to the new realities of the 21st century and an Army on continuous operations. It was also an important external message, as we needed the continuing support of the public. The diggers were proud of what they were doing and deserved recognition and support from all Australians.

Another aspect of readiness worth noting is the duration of deployments. We had decided early in the millennium that, because of the likely intensity of operations, six months was a reasonable time for each deployment. Clearly the longer you spend on operations the fewer troops required. As pressure came on from other quarters an immediate way of raising readiness was to extend the duration of the tour. This took some careful management and explanation.

Ready yet?

The Australian Army has certainly been through an era of intense operational demand over the last 15 years. Deployments have been global and continuous. They have varied greatly in nature and intensity. Overall they have been handled well and revealed the Army's capacity for innovation and acceptance of renewal. The Australian Army has been able to provide government with realistic options and combat ready forces. Risk has been managed but has become too focused on the soldiers rather than where it should reside – with government. This is particularly concerning because there is no foreseeable end to the requirement for ready, deployable and capable forces in Australia's nearer area of influence or in the Middle East. We remain in Afghanistan and Iraq, and have become militarily active into Syria, even as national security deteriorates across much of the globe.

Robert Kaplan in *The Coming Anarchy* and Paul Kennedy in *The Troubled and Fractured Planet* were right about the distressed nature of our world. There is more work to be done if the majority of the world's people are to enjoy peace and prosperity. It is clear that Australia will have a share in that work. Are we ready? The lesson of the last 15 years is that we aren't – yet.

PART 2: VIEWS FROM THE OTHER SIDE OF THE HILL

4

LESSONS FROM EAST TIMOR

CRAIG STOCKINGS

In my experience the capacity for true, honest and objective self-reflection is a rare gift, and not a very common human trait. To be self-critical, in the sense of self-analysis rather than self-censure, is demanding. It requires an uncommon degree of internal confidence, resilience and detachment. It can certainly cause pain on an intellectual, psychological and even emotional level. Not one in ten students that come to me in a university context after failing an assessment task, for example, are able to point to themselves as the primary cause. It is far easier to identify explanations that do not involve lack of internal personal drive, effort or ability. Continuing this theme, and if theories of group behaviour are any guide, then what is hard for an individual is harder still for an organisation. Here the issue is compounded by factors such as institutional cultures, aspirations, patronage networks, traditions and, for that matter, simple inertia.

Such considerations are important when considering the capacity of organisations to learn from their experiences – in this case, how the Army learns lessons from operations. One can see the temptations from *within* the system, for example, of using 'lessons' to affirm existing policy agendas or as a basis for arguing for additional resources. On the other hand, it might be much more difficult, on an institutional cultural level, to draw lessons that point to *reductions* in force levels or to the unsuitability of certain capabilities or even weapon systems. This is not to suggest for one moment that the Army has not made honest and extensive efforts at lesson-learning – certainly from the intervention in East Timor onwards – but rather that conclusions about the system, coming from *within* the system, will always be difficult, fraught, and fundamentally different from observations made from the outside looking in.

A new perspective on a turning point

In identifying some of the ways that external agencies, in this instance university-driven research, can feed into and perhaps add value to the military 'lessons-learned' process, I will draw examples from the International Force for East Timor (INTER-FET) deployment. The reason for this approach is straight-forward: I am leading a research team that has recently begun a three-year project with INTERFET at its centre. In any case, it is a useful case study not only because the Army instituted a lessons-learned policy as one of the outcomes it wanted to derive from the deployment but also because sufficient time and space now exists for outsiders to access operational data, make objective observations, and come to reliable conclusions with confidence. Moreover, the mission was a success – a success that, in many ways, masked problems, hid deficiencies and obscured failures. Observers are now aware of weaknesses that have *not* been consistently re-tested in subsequent operations when Australia has been embedded within larger coalition logistics and command infrastructures.

Given editorial constraints, and noting that INTERFET was such a complex undertaking that proved to be a watershed moment for the post-Cold War Australian Army, observations will be limited to the first week of the deployment, 20 to 27 September 1999. Just as profitably, lessons learned from the pre-deployment phase or, for that matter, any other period from October 1999 to late February 2000 could have been examined, but late September 1999 has been chosen because the benefits of the approach are readily apparent in this period. One of the most significant advantages for an observer in my position, looking back in a forensic manner at an operation that happened more than a decade ago, is the ability to survey, compare and synthesise a wide range of material not available to commanders and internal analysts who were under the pressures of immediacy and time, quite apart from the essential compartmentalisation of the organisation precluding an overall view of what occurred and why. I am also free of institutional constraints and political pressures militating against a candid and critical appreciation of the Army's performance. There is much to be said for an outsider's perspective, something I will demonstrate with respect to the example and themes I have described.

Movement command and communication

The landings at Dili, the capital of East Timor on 20–21 September 1999, and the consolidation that followed, revealed some serious command and control challenges for the ADF. One of the most controversial involved the air bridge from Darwin and Townsville into Comoro Airfield on the outskirts of the East Timorese capital. For a range of quite valid and understandable operational imperatives, the senior Australian commanders,

Major General Peter Cosgrove of INTERFET and Brigadier Mark Evans of 3 Brigade, sought to flood Dili with combat troops as quickly as possible. The plan was to get the 2nd Battalion RAR on the ground as a priority, and RAAF C-130 Hercules transport aircraft load lists and sorties were planned with this in mind. Yet the limited capacity of airport and the number of available aircraft led to conflicting priorities. Defence Headquarters, for example, again for outwardly sensible strategic and political reasons, wanted to insert a media element and United Nations Mission to East Timor (UNAMET) assets back into Dili as soon as possible. Likewise, Headquarters INTERFET wanted its Joint Support Unit (JSU) on the ground as soon as practicable. Thus, of the limited airframes scheduled for the first day of the lodgement, six were off-loaded with 3 Brigade designated stores and equipment and replaced with alternate loads. As a result the second half of 2 RAR, and 3 Brigade's logistic tail, were shifted backwards in the queue. This re-tasking and re-sequencing, literally conducted as the operation was launching, was done without reference to Headquarters 3 Brigade, the organisation responsible for the initial operational outcome.[1]

The important question, however, is not whether the Media Support Unit and 40 accredited journalists ought to have been landed before the arrival of 2 RAR was complete, or even if it was appropriate for such a unit with personnel not appropriately trained or prepared for operational deployment – and for that matter largely non-compliant with readiness and even medical requirements – to be in such a situation at such a time.[2] The issue is not even – though under different circumstances it might have been – how much operational risk was accepted in that for the first crucial 24 hours of the deployment combat power equated to only two infantry companies and two armed personnel carriers (APCs), when available. The question, rather, is what does such friction say about the complexity and effectiveness of command and control at such a crucial point? What did this issue reveal of chains of authority and communication? It strikes me that the reduction to airframes available to the 3 Brigade lodgements would have been more acceptable (given that contingencies always arise), providing the formation most effected was advised with sufficient notice to amend its plans. A failure to even notify the units relying on those aircraft for support in what was a hot and to some degree hostile operational environment, however, placed them at undue risk and had, to some degree, at least the potential to imperil the mission. Moreover, such requirements as a media presence in the first sorties must have been known, or at least forecast, by some responsible agency. How well then were those chains of higher command and communication functioning? How unfettered was the flow of information?[3]

Taking a step back, one of the larger problems made glaringly obvious in the first few days of the deployment, and one underpinning the difficulties associated with sequences of arrival in Dili, was the 'movements nightmare' from Darwin.[4] Agencies involved in providing movements support to the deploying force included the Joint Movements Group, Headquarters Northern Command (NORCOM), Joint Logistics Unit (JLU) North, and to an extent 1 Brigade, which was providing accommodation and some administrative support. Everyone was working at a very high rate of effort, but no single organisation appeared to exercise command/control over all these agencies, denying 3 Brigade, for example, a single point of contact where problem solving or issue clarification was required.[5]

Nor did the problems stop after initial sorties had landed at Comoro Airfield. In fact, competing priorities largely collapsed movement co-ordination in the first few days. It took up to a week to lodge sufficient vehicles and stocks in theatre. There were simply not enough movement assets, staff or handlers at ports and airports to feed through all that was required. During the initial period of build-up, one particular point of weakness was the extremely limited Army terminal capability.[6] The 18 staff on hand were overtasked. There was neither redundancy nor ability to rotate such people out of theatre. Back in Darwin there were instances where personnel consignments were waiting to load but the next available deployment aircraft was configured for cargo; the movements organisation then loaded for cargo rather than reconfigure for personnel, and further compromised the sequence of delivery. In another example a senior air trafficker arrived in Dili without communications equipment (due primarily to chaos in Darwin over movements) and began directing aircraft using Indonesian radios.[7] This and other workarounds succeeded but these effective innovations and successful improvisations cannot be allowed to mask obvious organisational weaknesses.

To be fair on the movements organisation, however, the absence of any real or effective plan to co-ordinate the movements effort and actions was a result of the inability of the highest levels of the ADF to decide upon, or more accurately to release, the details of the plan to be supported. These officers were stifled by a deliberately restricted trickle of information from government, and perhaps an overly heightened perception of the need for secrecy, even as the deployment grew close. Although my research is at an early stage and any assertions ought to be guarded, I have interviewed a sufficient number of commanding officers and reviewed enough documents from the period to contend with confidence that the 'big picture', as well as parts of the 'little picture', were far from clear to many of the men and women charged with implementing the 'plan'. In this instance it is fair to say that movements systems do not determine priorities; these are set by operations planning staff (at whatever level they are involved) and are only then implemented by movements agencies. If the operational planners could not discern or disseminate courses of action with appropriate lead times, or enunciate the plan at hand, the movements system could hardly excel at implementing their instructions. As with any logistic function, if demands cannot be articulated, the system cannot be expected to perform.[8]

Logistics on the run

Nonetheless, the initial lodgement of forces into Dili heralded a succession of logistic difficulties destined to plague the entire INTERFET deployment. Not unlike the movements conundrum, there were certainly deep and wide-ranging issues associated with logistics management. Many of the problems encountered were associated with compressed pre-deployment planning and compartmentalisation of information that set the scene for future difficulties. Editorial constraints do not allow me to digress but I need to mention that the morphing of Operation Spitfire into Operation Warden/Stabilise at the eleventh hour revealed serious logistic weaknesses. A deployment on 'light scales' always made more sense in the context of a services-protected/services-assisted evacuation type of operation than it did for a longer-term lodgement.[9]

In any case, the sustainment plan devised by 3 Brigade Administrative Support Battalion (3 BASB) had been largely abandoned by the late morning of 20 September. An aircraft with water and food was delayed and trucks that were to distribute water failed to arrive. Also delayed were medical personnel and supplies, even as the security situation remained uncertain. These challenges were only partially surmounted by the unplanned, fortuitous commandeering of a fleet of UNAMET Land Rover Discovery vehicles left behind at the United Nations compound in Dili. Contingency water stocks were rapidly consumed and logisticians were forced to seek bottled water from HMAS *Success*. Water concerns were alleviated only temporarily with the arrival of 3 RAR on 21 September in HMAS *Jervis Bay*, which was carrying 500 more cartons of bottled water.[10] As a result of such confusion and priorities, 3 BASB, the key logistics unit in Dili in the first few days, felt its relative priority for deployment had eroded. This unit's B vehicles were complete on the ground in East Timor at the same time as those belonging to 10 Force Support Battalion (10 FSB). Prioritisation of competing needs seemed, in many ways, beyond comprehensive. The process for determining what was really urgent was plainly broken.[11]

Once the leading INTERFET elements were firmly on the ground (22 September), a week of important consolidation work followed in Dili. Here too, however, some of the difficulties that had emerged during the initial landings not only carried over to the consolidation phase but, in some cases, the problems multiplied. In terms of command and control, the lack of deployed fixed-wing Command and Control (C2) was felt. The absence of an Aviation Task Force Headquarters hindered the planning and synchronisation of aviation subunit activities during major air operations as well.[12] The lack of peacetime training exercises between key force elements quickly emerged as a point of difficulty in terms of co-ordination and collaboration. The Military Information Support Contingent, based largely on the First Intelligence Company, described its interaction with intelligence staff on HQ INTERFET as 'rather less successful' than it might have been.[13] Meanwhile, at the 'front', 3 RAR complained about repeated instances of INTERFET contingents, particularly Special Force elements, moving through its area of operations

(AO) without the battalion's knowledge or permission. Given the fluid and dangerous environment in Dili at the time this was a potentially dangerous practice. Yet, it was an issue that raised its head many times between 3 Brigade and Response Force in the ensuing weeks.[14] Simultaneously, multinational issues began to emerge in the apparent void of ADF doctrine concerning the conduct of such operations. Different C2 definitions with other nations were an early issue for 3 Brigade, for example, particularly with the British contingent.[15]

Logistics remained an area of concern even after the initial lodgement proved, in Headquarters INTERFET's words, 'somewhat different to the plan.'[16] The consequences of coalition leadership, the scale of support arrangements required in an austere theatre, and the practical problems of maintaining a substantial line of communication from Australia proved to be challenges well beyond routine ADF logistic capabilities. Logistics structures were fluid and what can only be described as tenuous. A newly raised Force Logistics Support Group (FLSG), based largely around 10 FSB, struggled to establish itself by the end of September and to relieve a beleaguered 3 BASB, which had to this point provided logistics support not only for 3 Brigade (for which it had been designed) but also to the larger INTERFET force. Meanwhile, an ad hoc Force Support Group (FSG) in Darwin, based on 9 FSB (a distribution not an acquisition organisation), again raised to support the very different requirements of 'Operation Spitfire', struggled mightily to funnel supplies into Dili with overworked staff who were mostly unqualified on the information systems being used for the tasks at hand.

Once more, command and control issues emerged. The theatre-level Logistics Component Commander at Headquarters Australian Theatre (HQAST) was responsible for managing the supply chain into Dili, leaving Support Command–Australia responsible for strategic materiel acquisition and management, including the supply chain within Australia. Yet the appointment of a Logistics Component Commander at HQAST at the operational level in Australia also required logistics relationships to be defined and refined as the operation unfolded. Both the Force Logistics Support Group (the organisation which eventually took over force-level logistics from 3 BASB in Timor and whose commander was appointed the INTERFET Logistic Component Commander) and AST Logistics Component Commander represented new organisations attempting to operate under arrangements that had not been practiced previously – quite apart from the fact that there were not enough qualified staff on hand. LSF officers, for example, were stripped to meet responsibilities of the AST Logistic Component Commander. Indeed, logistics officers were actually loaned from Staff College to help draft the Commander's logistics operation orders.[17]

The logistics task was no easier for the units chosen to make the dangerously ad hoc and scrambling system work. Four days after the initial lodgement, 10 FSB – the key FLSG unit and a vital link in the logistic chain (yet a 3 Brigade-centric unit now asked to provide a force-level capability) – was still in Townsville as the Joint Movements Office was unable to secure commercial transport for its vehicles and stocks. This situation was only resolved through personal contacts and as a consequence of the coincidental and fortuitous discovery of Norwegian freighters in waters off North Queensland. These ships were hastily chartered. Meanwhile, 10 FSB struggled to build-up the required level of stocks for deployment. It was apparent that successive years of Support Command cost cutting had forced down stock levels, relying upon a 'just-in-time' approach, in order to realise financial savings for the taxpayer. The quest for long-term savings had produced a series of deficiencies that were not easily rectified.

10 FSB sought guidance from HQ LSF on the deployed dependency, guidance that was never forthcoming. The unit threatened to deploy without stocks and to in-load its complete requirement. In the absence of viable alternatives, HQ LSF could do nothing but acquiesce.[18]

Even after the lead elements of 10 FSB and HQ FLSG began arriving in Dili (two days after the INTERFET postal detachment) a series of new problems were replacing those that had been resolved. Command relationships remained cumbersome between the new Headquarters FLSG and the logisticians on Headquarters INTERFET.[19] 10 FSB soldiers could not get ballistic vests or Kevlar helmets because the unit was apparently 'not entitled' to the items.[20] Logistics systems themselves were also broken, particularly information management systems. Significantly, this sad fact had been known for years. The Cargo Visibility System (CVS) was considered a hindrance not a help and was often not used when demand was at its highest. In any case it relied on barcodes but not all points along the supply chain had barcode reading equipment.[21] Nor were CVS operators trained adequately. There were also difficulties with the Standard Defence Supply System, the primary means by which units in East Timor requested most items. The system was not designed to be taken overseas and was not used uniformly across the ADF. Units were not confident in using the system. Demand satisfaction measures were ignored.[22] Meanwhile, combat troops dealt with the realities of a creaky logistics system that could not, for example, resupply 3 RAR's medics with medical supplies to meet initial demand. Soldiers ransacked abandoned Indonesian Army (TNI) barracks for bandages, picked over the ruins of clinics that had previously been operated by aid agencies, and sourced supplies from Dili General Hospital.[23] Elsewhere, the aviation group soon realised the RAAF could not provide enough fuel, leaving naval assets to fill the gap, despite obvious inadequacies in the ability of the Navy's vessels to transport bulk liquid ship-to-shore.[24] The list of difficulties and deficiencies could go on – and on.

Getting the better of the situation

Sustainment was finally achieved at the end of the first week in East Timor by pushing through supply of the highest priority items, such as food, water, and ammunition, and by drawing on allied and commercial logistics support and improvised arrangements (such as loading 11,000-litre Mack fuel tankers into LCM-8s for the ship-to-shore fuel transfer). The processes, as they were, relied on the good judgement of operational and logistic commanders. Accolades were well deserved by these hard-working, flexible and professional individuals. But the situation should never have relied upon them as individuals. Rather, reliance on tried-and-tested systems ought to have prevailed and ensured success. This did not happen. Of course, logistic difficulties would have become a good deal worse if a plane crash had put Comoro Airfield out of action, if HMA ships *Tobruk* or *Jervis Bay* had broken down, or if the force had met armed resistance. The latter would have led to a tragedy given that stocks of formation level ammunition did not arrive in theatre until six days after the initial lodgement.[25]

Further, when considering logistics problems it should also be kept in mind that East Timor was as easy as it can get, and will ever get, in terms of a large Australian deployment supported by an Australian supply chain. It was close to Australia, the territory in which Australian forces operated was small, there was no large-scale manoeuvring of forces, there were no high-level combat demands nor was there any real enemy interference. Certainly, East Timor had its distinct challenges. There was little infrastructure in the host nation as a consequence of the Indonesian Army's 'scorched earth' policy. The geography was less than ideal with rugged central mountains, poor roads that washed out in wet season, few beaches suitable for over-the-shore operations, one deep port at Dili, and only three usable airfields. Yet, as author Bob Breen and others have pointed out, many of the problems that surfaced in East Timor had been identified on earlier deployments, such as Operation Lagoon in Bougainville in 1994. Here, too, logistics elements were excluded from planning and given minimum time to mount a multinational operation. During Operation Bel Isi II in Bougainville during 1998–2003 and Operation Solace in Somalia 1993 the logistics system had been reported as slow, inefficient and unable to deliver priority supplies (like vehicle parts) as fast as were needed. Somalia also showed the need for larger bulk liquid storage and movements capacity, paucity of stockholdings and inadequate cargo visibly. Problems and mistakes are one thing, repeating them is quite another.[26]

Just as surely as one might readily identify logistic and higher command difficulties in the early INTERFET deployment, so too there were many points of operational and tactical friction. As noted, the absence of big picture information or context at the lowest level left many combat troops in a vacuum, with little more than rules of engagement by way on an indication of what to expect on arrival. The risk here was that many were geared up and prepared to face serious opposition on arrival. In some cases early 2 RAR platoons deployed from C-130s, and 3 RAR platoons deployed as the ramps went down from *Jervis Bay* and their LCHs. These units deployed a tactical posture – possibly the opposite of the image of calmness and composure that ought to have been portrayed. Tactical operations began in a tense environment with many Indonesian soldiers and militiamen embarked in civilian vehicles, making the situation more tense with throat-cutting gestures. There was also a lack of forethought about the handling of detainees. Inadequate processes and ill-suited facilities proved frustrating.[27]

Information black spots

In a similar manner, the all-important intelligence battle got off to what can only be called a rather shaky start. The INTEFET field intelligence capability discovered it did not have its own processing and analysis capability. Nor did it have an internal communications or even an intra-detachment communications (such as 'Pintail') capability. There was no redundancy or spare capacity in computers and cameras (digital and video), and no night vision equipment. Perhaps more prosaically, field intelligence operators struggled to secure for themselves Kevlar helmets, flak jackets, and even Camelback water packs.[28] INTERFET's counter-intelligence capability deployed without any counter-intelligence 'estimate' with which to shape its operations, and nor does it appear to have asked for one. This lack of a starting point was perhaps the beginning of an explanation of what appeared to be a general weakness in INTERFET's general counter-intelligence effort.[29]

Communications, too, were a clear point of initial operational weakness. In the early days, it was apparent that 1 JSU could not easily support INTERFET requirements and various workarounds had to be used. These ad hoc measures included use of telephone data transfers and Joint Command Support System (JCSS) messaging. Only by mid November 1999, and after considerable effort, was connectivity through 1 JSU considered as generally good. Meanwhile, tactical Navy–Army communications were not always compatible since some RAN units were not fitted with Army Wagtail radios.[30] In the air, Black Hawk communications were erratic as well. Helicopter high frequency communications were unobtainable across most of the island and ground units were regularly unable to achieve VHF communications with Black Hawks until they were very close.[31] Perhaps the most serious communications failure during the early part of the operation was the inability of HQ INTERFET to receive some types of highly classified information directly. This necessitated the daily transfer of personnel to HMAS *Success* to receive intelligence briefs.[32]

None of these issues should be seen as purely technological shortcomings. I refer once more here, for example, to the passage of information and the reading-in of tactical units into the larger operational picture. One rather tense set of experiences at some 2 RAR roadblocks on the night of 21 September may well have been avoided had someone told the battalion of the approach of large numbers of Indonesian territorials intending to pass through its position.[33] Even back in Australia, 5/7 RAR felt its planning for a deployment to East Timor was severely hampered throughout September by a lack of direction from higher headquarters. Access to classified information was denied to the battalion, despite knowledge of various plans and contingencies that might have involved the unit.

Language barriers

Difficulties with the early engagement of the human or humanitarian situation in East Timor were perhaps another problematic operational aspect of the deployment. In the first instance many units indicated that their ability to engage and gain the confidence of the local community and refugees was initially difficult due to the lack of Tetum language proficiency and East Timorese cultural awareness. This problem was further compounded by a lack of extra-unit linguistic support at the appropriate level, and the lack of English-speaking Timorese who could be employed as interpreters.[34] 3 RAR certainly lamented that it never had sufficient numbers of interpreters to go beyond the one-per-company level (which was the best case), despite the fact that platoons and sections were required to operate regularly on an independent basis. The unit was fortunate enough to possess two soldiers who spoke Portuguese from within its own ranks, which helped the situation immeasurably. The unit felt the conduct of its operations would have been all the more difficult had this not been the case.[35]

Beyond the language barrier it is fair to suggest that neither Deployable Joint Force Headquarters (DJFHQ) nor 3 Brigade were well structured to conduct humanitarian operations, despite this requirement being made clear in the INTERFET mandate provided by the United Nations. There was only one officer within Headquarters 3 Brigade tasked for civil–military and humanitarian operations, for example, and the default use of artillerymen for humanitarian support was always a dangerous premise. There is no Civil–Military Affairs Unit on the brigade order of battle, which seems like a major flaw in the prosecution of peace support operations.[36] American support in this area would eventually be forthcoming but it took time to arrive and become effective. It is worth noting that the British contingent later grumbled that, 'The humanitarian line of operation was a notable omission from what constituted the INTERFET campaign plan at the commencement of the deployment ... the ADF had little or no experience of the utility and requirement for humanitarian operations.'[37]

Insight from analysis

Overall, what might be said of the sample of problems and difficulties outlined of the last week in September 1999 in East Timor? The purpose here is not so much to delve into lessons learned from this period in any significant manner, due to space constraints and an awareness that some of the issues raised have been discussed at length and addressed by the Army, while others, perhaps, have never received the attention they deserve. The main purpose is to provide some insight into what might be accomplished by the application of *external* research and analysis to *internal* Army issues (such as lessons learned) by informed and disinterested observers. With appropriate access to records, space and time plainly much more could be done. With research methodologies, connections and resources not available to the Army with which to examine data, new opportunities and fresh avenues of investigation are opened. In this case, for example, but might include not only data from the other services and government departments but international military partners and organisations like the United Nations, Red Cross and even the Falantil (the military wing of the main East Timorese political party, Fretilin) and the National Council of East Timorese Resistance (CNRT).

The bottom line is that there is capability available that *cannot* come from within the system. And this is not an East Timor issue – it is equally true of any and all operations and activities the Army might chose to name. The central point here is what was flagged at the beginning: that the limitations of an organisation reflecting on itself from the inside preclude the depth, width and possibilities open when standing on the outside, looking in.

5

ISLANDER PERSPECTIVES: BOUGAINVILLE AND THE SOLOMON ISLANDS

REUBEN BOWD

Over the past two decades the Australian Government has tried to contribute positively to the internal stability of several Pacific Island states that have endured civil and domestic unrest. How has Australia's contribution been viewed from 'the other side of the hill' and how effective has Australian assistance been? This chapter considers these questions from the Islander perspective of the Australian Army's participation in Operation Bel Isi II[1] (the Australian Defence Force (ADF) contribution to the Peace Monitoring Group (PMG) on Bougainville) and Operation Anode' (the ADF's contribution to the Regional Assistance Mission to Solomon Islands (RAMSI, also known as Operation Helpem Fren[2]). Although these deployments were mounted and sustained predominantly by the Australian Army, the Royal Australian Navy (RAN), the Royal Australian Air Force (RAAF) and a number of other government organisations, such as the Department of Foreign Affairs and Trade, AusAid and the Australian Federal Police (AFP), made critical contributions. These were also military and, in the case of RAMSI, police contributions from a number of Pacific states. Although these organisations had different remits and operating procedures, their impact needs to be assessed collectively.

The people

The people on that other side of the hill are Melanesians. They inhabit the Solomon's Archipelago – a double chain of seven large and numerous small islands that extend for about 1400 kilometres and have a land area of 37,500 square kilometres.[3] The population of Bougainville is 249,358[4]; the Solomon Islands has a population of 515,870.[5] The Islander societies here consist of a loose association of fragmented and culturally diverse clans and tribes with deep-seated rivalry, tribal violence and territorial warfare. Until the recent development of Melanesian Pidgin, they had no common means of communication – there are around 100 languages spoken in the archipelago,[6] and many more dialects, that are local and not commonly understood.

Unlike other areas of the Pacific, the people do not generally recognise hereditary chiefs or rulers but are, instead, influenced by 'Big Men' who compete to acquire and maintain their influence and are often motivated to do so through self-interest and the promise of personal gain. The people are yet to embrace fully the Western concept of nationhood. Instead, they identify themselves with a language group, clan or religion. This 'Wantok' culture is fundamentally inconsistent with nation building because it serves to reinforce traditional rivalries, jealousies and long-established distrust. These long-standing tensions provide the necessary context to Australian involvement. It was the deep-seated nature of the conflict that required a nuanced and creative

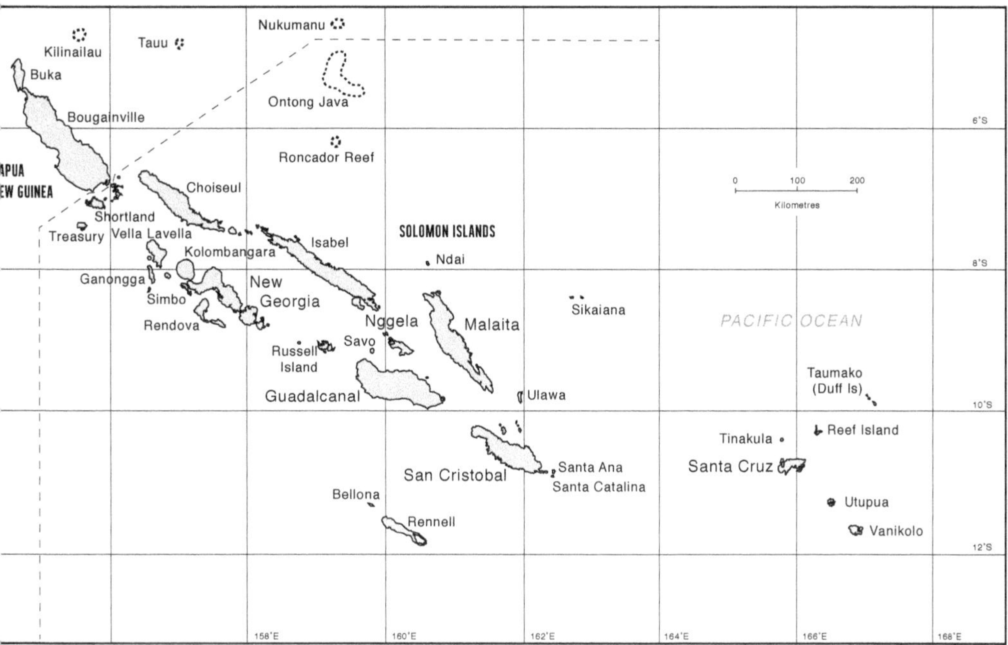

THE SOLOMONS ARCHIPELAGO

response from nations seeking to provide the conditions for a permanent peace.

It is, of course, an unfortunate accident of history, politics and geography that the Solomons' Archipelago was divided between the nations of Papua New Guinea (PNG) – which incorporates the North Solomons' Province of Bougainville, now the Autonomous Region of Bougainville – and the Solomon Islands. This has contributed to unrest and tension, especially because the 'dark-skinned' people of Bougainville and Buka share a closer cultural affiliation with the Solomon Islanders than they do with the 'red-skinned' people of PNG.[7] The troubles that have beset the archipelago are long standing highly complex and multi-faceted in origin. Bougainville's nine-year civil war was fuelled by competing interests over the copper mine at Panguna. It is estimated that the conflict directly and indirectly claimed the lives of over 10 per cent of the Bougainville's population.[8] In the Solomon Islands, social divisions, corruption and poor governance led to an armed coup in June 2000. The coup was followed by a low-level civil war driven by ethnic-based violence, particularly between the inhabitants of the large neighbouring islands of Guadalcanal and Malaita.

Operation Bel Isi II
(1 May 1998 to 30 June 2003)

The PMG succeeded the New Zealand-led Truce Monitoring Group (TMG) that had deployed to Bougainville on 6 December 1997 to observe the Burnham Truce signed on 10 October 1997. The truce promoted an immediate return to normality on Bougainville, including a lifting of the blockade that had been imposed by PNG. The TMG's mandate was set out in an agreement between New Zealand, Papua New Guinea, Australia, Fiji and Vanuatu concerning the neutral TMG for Bougainville on 15 December 1997 (the TMG agreement).[9] The ADF's contribution to the TMG was known as Operation Bel Isi I.

The TMG transitioned to the PMG on 1 May 1998 after the key disputants signed the Lincoln Agreement on 23 January 1998. The Lincoln Agreement provided 'a permanent and irrevocable ceasefire takes effect in Bougainville at midnight on 30 April 1998'.[10] To formalise the legal basis of the PMG, an amending 'Protocol Concerning the PMG' was made pursuant to the TMG Agreement on 29 April 1998. The PMG's mandate was broadly aligned with the mandate contemplated in the Lincoln Agreement. The PMG was to:

(a) monitor and report on the compliance of the parties
[involved in the Bougainville peace process] to all aspects
of the ceasefire

(b) promote and instill confidence in the peace process
through its presence, good offices and interaction with
people in Bougainville

(c) provide people in Bougainville with information about
the ceasefire and other aspects of the peace process

(d) provide such assistance [in implementation of the
Lincoln Agreement] as the parties may agree and
available resources allow

(e) deal with such other matters as may be agreed by the
parties to the amended TMG Agreement that will assist
with the democratic resolution of the situation.[11]

The PMG initially consisted of approximately 300 military
and civilian personnel. From late 2000 its size steadily reduced,
initially to 195 but by the time of the mission's withdrawal there
were just 75 personnel remaining.[12] In total, over 5000 personnel,
including more than 3500 ADF members and 300 Australian
civilians, served with the PMG.[13]

Weapons disposal

The PMG's initial main effort was the 'monitoring and reporting functions' of its mandate. This changed after the signing of
the Bougainville Peace Agreement (BPA) on 30 August 2001, an
agreement that had, at its heart, a three-stage weapons disposal
program (see Table 1). From December 2001 the Commander,
Australian Strategic Theatre tasked the PMG with 'supporting
the United Nations Political Office in Bougainville [UNPOB] in
addressing Weapons Disposal ... [and directed that this task was]
to be the PMG's first priority'.[14]

STAGE	REQUIREMENT	TARGET DATE	DATE COMPLETED
I	Weapons handed in to Bougainville Revolutionary Army (BRA) and Bougainville Resistance Forces (BRF) unit commanders, who will store them in sealed containers for the purposes of verification by UNPOB.*	12 June 2002 (deferred to 31 August 2002)	December 2001 to October 2002: 1625 weapons (304 of which were high powered) were handed in.[16] Eventually, over 1900 weapons were contained and destroyed.[17]
II	When/if amendments to the PNG Constitution to implement the BPA are ready for certification, weapons will be held in secure, double-locked containers under UNPOB supervision with one key held by the relevant BRA/BRF commander and the other held by the UNPOB pending a decision on the final fate of the weapons. Legislation amending the PNG Constitution to take effect on verification of Stage II by UNOMB.**	30 September 2002	The PNG Parliament passed the following legislation (first vote 23 January 2002, second vote 27 March 2002): (1) Constitutional Amendment No. 23 – Peace-Building in Bougainville – Autonomous Bougainville Government and Bougainville Referendum 2002 (PNG) (Constitutional Amendment); and (2) the Organic Law on Peace-Building in Bougainville – Autonomous Bougainville Government and Bougainville Referendum No. 29 2002 (PNG) (Organic Law) (certified 25 June 2002). 30 June 2003: PMG officially ceases operations. 1 July 2003: Small civilian Bougainville Transition Team (BTT) commences operations. 23 July 2003: Last PMG elements depart Bougainville. 30 July 2003: UNPOB verifies 'substantial compliance' by the BRA/BRF in the handing in of weapons.[18] 7 August 2003: Constitutional Amendment and Organic Law commence.

* United Nations Political Office in Bougainville
** United Nations Observer Mission on Bougainville

STAGE	REQUIREMENT	TARGET DATE	DATE COMPLETED
III	Decision on the final fate of weapons. Request that the PMG and the UNOMB continue until the decision (anticipated to be not later than end 2002).	Within four months of constitutional amendments that will be introduced on verification of Stage II	30 November 2003: BRA and BRF resolution declaring that the final fate of weapons will be destruction, to occur following inter alia the Bougainville Constitution coming into force (confirmed at 17 December 2003 meeting of the Peace Process Consultative Committee).[19] 31 December 2003: BTT ceases operations. 1 January 2004: UNPOB (that had operated since August 2008) is succeeded by the United Nations Observer Mission in Bougainville (UNOMB).[20] The PNG Parliament enacts the *Constitution of the Autonomous Region of Bougainville 2004* (PNG) (effective 12 November 2004; certified 21 December 2004). End May 2005: UNOMB verifies destruction and determines that the level of security makes it conducive to holding elections for an Autonomous Bougainville Government (ABG).[21] June 2005: Election of the first ABG; UNOMB ceases operations on 30 June 2005.

The PMG's success in meeting its mandate silenced even the most strident critics of the deployment. Many civilian commentators had thought the military was fundamentally unsuitable for such a role, while military people questioned the wisdom of sending a contingent that was unarmed into a conflict zone. Within months, however, many of the most vocal critics became avid supporters asserting that the PMG was the most effective peace-support operation conducted anywhere in the world.[22]

The PMG's local reception

The PMG was broadly embraced by all Bougainvilleans. There were some who deliberately disengaged from the peace process, namely the secessionist leader Francis Ona and members of his so-called Me'ekamui Defence Force (who retreated into a no-go zone centred on the Panguna mine site they had proclaimed) and criminal elements in the local community who tried to steal from the PMG. There were numerous break-ins and thefts at the PMG compound at Loloho. In the final stages of the deployment a number of strategies were employed with some success to mitigate the risk, including the engagement of the Joint Bougainville Law Enforcement Body (comprised of ex-combatants) to provide additional security and the promotion of the PMG's safety as a shared community concern.[23]

Most Bougainvilleans saw the PMG's presence as a significant obstacle to a return to violence and believed its continuing presence guaranteed the peace. There was, not surprisingly, considerable concern among the local population about what would happen when the PMG was withdrawn. Would the peace collapse? Would respect for law and order deteriorate? Unlike for RAMSI, there had been no surveys canvasing popular support for the PMG. Fieldwork and interviews conducted on Bougainville as part of the Australian National University's (ANU's) Peace-building Compared Project observed that the PMG was 'overwhelmingly acclaimed for the sensitive and helpful job' it did. The interviewers were unable to elicit any local criticism of the PMG, although the people did think that it should have stayed longer or until all privately held weapons were surrendered.[24]

The PMG's withdrawal

The duration of the mission was determined at the strategic–political level. It was beyond the control of the PMG itself. As a lesson learned, there was a disconnect between the strategic, operational and tactical levels with respect to the end-state that the PMG was established to achieve. At the military–strategic and operational levels there was a perceived focus on the withdrawal of ADF elements by a specific date, whereas, at the tactical level, the focus was on weapons disposal and the need to eliminate private possession of firearms.[25] Different perceptions of what the PMG needed to achieve meant that the group's personnel might be withdrawn before the mission's main task had been completed. The risk of the gains made being lost was most apparent when the PMG ceased operations and withdrew *before* the UNPOB had officially verified completion of Stage II of the weapon disposal process and *before* a decision had been made on the final fate of the weapons (Stage III). Had the situation not been managed well, and it was with the timely deployment of the Bougainville Transition Team in mid 2003, the decision to withdraw the PMG at the end of June 2003 had the potential to affect adversely the local perception of the broader operation. The PMG pursued a number of lines of effort to ensure that the view from the other side of the hill was the right one.

First, neutrality was the PMG's centre of gravity.[26] The PMG did not take sides and avoided the temptation to play a more active role in the peace process. At all times the ex-combatants had full ownership, and dictated the tempo, of their peace process while the PMG limited its part to providing logistical support, monitoring and investigating ceasefire violations, promoting reconciliation and negotiations, disseminating information, and disposing of weapons. To obviate any perception of

Australian dominance and possible bias toward PNG, the PMG used junior leaders of the Pacific Islands Contingent (PIC) to fill various forward-facing command positions. This reinforced the local perception of the PMG as a multinational team. Given the differing levels of (often lesser) experience of the PIC personnel, these officers were often paired with an ADF or New Zealand senior and more experienced non-commissioned officers or commissioned officers who provide guidance and advice.[27] A similar approach was adopted during Operation Anode.

Second, the members of the PMG were highly disciplined. There was a zero tolerance of fraternisation between the PMG and the civilian population to avoid creating resentment. In this regard, a leading Australian intelligence official was reported to have observed that 'unlike so many United Nations operations, there was none of that frequenting of brothels. Monitors were highly disciplined and that was a key to success … it worked well because [from early on] they set … strict rules on fraternisation.'[28]

Third, the PMG established effective lines of communication with key stakeholders in the peace process and the local population. Its focus was on 'push shaping operations', which took its message to the villages across Bougainville. It also communicated its message by publishing and distributing tens of thousands of copies of the PMG fortnightly newsletter, *Nius Bilong Peace.* It was often the sole source of information about the peace process in remote areas. Additionally, the PMG sponsored a segment on Radio Bougainville (located in Buka) and monitored Radio Free Bougainville (in Panguna).[29]

Fourth, given that the PNG's force protection was underwritten by the maintenance of good relationships with the Bougainvilleans, military participants were constantly reminded that whatever their role, they were principally monitors with responsibility for enhancing the PMG's collective reputation. The analogy of a force protection 'bank' was used. Each individual had the choice of either making a deposit or a withdrawal of goodwill from the bank based on how they behaved towards Bougainvilleans. Every positive contact, such as a wave or a smile, a greeting or playing sport, was a deposit in the bank. Conversely, every time a member ignored a Bougainvillean, looked angry or was distant they made a withdrawal from the bank and potentially endangered the lives of their mates.[30] Fortunately, the PMG's bank balance was always maintained at healthy levels, although the potential to overdraw was an ever-present reality.

Every opportunity was taken to build positive and productive relationships. For example, prior to his deployment, the PMG's last Chief of Staff took advantage of a prominent Bougainvillean, Joseph Kabui, being in Brisbane by inviting Kabui to his family home for dinner. This gesture was reciprocated by Kabui in Bougainville and served to cement the important strategic relationship between the PMG command team and the provincial leadership.[31] At the tactical level, the PMG built relationships through active patrolling programs and by operating shop fronts and patrol bases. Significantly, the patrols included women who were vital to engaging with Bougainvillean women. The PMG was also represented in community events and used the local passion for sport, religion and music to maximum effect (the Australian Army Band toured Bougainville on at least two occasions).[32] PMG assets such as helicopters were used to transport community leaders to peace meetings and the medical element provided emergency support to locals and was credited with saving a number of lives.

Fifth, the participation of unarmed military personnel was central to the success of the PMG. That the PMG's members did not bear arms had immense symbolic value.[33] Bougainvilleans recognised the risk PMG personnel were facing and responded positively. In being unarmed, the PMG led by example. The message to all Bougainvilleans was that the PMG had such confidence in the Bougainville peace process that it did not need weapons. Conversely, the people of Bougainville should also have confidence in their peace process and reject the use of force. The understanding was that, so long as the PMG did not take sides, its members would not be harmed. As a lesson learned, the symbolism of being unarmed may, in certain circumstances, be transferable to other environments where the objective is to instill confidence in the Australian Army's message and intention.

In reality, the situation in Bougainville was volatile and the PMG was constantly exposed to risk. It had no night-flying capability, possessed only a rudimentary ability to conduct low-level recovery and search-and-rescue operations, and no real intelligence analysis capability that would have given the group a greater appreciation of the local landscape. The risk of a member finding themselves in the wrong place at the wrong time was minimised by curfews and movement restrictions.[34] In the final weeks of the operation, PMG personnel travelled in pairs and carried a radio, body armour, helmet and a pick handle as the most rudimentary protection.

There are useful lessons to be learned about the way in which actions external to the theatre of operations have the potential to affect the security environment and local relationships unintentionally. For example, in the final weeks of the deployment leaders at the military–strategic level were slow in approving the PMG's gifting policy. This delay caused some anxiety, especially among interested Bougainvilleans who wanted to know what the PMG would be leaving behind once it withdrew. The risk was that the Bougainvilleans would become impatient, take matters into their own hands and resolve the uncertainty by taking whatever they wanted.[35]

Operation Anode
(24 July 2003 to 1 July 2013)

The military component of RAMSI was known as Combined Task Force 635 (CTF 635). It comprised military elements from Australia, New Zealand, Fiji (until the military coup of 2006), Tonga and PNG. The CTF 635 mission was 'to provide security and logistic support to the Participating Police Force [from 11 Pacific nations] within the DFAT led mission to restore law and order in the Solomon Islands'.[36]

Approximately 7270 Australian personnel, predominantly Army, deployed on Operation Anode. Of that number, about 2112 were Australian Army Reservists who would provide the bulk of the Australian commitment after 2006.[37] At its height, CTF 635 comprised approximately 1800 military personnel in support of over 200 participating police force personnel.[38] The rapid successes of RAMSI in restoring law and order, combined with its clear policing focus, as opposed to military focus, meant that by mid 2004 CTF 635 had significantly downsized. It eventually comprised about 160 (mainly Australian) personnel, organised as a multinational headquarters commanding a light infantry company.[39]

Assessing perceptions

Attempts to assess objectively the local perception of RAMSI were focused on a number of nationwide surveys undertaken by independent bodies (see Table 2). The survey results indicate that at all times prior and during its deployment, RAMSI consistently enjoyed the broad popular support of the local people. It had high levels of approval for its role as a security force, a role that was fundamentally a responsibility of the military contingent. These surveys are consistent with my own experience that the

POLL/SURVEY	DATE	QUESTIONNAIRES/ RESPONDENTS	PROVINCES/ LOCATIONS SURVEYED	QUESTION	APPROVAL RATING
SOLOMON ISLANDS DEVELOPMENT TRUST (SIDT) [40]	July 2003 (pre-deployment)	2100	Unknown	'Do you support RAMSI security effort?'	94%
	February 2004	2341	Unknown		88%
	July 2005	Unknown	Unknown	'Should RAMSI leave?'	71% disagreed (mostly just 'a little bit')
ANU ENTERPRISE/ ANUEDGE 'PEOPLE'S SURVEY'[41]	2006 (pilot)	1085	5	'Support the presence of RAMSI in Solomon Islands?'	Not asked
	2007	5154	9		90%
	2008	4304	6		89%
	2009	5035	8		88%
	2010	4939	8		84%
	2011	4972	8		86%
	2013	3405	5		86%

RAMSI military component seen from the other side of the hill was overwhelmingly positive.

The ANU Peacebuilding Compared Project observed that RAMSI personnel did, however, attract much more criticism from locals than the PMG. This was largely because the PMG was seen as being much closer to the local community, whereas RAMSI was perceived to be segregated in compounds well out of town or in white enclaves, with its personnel seen driving with other expatriates in air-conditioned cars or sitting together in air-conditioned restaurants 'such as the Lime Lounge, with its almost exclusively white clientele'.[42]

From a military perspective, the location of the RAMSI compounds did not have any negative affect on local perception.

Locations were chosen on the basis of military and strategic considerations, including a site's ability to accommodate the force and its assets. Locations like Henderson Field were out of the public eye, assisted with force protection and delivered the unexpected advantage of creating a mystique among the local population about its activities.[43]

The Peacebuilding Compared Project offered another three observations that are relevant to the conduct of CTF 635 and public perceptions of its work. The first observation was that the RAMSI military was more popular with locals than its police 'because they walk the streets and talk to people'.[44] The blue uniforms of the Royal Solomon Islands Police were associated with corruption, misconduct and various atrocities. In the eyes of the locals, all police, regardless of their nationality, were tarnished with the same brush. Furthermore, civil policing is not commonly regarded as a 'friendly' interaction and police, often deliberately, keep a distance from the community.

Second, it was noted that 'some of the early RAMSI military personnel transgressed local cultural codes by their involvement with prostitutes and local women'.[45] Fraternisation has the ability to erode the local perception of the collective effort quickly. While Australian military personnel were not seen to have been involved in such fraternisation, the lesson remains relevant for future operations.

Third, the ANU study claimed that RAMSI's best work was its 'announcement effect' with stolen cars and other property returned to their owners and most of the surrendered weapons having been deposited with the National Peace Council (NPC) before RAMSI landed.[46] While the impending arrival of RAMSI undoubtedly had a profound psychological effect on the people and their behaviours, the assertion in the ANU study regarding weapons collection is not supported by the facts (see Table 3). Furthermore this assertion unjustly detracts from RAMSI's major achievement in disarming the Solomon Islands. The disarming of local factions was critical in shaping local perceptions of the mission.

Weapon collection

TABLE 3 **WEAPONS COLLECTION AND DISPOSAL 2000-2003**

ESTIMATED WEAPONS (OCTOBER 2000)	ESTIMATED WEAPONS SURRENDERED (NOVEMBER 2000-JULY 2003)	ESTIMATED WEAPONS (JULY 2003)	WEAPONS SURRENDERED AND DESTROYED DURING FIRST 120 DAYS OF RAMSI
4300–6100[47]	2255 (including 274 high-powered)*[48]	2640–3520 (including 1,010–1270 high-powered)**[49]	3800 (including almost 700 high-powered)***[50]

*   Most weapons were surrendered to the International Peace Monitoring Team.

**   The number of high-powered weapons commonly reported was 500 to 700 although the Small Arms Survey considered there were significantly more.

***   RAMSI estimated that this constituted between 90 to 95 per cent of all weapons. Approximately 3700 of these weapons were surrendered during the amnesty.

Most weapons were collected during the August 2003 weapons amnesty, which was declared in recognition that the most immediate impediment to the nation's recovery was the presence of illicit firearms in the community. CTF 635 assisted in formal weapons handback and destruction ceremonies that acknowledged the importance of the locals seeing them destroyed. These public acts dispelled any concerns that they would fall back into criminal hands.[51] CTF 635 also organised a series of events to showcase the military capability that supported RAMSI policing operations. For example, an open day was held in Honiara in early August 2003 to demonstrate and, in some cases intentionally overstate, the military search-and-detection capabilities, such as working dogs, night vision, ground detection radar and tactical unmanned aerial vehicles. Post the amnesty, a second open day was held at Honiara that sought to encourage the reporting of those concealing weapons. These events drew crowds of over 10,000 people. Rumours spread and myths arose around the CTF's alleged successes with weapons detection. In reality, there is no evidence that these capabilities actually detected any weapons during the amnesty, but the mere fact that they existed met the need. CTF 635 also developed a rapport with the local population through community events like sports days, public concerts and a Clean-up Honiara Day.[52]

CTF 635 deliberately set out to ensure that RAMSI was not perceived as an invading force. It did this by taking a back seat to the policing effort while presenting itself as a force with the necessary muscle and the technological edge needed to overcome any adversary. Reinforcing this perception, it arrived by air and sea in a carefully balanced spectacle that made it clear to any challenger that it meant business. Because the force landed without body armour or weapons slung, however, the friendly but professional demeanour of its members militated against the notion that it was an invasion force.[53]

RAMSI personnel learned early in the mission that affording disproportionate attention to any one stakeholder was a serious mistake. For example, there was some anxiety among the Malaitan population because RAMSI had focused most of its initial efforts on the island of Guadalcanal, where the capital of Honiara is located. This anxiety encouraged misinformation and biased some Malaitans against RAMSI, creating suspicion of its intentions and objectivity. RAMSI's response was the Malaitan Engagement Strategy, which included open days on Malaita and other targeted, whole-of-RAMSI, community engagement activities.[54]

Within 120 days, RAMSI's efforts had resulted in the surrender and subsequent destruction of over 3800 weapons. Additionally, over 300,000 rounds of ammunition were handed in, combatants neutralised, law and order restored, 16 police outposts established, and a number of key criminal figures, including Harold Keke, in custody.[55] From the start, the view from the other side of the hill was that RAMSI could get the job done.

Providing real local support

Many approaches to maximise local support were tried and tested on both operations. One more warrants mention. Engaging locally employed civilians (LECs), who benefited from employment and on-the-job training by performing functions such as maintenance, security, laundry and kitchen tasks, also worked to enhance the relationship between Australian personnel and local populations. But there is a risk that, once the initial phases of these kinds of operations are completed, the push to commercialise the support function could adversely affect local perceptions of the military effort. In brief, civilian contractors can behave in a manner that quickly undermines any goodwill established by uniformed personnel. For example, Patrick Defence Logistics, which was contracted by RAMSI, was accused of cutting the wages of its local workers 'from $70 a day to $32. No dialogue, no discussion, no comprise'. This was purported to have contributed to labour disputes in Honiara.[56] The interests of contractors and the expectations of local populations need to be carefully balanced if the national intent implicit in such operations is not misunderstood. If Australia seeks to help its neighbours, uniformed personnel and civilian contractors need to communicate the same message by their actions and attitudes.

A final lesson for the ADF to learn from both operations is the importance of identifying the right personnel, with the right skillsets, to perform vital forward-facing roles at the right time. There is a standing need for skilled Australian negotiators and linguists. This provision will minimise Australia's historical reliance on Pacific Islander personnel for vital interpreter functions and enhance opportunities for Australians to get closer to the people and operating environment of this region. Force preparation training was light on when it came to language, cultural awareness and basic negotiation skills training. Wherever possible, greater time should be dedicated to these aspects to ensure that military personnel are equipped to fight and win the equally important battle for hearts and minds.

PART 3: OPERATIONAL AND READY?

6

AFGHANISTAN, IRAQ AND THE WAR ON TERROR

AMIN SAIKAL

The 2001 and 2003 United States-led invasions of Afghanistan and Iraq as part of what Washington declared to be the wider 'war on terror', a campaign that has involved Australian forces over more than a decade and has cost dozens of lives, initially generated much optimism about the future of those two countries and the region. A majority of Afghans evidently welcomed the overthrow of the Taliban's dreadful medievalist Islamic rule, and most Iraqis rejoiced over the demise of Saddam Hussein's dictatorship, in spite of widespread international opposition to the American invasion of Iraq. Concurrently, pro-democracy and liberalist forces in those two countries, and indeed in the Muslim world, could take solace in a view that now the United States and its allies could help them instrumentally to engage in transformative changes in their societies with the aim of limiting the space for extremist elements in their midst and changing their countries for the better. Yet, as the United States-led campaigns progressed, the initial optimism gave way to disillusionment and despair on the part of many Afghans and Iraqis in particular, and liberal and democratic forces in the Muslim world in general.

What went wrong between the invasions and withdrawal, and where are Afghanistan, Iraq and the war on terror heading? Whether one looks at the prevailing situation from the perspective of the Afghans and Iraqis, or assesses it from the vantage point of seasoned analysts and observers of the Afghan and Iraqi conflicts and the war on terror vagaries, the story is one of disappointment, to say the least. Both the Afghan and Iraqi people have many reasons to feel duped. They have been fundamentally failed by their leaderships and by the foreign actors that have backed and propped up those leaderships. The initial promise made by former United States President George W Bush that the goal of the United States was to bring peace, stability, security, prosperity and democracy to both Afghanistan and Iraq, and to free the world from what he called the terror by those elements who used and abused the religion of Islam,[1] rings more hollow now than ever before.

Afghanistan

Afghanistan is in the doldrums. After so much investment in blood and resources on the part of the United States and its allies, not to mention the incalculable loss of lives and property on the part of the Afghan people, Afghanistan today is far from being what the United States promised. This is not to claim that certain infrastructure, telecommunications and social and civil society developments have not taken place. To the contrary, Afghanistan has a large pool of educated and politically conscious youth who could prove to be capable of moving the country towards a better future, should they be given the necessary opportunity.

The country's smaller minorities – the Hazaras, Panjshiris, Uzbeks and Turkmen, who had historically existed as second class citizens, although in various degrees, compared to the larger ethnic Pashtun and Tajik groups – are more empowered now to play a greater role in their country than at any time in the past. The United States and its allies could also claim that Afghanistan has been put on a procedural or minimalist democratic path, as tenuous as it may be. Some seven million Afghans voted (noticeably in some areas along cross-ethnic lines) in the April 2014 presidential elections.[2] Although the May 2014 run-off between the two leading contenders, Ashraf Ghani and Abdullah Abdullah, was widely rigged in favour of the former, resulting in American and European Union intervention and the eventual formation of a National Unity Government, the first round reflected the majority of the Afghans' desire for a better future, and was a major credit to them. In addition, Afghanistan has achieved possibly the highest level of freedom of press and expression in the region.[3]

Even so, the country still remains mired in instability, insecurity, poverty, patronage, corruption, national divisions, a culture of drugs and deception, and appalling human rights violations, especially in relation to women. The influence of 'strongmen', who have traditionally featured in the Afghan landscape in different ways and forms, also remains pervasive throughout the country.[4] Meanwhile, there are doubts at this stage about the viability and effectiveness of the Ghani–Abdullah National Unity Government.[5] It has no constitutional and institutional bases, and Ghani (as President) and Abdullah (as Chief Administrator, a post that is supposed to be the equivalent of prime minister but which cannot be officiated as such until a change is enacted in the 2004 Afghan Constitution) come from very different backgrounds.

The American-educated Ghani, from a Pashtun heritage, is largely grounded in secularist politics. After spending most of his adult life in the United States, mostly as an academic and partly as an employee with the World Bank, he returned to Afghanistan following the United States-led intervention that toppled the Taliban regime and the formation of the internationally backed government of Hamid Karzai (2001–14). At first, he was attached to the United Nations Secretary General's Envoy for Afghanistan, Lakhdar Brahimi, and subsequently joined the Karzai team, serving as Finance Minister (2002–04). He was, however, dropped from Karzai's new cabinet, leading him to engage in different activities to raise his credentials as a Pashtun nationalist and reformer as well as an international actor for a future leadership role, including being appointed by Karzai to take charge of the transition of security from NATO to Afghan forces from 2010. He ran for the presidency in the 2009 election, but scored very poorly against Karzai and Abdullah, who were the two leading candidates, with Karzai finally being declared as the winner amid allegations of widespread rigging. This has meant that Ghani has had no strong national political and social base of his own, and this remains the case to a considerable extent to date.

In contrast, the Afghanistan-educated Abdullah comes from a mixed Pashtun-Tajik parentage. He can claim credentials as a participant in the Islamic resistance to the Soviet occupation of Afghanistan in the 1980s and subsequently to the Taliban regime, and his legitimacy is bolstered by the fact that he never left Afghanistan for any lengthy period of time. While closely associated with the late legendary moderate Islamist Mujahideen commander, Ahmad Shah Massoud, who fought both the Soviets and the Taliban, but was assassinated by Al Qaeda agents two days before 11 September 2001, Abdullah served as the foreign policy envoy of the Islamist Mujahideen government under

President Burhanuddin Rabbani (1996–2001). He was an active participant from Kabul in the December 2001 Bonn Conference that legitimised the formation of the Karzai administration. He is grounded in a moderate political Islam, with a strong social base of power and influence.

Further, the Taliban-led insurgency in pursuit of retaking power and reverting Afghanistan to a traditional Islamic Emirate, and Pakistan's interference in support of them, continue to seriously threaten Afghanistan's viability. The Afghanistan conflict has reached a point whereby, since 2010, the United States and its allies have abandoned their policy of rejecting the Taliban and some of their affiliates as terrorist groups. Instead, they have made strenuous efforts to reach out to them for a negotiated political settlement of the Afghan crisis. Their efforts have not paid off in any substantial way so far.

The death of the founding leader of the Taliban, Mullah Mohammad Omar, was announced in July 2015 in Pakistan, despite claims by the Afghan Directorate of Intelligence that he actually died in a hospital in Karachi in April 2013.[6] Omar was replaced by his deputy, Mullah Akhtar Mansour, who has declared a willingness to negotiate, provided that all foreign forces leave Afghanistan and that the country be declared as an Islamic Emirate, with Sharia or Islamic Law underpinning the operation of state and society[7] – demands that the Taliban have long insisted upon. At any rate, the change to Mansour, whose succession was initially disputed by dissenting elements within the Taliban, has made no difference to the operations of the groups and their affiliates, especially the deadly Haqqani network, which the United States has accused of being linked to Pakistan's intelligence service (ISI)[8] and has designated as a terrorist organisation, and Gulbuddin Hekmatyar's opportunist Hezbi Islamic groups. Afghanistan, and more specifically Kabul, experienced more fighting in the summer of 2015 than previously, and the insurgents made some important gains in the south and north of the country. As the insurgents believe that time is on their side, they have succeeded in forcing the Afghan National Security Forces to become over-stretched in the wake of the withdrawal of most of the United States and its NATO and non-NATO forces by the end of 2014.

Iraq

Iraq is in a worse situation than Afghanistan. It shares most of the problems that have bedeviled Afghanistan. After fighting a trillion-dollar war for nine years at staggering human and mate-rial costs for the United States and its very limited number of Western allies, Britain in particular, and for the Iraqi people, the United States finally made an unceremonious exit from Iraq at the end of 2011. It left behind a broken Iraq. The country is deeply mired in sectarian and ethnic violence as well as acrimo-nious political divisions, and highly vulnerable to interference by rival regional actors, especially the Shia-dominated Islamic Republic of Iran and the Sunni-dominated Kingdom of Saudi Arabia, turning Iraq into a zone of proxy conflict.[9]

Meanwhile, Washington's handpicked Prime Minister Nur al-Maliki (2006–14) turned out to be a very damaging and dubi-ous partner. Al-Maliki had his power base among Iraq's Shia majority, with a close affinity with Iran. He rapidly proved to be exclusionary towards Iraq's substantial Sunni minority, which had traditionally dominated Iraq's power structure until the over-throw of Saddam Hussein, and he was incapable of preventing Iraq's other substantial minority, the Kurds, from building a vir-tual state of their own in northern Iraq.[10] Against this backdrop and in the context of the Syrian conflict, the rise of the Sunni extremist group of the Islamic State of Iraq and Syria (ISIS), and its lightning defeat of what had been described as one of the best American-trained and -equipped Iraqi army, and declaration of Islamic State in June 2014, should not have come as a surprise.[11]

Whereas in the case of mosaic Afghanistan, where the country had historically been characterised as a weak state with strong societies, and where the United States-led intervention had done little to change it in this respect, the same could not be said about Iraq. Prior to the coalition invasion, despite having been limited by the early 1991 military defeat of Iraq over its occupation of Kuwait six months earlier and by severe United Nations sanctions on Iraq as well as by the Western air exclusion zones on northern and southern Iraq, Saddam Hussein still managed to maintain a personalised, repressive hold on his country. As such, while relying heavily on his Sunni minority sect, he was able to suppress any major challenge from Iraq's Shia majority and Kurdish populations.[12]

But the coalition invasion changed the character of Iraq from a strong authoritarian state with suppressed societies to a weak state with strong but hostile societies. The invasion created a massive political and power vacuum in the wake of destroying the Iraqi state in the process of eliminating the Saddam Hussein regime. In the absence of a viable American post-invasion plan to bring order to Iraq, the Iraqi societies found it opportune and necessary to fight one another to fill that vacuum. This was in addition to some of them resisting the American occupation in different times, with support by regional rival actors, although for different reasons. Whereas the Shia Islamic Republic of Iran sought to advance its standing with the Iraqi Shias, the Sunni Kingdom of Saudi Arabia took up the cause of the Iraqi Sunnis, who were marginalised in the Iraqi power structure with the removal of Saddam Hussein and the political ascendency of their

Shia counterparts under the American policy of democratisation of Iraq.[13]

Iraq no longer functions as a state. It is more violent and fragmented than Afghanistan, with little or no security for a great majority of its people. Although under pressure from the United States and its allies, al-Maliki was forced out of office in favour of Haider al-Abadi in September 2014. This predictably did not make much of a difference in regard to the Iraqi government being very inclusive towards the Sunnis, among which IS boasts a social base, and the Kurds for the sake of national unity. Al-Abadi comes from the same Shia group, Da'wa, with a close association with Iran, as al-Maliki. Like al-Maliki, al-Abadi's power base rests with Iraqi Shias.[14] He is not in a position to give a substantive share in the power structure to the Sunnis or to divert the Kurds from maintaining their extensive autonomous status, which is further reinforced by the United States and its allies providing direct military aid to the Kurdish sub-national militia, Peshmerga, in fighting IS. As time has progressed, al-Abadi has not been able to bring about the much-needed domestic structural reforms in order to improve governance, fight corruption, enhance security for a great majority of the Iraqi people, and achieve success against IS. In fact, IS has gained more territory in Iraq since the advent of the al-Abadi leadership, and has taken over Ramadi, the capital of the Sunni dominated Western Iraqi province of Anbar.[15]

The war on terror

Similarly, any claim of success on the part of Washington and its allies, including Australia, against the war on terror, targeting initially Al Qaeda network and its affiliates, including the Taliban, in the Muslim world falls flat in the face of the growth of extremist groups across the Muslim domain. Not only does Al Qaeda remain robust, especially in Syria, the Arabian peninsula and Libya, but more extremist forces, ranging from IS to Al-Shabaab and Boko Haram have now come to haunt the United States and its allies in many parts of the Middle East, the Horn of Africa and Africa. Paradoxically, the war on terror has done more to galvanise and empower Muslim extremist forces than to diminish their operational capacity or the arena for their expansion.

The Obama Administration in Washington initially sensed the ineffectiveness of the war on terror and advocated the use of the term 'counter-insurgency' as an integrated political, social, economic and security approach to stabilise Afghanistan and Iraq as part of an exit strategy. The administration still found it imperative, however, to keep the essence of the war on terror as a means to carry out operations against specific targets – whether in Afghanistan, Pakistan, Yemen, Somalia, Libya or Iraq – and to deploy drones as the preferred tool to do the job. Indeed, the use of drones has had its own drawbacks. Notwithstanding the legal controversy surrounding them, drone attacks have caused civilian casualties, which in turn have played into the hands of extremist groups and allowed them to widen their circles of popular support and recruitment.[16] Meanwhile, the rise of IS and its affiliates has driven Washington full circle. The United States-led air campaign, accompanied by thousands of American and Western allied forces on the ground in Iraq, ostensibly for training and support purposes but with authorisation to engage in defensive operations, amounts to little more than anti-terrorism action, and thus it is far from being a counter-insurgency operation.[17]

Common factors

Lessons to be learned are embedded in multiple factors that account for what is now an Afghan debacle, Iraqi fiasco and war on terror failures. Ironically, the factors that have thwarted American efforts and those of its allies in achieving their original Afghan, Iraqi and war on terror objectives are similar to those that were experienced by the Americans in Vietnam and the Soviets in Afghanistan. Four of these factors are worth stressing as common themes running through the United States' experience of Vietnam, the Soviet's Afghan quagmire and retreat, and the faltering coalition campaigns in Afghanistan and Iraq, especially when compared to the amount of blood and money invested in these campaigns.

The first factor concerns a lack of understanding of the complexity of the society and neighborhood of the invaded countries on the part of outside powers, and their failure to learn lessons from each other's invasion experiences. Former United States Secretary of State, Robert Gates (2008–13), captures this well in his 2014 biography. Commenting on Afghanistan, he states, 'Our lack of understanding of Afghanistan, its tribal and ethnic politics, its power brokers, and their relationships, was profound.' He further states that after assuming office as Secretary of Defense in 2008, he 'came to realise that in Afghanistan, as in Iraq, having decided to replace the regime, when it came to "with what?", the American government [had] no idea what would follow. We had learned virtually nothing about the place … since helping defeat the Soviets there.'[18] Gates's words also ring true about Iraq. His reflections can also explain the American misapprehension of the Vietnam situation and the Soviet miscalculation of the Afghan situation. His assertions have been reinforced with similar remarks by the former US Commander of NATO forces in Afghanistan, General Stanley McChrystal (2009–10).[19]

The second factor is the inability of the intervening powers to secure a credible and effective national partner to assist in implementing processes of stabilisation and transformation in Afghanistan and Iraq. The United States could not achieve this goal in South Vietnam, as the governments of Ngo Dinh Diem and his successors under Nguyen Cao Ky and Nguyen Van Thieu proved to be incompetent, dysfunctional and corrupt. This was also precisely one of the key factors that bogged down the Soviets and contributed to their defeat in Afghanistan. Soviet efforts to harness a united and effective People's Democratic Party of Afghanistan (PDPA) government in Kabul produced no enduring results. The USSR similarly proved unable to stop factional fighting within the PDPA, which continuously tore itself apart and could not survive even in name without massive Soviet support. The PDPA's collapse shortly after the disintegration of the USSR in December 1991 served merely as confirmation.[20]

The United States and its allies have suffered from a similar situation in Afghanistan. Former Afghan President Karzai, who was initially treated as a trusted ally of the United States and who led Afghanistan with the full support of the international community for nearly thirteen years, was not an effective American partner and state-builder. Skilled in the art of political survival, he acted largely in the manner of a tribal chief, presiding over a dysfunctional and corrupt government and relying largely on family, tribal, ethnic and factional connections and patronage to maintain power. He had limited writ over what became largely a narco-state and foreign aid-dependent rentier state.

Initially, when Karzai enjoyed a degree of domestic and international support that none of his predecessors could have dreamed of, he was in a position to engage in bold, visionary, and innovative policy actions. Instead of seizing this opportunity, however, he resorted to old traditional practices of patronage, corruption and power maintenance, and thus squandered a unique opportunity for effective and long-term state building. Essentially, he nurtured little more than a Karzai 'cartel' rule. An April 2014 confidential report written for the State Department in Washington concluded that the Afghan government was not ready to govern Afghanistan after the US withdrawal.[21] This goes to the heart of the difficulties that have now confronted the post-Karzai National Unity Government under Ghani and Abdullah, who have taken nine months to agree on a Minister of Defence in a country that is in the middle of a bloody conflict.

Karzai's position was very much mirrored by al-Maliki. His Shia-dominated administration proved to be as incompetent, corrupt, divisive and dysfunctional as that of Karzai. His pro-Shia but anti-Sunni stance, backed by the United States in fits and starts, caused as much damage to Iraq's national unity as the US 2003 invasion of the country had done.[22] This, together with the devastating and tragic Syrian conflict, has largely been responsible for heightened sectarian, geopolitical and humanitarian crises and the rise of IS, whose extremism has once again drawn the United States and some of its allies, including Australia, into another long and drawn-out bloody conflict in the Middle East. Like Afghanistan, Iraq has become a zone of conflicts within conflicts. Whereas in Afghanistan the fighting between the government forces and the Taliban-led insurgents is at least partly influenced by Indo–Pakistan rivalry, Pakistani–Iranian competition and Iranian–American enmities; in Iraq it is Iran and Saudi Arabia that have waged a proxy war along their geopolitically driven sectarian rivalries.

The third factor is the inability of the invading powers to successfully sell their invasions to the invaded people, their own constituencies and the international community. Just as the United States failed to garner the support of the Vietnamese people and the international community during the Vietnam War, and the Soviets could not enlist the support of the Afghan people and the outside world for its invasion, the United States has struggled to maintain support for its Afghan and Iraqi campaigns. Not only have a majority of the Afghan and Iraqi people grown disillusioned with the foreign occupation for failing to deliver on its promises, but also a majority of Americans and their Western counterparts have not been able to fathom the benefits of America's involvements. The narrative of the Afghan War as the 'good war' or 'war of necessity' as distinct from the 'bad war' or 'war of choice', with which the Iraq War was labelled by many, including President Obama, rapidly lost its gloss at home and abroad. A great number of Afghans and Iraqis rapidly lost their confidence in the United States and their American-backed national government.

The fourth factor is the failure of the invading or intervening powers to halt outside support for resistance forces. While the United States could not contain Soviet and Chinese assistance to the Viet Cong, and the Soviets could not prevent Western and Pakistani support to the Mujahideen, the United States and its allies have failed to neutralise Pakistan's support for the Taliban and their affiliates. The same applies to Iraq. The United States has not been able to contain either Iranian involvement in support of various powerful Shia elements and militias or Saudi-led Arab support for the Sunnis in Iraq. Despite their public condemnation of Islamic State, Riyadh and its Arab allies seem to be comfortable with the Salafist–Wahabi rooted IS as long as it is an anti-Shia and anti-Iranian force. The Arab position is paralleled by Turkey's treatment of IS as a counter to the Iraqi Kurds' efforts to gain an independent state in northern Iraq and to encourage the Turkish Kurds, who form some

20 per cent of Turkey's population, to bid for a similar development.[23]

Meanwhile, it is not surprising that the United States and its allies have not been able to build a regional and international consensus on either Afghanistan or Iraq. The Afghan and Iraqi conflicts have become entangled with conflicting interests of not only regional protagonists, but also international adversaries. Moscow's policy of reassertion and therefore support for Iran and the Syrian regime as part of this policy, China's growing quest for resources, and America's efforts to remain an influential player in the Middle East have made the region a fertile ground for major power rivalries, not seen since the days of American–Soviet superpower Cold War hostilities.

Can the conditions be changed?

The future of both Afghanistan and Iraq hangs in the balance, although in different ways. Both states are confronted with serious domestic challenges and foreign policy complications. Afghanistan faces an uphill battle to solidify as an effectively functioning state, with sufficient internal structures and sources of income to be able to stand on its own feet for years to come. The best that can be expected of the country under the prevailing circumstances is to muddle through until such time that it has acquired the necessary pre-requisites for peace, stability and security in a highly complex, volatile and contested region, provided that it does not fall apart in the meantime. Iraq, on the other hand, has sunk into such a state of inertia and fragmentation that it may not be easy to put it back together as a functioning state. Its geographical counters have already changed as its borders to the west with Syria have been demolished and to the north have been nibbled away by its

Kurdish population, which is determined to have at the very least an extensively autonomous enclave of its own.

As for the renewed war on terror, with its main target now being IS, it is unlikely to succeed in achieving its objectives, just as the Bush version had failed. Even if the United States and its allies manage to roll back IS, there is no guarantee that another extremist group will not emerge to replace it, as long as the right conditions for its existence persist. While the United States and its allies are struggling to put together a viable strategy, the widening power vacuum in the Levant has opened opportunities for not only America's regional adversaries, but also its international rivals. The Russian military intervention in Syria is a case in point.

The best way to deal with violent extremism in the Middle East and beyond is to change the conditions that give rise to such extremism. The region is haunted by authoritarianism, social and economic disparities and injustices and Western policies of demonisation and disempowerment of Muslims for domestic political gains and regional geopolitical ends. Military actions on their own cannot bring stability and security to the Middle East. A comprehensive political strategy is needed to deal with those root causes of violent extremism that defy military solutions. Tragically, such a strategy does not exist currently.

Lastly, there is opportunity for a concluding lesson for the Australian Army. Australia has had a minor role in making Iraq and Afghanistan into what they now are. As a junior coalition partner, the design and implementation of a high-level strategy is not within its purvey or ability. As a small actor in these tragedies, its role has been that of a supporting player. This does not mean, however, that these wars were not without their own effects on the organisation and institution of the Australian Army. Iraq and Afghanistan have been expensive in lives and treasure and the institution has responded, at times, only with difficulty. Even minor players, therefore, must be cognisant of a senior partner's ambitions and competencies and factor this into the decision to participate in a conflict and the extent to which it becomes involved.

7

IMPROVEMENTS AND CHALLENGES FOR ARMY'S ISR ENTERPRISE

SCOTT GILLS, BEN ALWARD
AND TIM RUTHERFORD

The Australian Army, after a long period of operational inactivity, has now completed 15 years of continuous operations and counting. Significantly, this era of high-operational tempo was largely unforeseen by strategic planners, with the result that the Army had numerous, substantial capability shortfalls when it readied for operations to East Timor in 1999, Afghanistan in 2001 and Iraq in 2003.[1] The experience of one part of the Army, its Intelligence, Surveillance and Reconnaissance (ISR) capabilities, like those of other Western coalition partners, were not initially ready to go to war and have had to spend the past 15 years adapting while fighting.[2]

The opening engagements of the present century were considered by many strategic theorists and commentators as the harbingers of an emerging complex security environment.[3] While the British Army's Chief of the General Staff, General Sir Nicholas Carter, described the future operating environment as 'uncertain',[4] it is unlikely that the messy, hybrid, counter-insurgency conflicts will suddenly end with the recent drawdown of forces from Afghanistan. In fact, some argue that the character of the operating environment is, for the time being at least, stabilising. For example, in a recent study commissioned by the Australian Army's Future Land Warfare branch, former Army officer David Kilcullen noted that three of the four features of the current operating environment are enduring and that only the fourth – connectivity – is new and transformative.[5] This provides a solid basis for the use of recent history to guide future thought on capability development objectives.[6]

Since the turn of the century, the exponential growth in connectivity has facilitated a more globalised approach to conflict and the creation of a new cyber domain has the potential to threaten national interests as effectively as the more traditional domains – only faster.[7] Inexpensive access to information has enabled entrepreneurs and innovators to collaborate on developing new technologies and improve existing ones. As the access to these technologies becomes more widespread, it is expected that the technological advantage previously enjoyed by Western militaries will diminish. In light of this, the Army's decision advantage will likely become its defining characteristic. Preserving that edge means that now, more than ever, the Army must come to terms with and be prepared to operate in an era of information manoeuvre.[8]

The ability to negotiate successfully in the information domain requires commanders and their intelligence staff to have instant access – at the point of need – to the widest array of relevant information in order to support fast and accurate decision-making. But this presupposes that the information collected is both needed and dispensed in a manner that is useful to the decision-making process. Since 1999, the Army has effectively binged on new technology and has arguably overwhelmed its analytical capacity and in turn decision-making processes, with terabytes of raw data, across the full spectrum of sensors.[9]

Given the scale of change experienced by the Army's intelligence and ISR capabilities over the past 15 years, there is merit in consolidating the many improvements and challenges encountered, to establish a new baseline of capability understanding. Accordingly, there is a need to examine the key lessons identified in the Army's ISR capability over the past 15 years across the broad themes of the collection/analysis imbalance and the need for an ISR enterprise. To do this, a review needs to be undertaken of the improvements made to the management of intelligence and ISR capability in the Army, before some thoughts on the challenges facing Defence in the management of a truly joint ISR capability into the future can be offered.

To establish a common basis of understanding, a few definitions are needed. Intelligence can be defined as the directed and co-ordinated acquisition and analysis of information to assess environment and threat capabilities, intent and opportunities for exploitation by commanders at all levels; and ISR is the activity that synchronises and integrates the planning and operation of dedicated collection capabilities, including the initial processing and dissemination of the resulting product.[10]

An age of change

The Australian Army has experienced significant technological improvements since the start of the new millennium. It has seen a proliferation of sensors, driven by an unquenchable thirst for information, which has seen its analytical capability overwhelmed. The result has been what one commander termed 'digitised chaos'.[11] To examine the imbalance in the Australian

Army's collection and analytical capabilities, a brief review of why the Army has felt the need to know so much is followed by a discussion on its technological addiction and what this has meant for the Army's ability to produce meaningful intelligence.

Since 1999 the Australian Army has seen the proliferation of the microprocessor, the global acceptance of the internet and the advent of nanotechnology – all of which have made possible smart cars, smart phones and smart watches. In effect we have, as individuals, become thoroughly digitised. But, the force that deployed to East Timor in 1999 was in many respects analogue, with few capabilities that would distinguish it from the task force sent to South Vietnam 35 years earlier. Since the East Timor intervention the Australian Army has worked hard to redress this technological deficiency. It is worth asking why.

The demand for an information edge may well be linked to the considerable military dominance enjoyed by Australia's allies since the end of the Cold War. Operation Desert Storm in 1991 could be seen as the culmination of several centuries of work towards perfecting the co-called 'decisive battle'.[12] Likewise, it could be seen as the trigger for the rapid rise in asymmetric forms of conflict.[13] As future adversaries continue to offset the Army's military strength by fighting from among the population, the need for accurate intelligence to guide its operations has increased exponentially. In the years since 1999, the quest for high-fidelity information to improve decision-making and reduce the risk to soldiers and non-combatants has driven a technological overhaul of intelligence and ISR capabilities.[14] This has been enabled by the continuing miniaturisation of computing systems,[15] allowing capabilities that were previously too big or complicated to exist below strategic levels to be devolved, in one form or another, to tactical elements. While technology alone is incapable of 'lifting the fog of war' or indeed achieving 'dominant battlespace knowledge',[16] it remains a critical component of successful decision advantage.

New technological advances have supported the proliferation of sensors to every corner of the battlefield. Since 1999, the Australian Army has introduced a plethora of collection devices, ranging from unattended sensors; remote optics; nano, small and medium unmanned aerial vehicles; man-portable radars as well as sophisticated miniature electronic eavesdropping and targeting capabilities, to name a few. The Australian Army is now capable of gathering more information, faster, than at any other time in its history. But the technological investment in collection capabilities has far outpaced the improvement of analytical capability. Simply put, the Army has allowed itself to be seduced by the technology of collection and forgotten that information aggregation is of equal importance.[17] A recent RAND study noted that as little as 5 per cent of information collected by ISR platforms in the US Navy is seen by an analyst let alone assessed.[18] Even if this number is inaccurate for comparative use in an Australian context where no such study has been undertaken, it provides a useful gauge on the disproportionate level of information collected to what can be meaningfully analysed.

The ability to manage the 'volume, velocity and variety'[19] of information efficiently has parallels with the big data challenge confronting the digitally enabled business community. While this has provided some insight to potential solutions for the Army, the idiosyncrasies of military operations, including the lack of standard information formats, fixed infrastructure, or predictable data flows, means leveraging a complete solution is unlikely – at least not in the near term. But perhaps the most complicating factor is Army's need to consider a fourth 'V' related to the information it processes – the 'veracity' of the information provided to decision-makers.

Managing the four Vs of information complicates the task of intelligence staff and poses a real risk to the Army's ability to make timely and accurate decisions. In a satirical poke at the oversupply of information in modern life, literary critic Linda Holmes once remarked that 'statistically speaking, you will die having missed almost everything'.[20] Her comments strike a chord with the military intelligence analyst who fears that soldiers will die precisely because they will have missed something. A solution lies in what the 2013 Defence White Paper referred to as the 'commensurate investment in analysis, and access to that analysed data'.[21] The combination of collection, access and analysis to information are the tenants that define the Army's second challenge: the need for an Army ISR Enterprise.

Needs and benefits

Harnessing the influx of sensor feeds has challenged the Army ISR community's ability to effectively store, manage, access, search and analyse information to produce timely and accurate intelligence for commanders. The scale of this challenge requires an integrated approach across Defence, government and the allied intelligence community and should not be limited to activities just prior to, or during, a deployment. This examination of the need for an Army ISR Enterprise, beginning with a brief review of the support provided to commanders on operations from 1999, is followed by a discussion on the Army ISR Enterprise and the benefits of analytical immersion.

The deployment to East Timor in 1999 was not anticipated by the Army, which had been structured according to successive White Papers around the defence of the continent, with a heavy reliance on the air–sea gap to act as a strategic moat.[22]

The Australian Army was essentially a force reliant on strategic lead times for mobilisation and was ill equipped for short-notice expeditionary operations.[23] Consequently, when troops deployed rapidly as part of INTERFET, there were no intelligence personnel in the Army dedicated to understanding the tactical land-operating environment of this near neighbour, much less other potential crisis points in the region. Not unlike the behaviour of poor students prior to a university exam, the Army's intelligence professionals had no alternative but to engage in cramming, given the paucity of known information about where they were likely to be deployed. Inhibited by both systematic and technological weaknesses, classified reporting by national and allied intelligence agencies was largely inaccessible to tactical commanders or their intelligence staff. In theatre, information was being collected, fused and analysed by under-manned and over-worked intelligence cells, rather than a dedicated all-source analytical capability.

As Australia transitioned to operations in Central Asia and the Middle East, the importance of intelligence and ISR collection was gradually realised as deployed commanders down to the sub-unit level were increasingly supported by a range of tactical collection and analytical capabilities, including unmanned aerial systems. With the positioning of national agency liaison personnel at unit level, commanders were now able to access unprecedented levels of intelligence to support decision-making. The proliferation of collection and distribution assets allowed commanders to broaden their focus from the immediate threat(s) to the more fundamental questions about the operating environment and the stakeholders they sought to persuade.[24] Along with its coalition partners, Australia learned that to fight a war among the people, one must first understand them and their aspirations. Australia was not intellectually prepared for the wars in Iraq and Afghanistan, which was not surprising given that neither country was considered a likely area of operation until shortly before each deployment took place. In both conflicts, a range of ethnic, religious, and cultural differences drove much of the fighting.[25] The expanded intelligence requirements and associated increase in information led to the reintroduction of a dedicated all-source analytical capability. Although the establishment of this highlighted that information collection and analysis was becoming more interdisciplinary, it continued to be challenged by both access to relevant reporting and the lack of a pre-conflict understanding of the operational environment. Importantly, the renewed emphasis on the human domain and human aspects of military operations should be reinforced and sustained over time.[26]

Culturally, as well as technically, an enterprise approach is urgently required to cut across specialisations, functions, organisations and echelons to support intelligence staff and resident ISR force elements in the provision of advice to commanders at the point of decision. Counter to the Army's hierarchical organisational structure, the flow of battlefield knowledge should not be constrained by a chain of command. The Army needs to effectively turn its disparate intelligence nodes into a mutually reinforcing enterprise, thereby optimising access a broad range of relevant information from every echelon – national to tactical – at the point of need.[27] The Army needs the ability to integrate information from all elements of the national intelligence community at the point of decision, where the line between strategic and tactical is becoming increasingly blurred.

The 2013 Defence White Paper noted that intelligence requires long lead times to develop, produce and catalogue reports. This correctly infers that a continual rate of effort is required in peacetime, to provide the quality and quantity of information required in wartime.[28] To facilitate this outcome, the Army ISR Enterprise needs to be 'always on',[29] constantly collecting, analysing and updating Army's understanding of the potential land tactical operating environment. This active status ensures relevant personnel are immersed in relevant geographical or thematic problem-sets, which allows them to continuously practice and hone their tradecraft. Immersion supports the intelligence professional's ability to provide a 'continuous intelligence study'[30] that is capable of answering the more fundamental questions about the potential operating environment, such as the context in which adversaries operate, the institutions within which they live, as well as detailed information about their cultures, fears, perceptions, motivations and history.[31] To achieve this level of insight, the Army arguably needs to review its current bias toward a bespoke force generation model, to one where intelligence and ISR capabilities have the flexibility to operate in the same manner whether they are deployed or not. Underpinning the always on philosophy is the seamless access to relevant information through habitual use of familiar systems, applications and databases that are able to be employed both in-barracks and upon deployment.

In order to provide decision advantage to the Army's commanders, the Army ISR Enterprise – as part of a broader joint, coalition or national context – must integrate disparate intelligence capabilities into a mutually reinforcing whole, generating an enduring understanding of the region and the potential operating environment(s) from pre-crisis or conflict through mission initiation to mission completion.

Achieving the vision

Western military doctrine maintains that the commander directs the intelligence effort and it is the principal intelligence officer, regardless of his or her level, who manages that effort on the commander's behalf.[32] This responsibility includes acting as the commander's principal advisor for ISR and implementing activities that meet the commander's intelligence requirements. A review of the improvements made to the provision of professional intelligence support in the Army since 1999 offers some perspectives on the challenges now facing Defence in the management of a truly joint ISR capability into the future.

In 1999, the Army's intelligence and ISR collection capabilities were suffering from years of neglect. The decision to abolish the Directorate of Military Intelligence as well as the Directorate of Electronic Warfare and Special Intelligence during the Strategic Reform Program in the mid 1990s depleted what little ability the Army had to develop and manage a capability that was rapidly becoming specialised.[33] While commanders in Headquarters 1st Division and the now defunct Land Headquarters were staffed with intelligence professionals, the practice was not consistently applied across the Army's brigades or units, where intelligence functions were often performed by personnel as extra-regimental appointments. Workforce pressure continued as the Army attempted to consolidate its disparate specialist intelligence capabilities into the unit now known as the 1st Intelligence Battalion. During this period, the Army's concept for intelligence support had arguably become increasingly myopic, focusing singularly on the provision of intelligence advice and not the complementary task of advising on capability development and force modernisation. This changed with the deployment to East Timor.

The need for accurate intelligence to support decision-making during operations stimulated a surge in investment that was needed to mitigate the neglect of the 1990s. Since the INTERFET deployment, the Army has expanded its tactical human intelligence capability, introduced a range of unmanned aerial system capabilities,[34] improved the tactical signals intelligence capability, and increased the level of dedicated combat intelligence staff support to units and, in some cases, sub-unit levels. Improvements have also been observed at an organisational level. In March 2010, the Army grouped its specialist intelligence and ISR units into the one formation, the 6th Brigade. Finally, in order to undertake the complementary task of advising capability development and force modernisation within the Army, the Directorate of ISR was established in Army Headquarters during May 2014. This was a significant step forward.

If the future joint force aspires to achieve decision advantage over adversaries, continued investment must be made in the professional representation and in the quality of intelligence advice and ISR capabilities at the most senior levels of Defence. Applying the doctrine that intelligence should be centrally controlled and co-ordinated,[35] it could be argued that Defence currently lacks the structure and, more importantly, suitably qualified senior intelligence professionals to provide optimal advice to ADF senior leadership. This is a lesson hard learned by the Army over the past 15 years. Of critical concern is the lack of an advocate for the development and management of a truly joint ISR enterprise. As the source of information becomes less constrained by service affiliations a need exists for Defence to appoint an officer responsible for prescribing the requirements, policy and standards for the groups and services, across multiple classified systems, for the various intelligence and ISR collection capabilities at every level. The recent publication of the First Principles Review provided such an opportunity, with the Vice Chief of the Defence Force (VCDF) appointed the 'C4ISR Design Authority'.[36] While there is a debate currently underway on what this innovation means, a window exists to appoint a senior intelligence professional, supported by suitably qualified and experienced staff, to advise the VCDF and the service chiefs on the intelligence and ISR-related capability development aspects of the new role.

The management of intelligence and ISR-related capabilities in Defence is currently complex and plainly disjointed. Appointing a principle intelligence advisor to the VCDF could address this deficiency through the provision of joint intelligence and ISR strategy, capability development guidance and related policy advice to the groups and services. Ideally, this position would facilitate the effective synchronisation of intelligence and ISR capabilities across the Defence Department and throughout the ADF.

Adapting to future needs

If we assume the trajectory of technological change will continue at something like its current rate, then uniformed personnel are truly in the middle of an historic period of change. The Army, like all global actors, has needed to adapt while continuing to function during the longest and potentially largest commitment of forces in its history – the Iraq and Afghanistan wars. By adapting in this manner, the Army has adopted a number of valuable innovations, more often than not through trial and error.

The first observation is that collecting information is easy. But unless time sensitive and from a reliable source, information alone does not effectively support the decision-making process until it has been validated and analysed. The Army's predilection for collection has the potential to stifle decision-making and waste resources. Collection should be a co-ordinated process that is matched with an appropriately resourced analytical capability. The requirement for the Army to adopt an enterprise approach to ISR will facilitate seamless access across a range of classified and unclassified systems throughout every echelon, including allied intelligence partners both in-barracks and on deployment to support commanders at the point of decision. Furthermore, the Army has learned that an organisation cannot cram an under-standing of the operating environment. Information and the insights drawn need to be discerned over time so that nuances and subtleties can be identified. For the Army's ISR Enterprise to provide timely and relevant support to the decision-making process, when the crisis happens, the intelligence capability must be considered as always on. Applying this philosophy is a work-in-progress and may require a review of the balance between the analytical and the collection capabilities within the force gen-eration cycle. Finally, a joint capability development and force modernisation approach to manage the increasingly compli-cated requirements of the intelligence and ISR capabilities across Defence needs to be considered. The VCDF will require the sup-port of a suitably qualified and experienced intelligence profes-sional in order to assist in the ISR-related aspects of the VCDF's role as the C4ISR Design Authority.

Over the past 15 years the introduction and maturation of a new range of organisations and capabilities underpinned by a depth of operational experience throughout all ranks has pro-vided a solid platform from which to continue ISR develop-ment. Like many Army capabilities, intelligence faces challenges into the future. As the eminent British military historian Sir Michael Howard observed, no matter how clearly one thinks it is impossible to predict precisely the character of future conflict.

The key is to come close enough to be able to adjust rapidly as new challenges to security emerge.[37] Although technological solutions alone will never provide all commanders with what they need to know about the threat and the environment, if the Army aspires to achieve enduring periods of decision advantage in the future battlespace, ISR will be crucial to offset the size of the ADF and enable a competitive warfighting advantage over Australia's adversaries.[38]

8

LOGISTICS AND THE FAILURE TO MODERNISE

DAVID BEAUMONT

Irrespective of the way in which logistics is described, either abstractly as a component of the art of war or as a mere administrative science, it is fundamental to an army's combat potential, its survivability and, above all else, its ability to accomplish its mission. A cursory examination of the last 15 years of operations suggests that the Australian Army understands this truism, given no major incidents can be attributed to a systemic failure of logistics. But this logistic success may have been more a factor of good luck than good planning, however, as the Army has consistently deferred investment in logistics, giving preference to other areas. Not only does this practice of prioritising resources and attention away from logistics risk limiting government options, it can also have fateful consequences.

Writing soon after Australia's leadership of the International Force for East Timor (INTERFET) concluded in 2000, Lieutenant Colonel Susan Smith, Chief of Army Visiting Fellow at the Australian Defence Studies Centre, declared that the practice of casting logistics as 'an enabler' had left it a 'handmaiden to the politically appealing warfighting technology that dominates capability considerations'.[1] Unsurprisingly, the Army's first operation of the last 15 years revealed how operationally defining this handmaiden could be. But looking back on this operation that many years later, and despite the lessons observed elsewhere, there are worrying signs Smith's observation remains true today.

The chronically low priority afforded to the Army's logistics over the last 15 years has created an inappropriate level of risk in the force's operational sustainability. This is seen in an analysis of operations that on the surface appear distinctly different, an operation where the problems were patently obvious, and a series of operations in which old habits and preferences subdued the need for change in the Army's logistic habit. After examining the Army's recent attempts to modernise logistics it is clear that to fundamentally revise logistics concepts, capability and force structure in order to ensure the Army is operationally ready and operationally sustainable is imperative.

Lessons from an absence of failure

The INTERFET Commander, Major General Peter Cosgrove, remarked:

> In the past the Australian armed forces have not had to invest
> in substantial deployable logistic capabilities. Our forces
> have relied upon major allies such as the US and Britain.
> The logistic support for INTERFET was magnificent,
> but sustainment was not achieved without frustration and
> some failures. Frankly, if the ADF is required by the nation
> to go offshore again in a lead role or as a contributor to
> international military action, we will have to underwrite our

operations with a responsive and effective logistic system
with stamina. At the moment there is room for enhancement
of our capability to support offshore operations. We
succeeded in East Timor but our logistic engine was under
extreme pressure most of the time.[2]

The Army's logistic capability in 1999 was in a parlous state.
Speaking to the Australian National Audit Office (ANAO) soon
after the completion of Operation Warden to East Timor, General Cosgrove reflected on operational issues that revealed much
about the endemic fragility within the ADF's capacity to sustain
large land forces. He had experienced an operation in which the
ADF had been expected to conduct without being logistically
underwritten by major allies, and where 'frustration' and some
'failures' caused by deficiencies in sustainment capabilities had
been starkly revealed. Most importantly, Cosgrove confirmed
that substantial work was required to remediate logistic weaknesses that had affected the ADFs ability to support 'offshore
operations', as a leader of coalition military action or independent deployments.

INTERFET is the exemplar of the potential regional missions the Army must be prepared for, and a benchmark upon
which its deployable capability should be based. While today's
Army struggles with the difficulties of sustaining a battalion-sized
amphibious operation, INTERFET saw the force projection of
nearly one division of coalition troops by sea and air and a sustainment effort involving every logistic capability the Army could
muster. As a consequence, its lessons have been repeatedly revisited as the Army develops responses to contemporary strategic
policy imperatives. Yet hidden behind the thin veneer of operational success INTERFET starkly revealed how the preferential
allocation of resources to combat capabilities and the acceptance

of risk in logistics functions brought the Army to the precipice of operational failure. Moreover, it revealed the importance of the Army's logistic capabilities that existed outside of the purview of its favoured units of action – the brigade or battalion. These were capabilities underwriting leadership of regional coalitions, and the performance of the joint force.

Given the extreme challenges this operation placed on the Army's logistic elements, it is unsurprising that a number of well-known reviews and academic papers were writing as warnings to the contemporary Army. The ANAO study, Management of Australian Defence Force Deployments to East Timor, observed that logistics should have been 'as easy as it gets', given the proximity of East Timor to Australia and the absence of the 'stresses and demands of sustained combat'. The study confirmed significant limitations on the then ADF to sustain forces in arguably 'low-intensity' conditions.[3] Bob Breen outlined numerous shortcomings in logistic planning and execution, the *ad hoc* and inefficient nature of logistic arrangements, and the importance of the embryonic operational and strategic approach to logistics of the time.[4] However, it was predominantly issues of function, not form or process that had left Army logistics in a perilous state prior to the East Timor deployment.

The INTERFET deployment confirmed a rule of war that despite its obviousness is often forgotten by force designers. The force structure decisions of the past determine the operational options of the future. The logistic challenges of INTERFET were largely the consequence of well-intended decisions made by the Army's senior leadership in an arguably difficult period. The 1990s was a time in which government compelled the ADF to reapportion funding to support the introduction into service of new capabilities. But in order to preserve combat capability, the Army's leadership made the choice to direct cuts to logistics and support areas.[5] The capacity of the Army's logistics capabilities were severely constrained by the resultant reductions in numbers, and pressured further by the 1991 Force Structure Review and government direction that sought to commercialise significant components of military logistics.[6] There were substantial, immediate and financial benefits to Defence in embracing logistic jointery and commercialisation. However, the comprehensive approach undertaken to the outsourcing of logistic capabilities had significant operational consequences.

Commercialised logistic arrangements proved a marginally sufficient response to operational needs on the mainland, but within the operational environment outsourcing logistic responsibility proved problematic. As INTERFET deployed, Australian industry lacked the commensurate responsiveness necessary to support the unfolding situation, and economic infrastructure did not exist in East Timor to establish a commercial base useful to INTERFET. When the assumed contractor support failed to materialise, the Army's capability gaps became starkly evident. The Army faced immense logistical challenges in the assumption of operational leadership. In some cases, as recounted by Cosgrove, coalition members were allocated to areas of operations on the basis that they could not be sustained otherwise.[7] In 2000, the Chiefs of Staff Committee noted the root of these problems:

> Ongoing organisational rationalisation, particularly at force
> level, has resulted in severe limitations in critical skill areas,
> such as [sea and air] terminal operations, which are virtually
> impossible to reconstitute for short warning contingencies …
> There is an imbalance between the ADF's combat capability
> and its organic logistics support capability.[8]

In review of the lessons of INTERFET, the Army reinforced several of its logistic capabilities that had proven particularly vulnerable. After returning from command of Joint Task Force 631 (JTF 631) during Operation Astute, Brigadier Mick Slater noted these changes were critical to the success of his mission. Significant improvements in joint capability, deployability and readiness encouraged him to assert 'that we have largely solved the deployable logistic problem since 1999'.[9] He noted that the ADF had 'poured resources into rectifying the problems we had in getting water, POL [petrol, oils and lubricants] and key war stocks into theatre and sustaining ourselves away from our Australian bases' and that 2500 people were sustained 'superbly'.[10] JTF 631 was the beneficiary of significant reforms undertaken in joint strategic logistics and operational command and control, reforms that arguably enhanced the efficiency and effectiveness of the supply chain into theatre. Yet it was a smaller and less risky operation than INTERFET in an environment that was now familiar to the ADF. The success of JTF 631 suggests that the Army's deployability had been improved, but in this context the outcomes of change seems to be of a much lesser order.

The passage of time might prove the INTERFET operation an aberration, an exceptionally sized deployment that is unlikely to be repeated in the foreseeable future. Even if this was true, and despite proclamations that maintain otherwise, it should be a concern that a number of problems in this deployment remain unresolved. Specialist capabilities resident within the 17th Combat Service Support Brigade remain hollow and are a well-known risk to the operational sustainment of the combat brigades intended under Plan Beersheba. The assumption that contractors can mitigate hollowness in the Army's deployable logistic forces remains a theme of force design, as does the centralisation of logistics functions to achieve efficiency improvements in the 'raise, train and sustain' environment. It is yet to be seen whether either of these approaches will be successful in sustaining a major combat operation. The Army is on the cusp of a period in which the block obsolescence of its combat systems is likely to necessitate the prioritisation of funds most probably away from the very few logistic programs currently evident in the Defence Capability Plan as has been done so in the past. The chance of another INTERFET-type deployment might be low but the need to prepare the Army to lead and sustain major operations independently within the region remains real. If this requirement manifests, it would be unsurprising to see a reappearance of some unfortunately familiar operational challenges with it.

New logistics and old habits

In the wake of the ADF's largest deployment since the Vietnam conflict came a series of operations that formed Australia's longest continuous wars fought in an unexpected region and with conditions markedly different from that experienced during INTERFET. With different sustainment logic to East Timor, many of the concerns expressed following INTERFET were muted as the Army shifted its focus to different operational challenges. These new operations echoed Australia's expeditionary traditions, and the problem of force deployment and sustainment was deferred to externally sourced support. With forces deployed as self-contained, specialised task groups or units, lodging within a coalition force and largely independent of one another's activities, it was expeditious – even necessary – for these units to be sustained under the auspices of a larger benefactor. Constrained by arbitrary manning caps, with a desire to keep the logistic footprint small, the Army's logistic support instead reflected the sustainment trinity of coalition, host-nation and contractor support.

With operations continuing to this day, it is difficult to openly study the Army's logistic performance or its impact on subsequent modernisation. Operations in the Middle East have not revealed logistic problems in the same manner as INTER-FET. Aside from a classified history, circumstances have not compelled either an audit or an external review that might have served to prompt discussion. Once again, we can look upon this as a measure of success. If we do consider it a success, it has been a success fundamentally delivered by the ADF's ability to attract logistic support for its operations rather than its integral capacity to provide adequate logistic support. In comparison to its regional operations, the Army's deployed units have enjoyed a logistic abundance enabled by the ready availability of coalition and contractor support. Indeed, if one examines the ratio of logistics personnel, including contractors, to combat troops in recent Middle East operations, support personnel reflected around two-thirds of the total force.[11] In such an environment it was possible for the ADF to deploy with a force structure whose composition was the inverse of most nations participating in the wider coalition.

The ADF's sustainment methodology looked like a patchwork of specialist capabilities that offset gaps in problem areas. These were largely centralised into joint, force and logistics units. Integral echelons were factored into the structures of deployed battle groups, although the manning cap did force compromises, often at the expense of logistics manning. These compromises contributed to a number of problems that presented at the tactical level, ranging from concerns over logistics governance systems for stores and equipment to the inability of logistic convoys, also known as combat logistic patrols, to protect themselves without external assistance. The provision of combat health and distribution was predicated on coalition support, especially in Uruzgan, Afghanistan, where US Army vehicles were assigned to local Australian logistic units. When problems emerged, the ADF response was principally one of fault correction as evinced in the deployment of caterers to Uruzgan as a response to dissatisfaction with contracted service providers. Although armies rarely deploy with all the logistics capabilities they want, the structure of Army forces allocated to these operations was a conglomeration of specialists filling gaps that coalition and contractor could not provide.

The conduct of these operations paralleled the maturation of joint agencies involved in the sustainment of deployed forces, organisations that were in their infancy during INTERFET. Jointery leverages efficiencies gained when the Army, Navy and Air Force work collectively in the sustainment of a force. The development of Joint Operations Command, Joint Logistic Command, Joint Health Command and other operational strategic agencies has been undeniably beneficial to logistic outcomes at the strategic and operational level. Unlike the relative chaos of the INTERFET supply chain, the ADF's most recent operations are now governed by a generally responsive strategic logistic infrastructure. Defence logistics more effectively captures military sustainment from acquisition to the end-user, enabling the rapid deployment of new equipment to the soldier.[12] The Army, as part of greater adaptations underway in the ADF due to wartime experiences, is the beneficiary of a strategic sustainment system perfectly suited to its current operations.

Yet these successes hide a number of weaknesses – imbalances left unresolved since they were revealed during INTERFET. Just as there was an institutional imperative to embrace shared services in the 1990, a similar attitude permeates the current approach to logistical jointery. Jointery is, first and foremost, about improving interoperability, productivity and efficiency in operational effects by sharing capability between the services. Properly employed it leverages trade and professional strengths that are evident in individual services and absent in others.[13] But jointery can be seen as a panacea for costly investment in disaggregated logistics capabilities within the services, a continuation of a government-induced inexorable trend toward organisational centralisation that began in the resource-constrained 1980s. Just as the Army prioritised its resources towards programs such as 'Hardening and Networking the Army' or the 'Enhanced Land Force', it embraced efficiencies and effectiveness through the joint force.

The Army was compelled by the government to resource joint logistics agencies and, as its largest contributor, should and quite rightly did expect a return from its investment. This expectation should not, however, have deterred investment in the Army's integral logistics for use on operations. Indeed, the assumption that joint agencies can fulfill the Army's tactical logistic requirements is a perilous one. If the joint capabilities transferred from the services do not effectively account for all operational logistic requirements, risk is ultimately transferred and the problem only temporarily deferred. The Army learned this lesson in the late 1990s with the transition of Logistics Command into the joint force as Support Command – Australia. This 1997 Defence Efficiency Review outcome affected the quality of support by stretching already hollow logistics capabilities even further in requiring them to support the entire ADF.[14] The quality of the operational joint effect is dependent on availability of robust commitments from the services – militaries often tend to forget that the precondition for effective joint interdependence is joint independence, especially at the tactical level.[15]

When it came to tactical and operational logistics functions in the Middle East, despite the joint moniker, the Army's logistics forces largely shouldered the burden of sustainment. Although supported by other services, the Force Support Unit and its ancestors were based upon Army logistics units, and it is unclear whether the resultant effect was greatly beneficial to the Army. Much of the time spent by these joint units was in addressing the capability gaps induced by the under-resourcing of single-service battle groups in functions such as transportation, medical, maintenance and catering. In the end, it was virtually irrelevant where land logistics capabilities were deployed, to the joint force or the Army, as the majority originated from exactly the same source, and ultimately with the same effect.

The Army must therefore be cautious about basing the modernisation of its logistics upon its experiences in the Middle East. From operations in East Timor where logistics capabilities and resources were scarce, the Army was well supplied by generous coalition benefactors, and was supported by a level of local contracting unlikely to be available in Australia's own region as INTERFET showed. Even then there were problems, and logistics remained the 'overcoming of an endless series of difficulties'.[16] Once again, it is tempting to look back upon this period of operations and describe the absence of failure as a significant success for the ADF, and a validation of transformational change in the way deployed forces were sustained. For the Army, however, we must see the deployment for what it was: a relatively small, low-intensity operation, logistically underwritten by a major ally with a prodigious capability to deploy expeditionary forces. In a testament to the adaptability of the Army and its soldiers, these operations have been successful not because of the Army's integral logistic capabilities, but in spite of their limitations. Furthermore, the operations show that despite the promise of jointery, the Army must integrally possess the capability and capacity to support the joint force on land. As the Army postures itself for the future by modernisation on the basis of lessons observed on operations, it must therefore be extremely careful about basing its force development on such a logistically 'safe' series of operations.

Logistic capability for the future

According to an Australian Army report:

> The upgrade of existing Land-based systems, acquisition of new combat capability and developing concepts, such as NCW (network-centric warfare) and FLOC (Future Land Operating Concept), are likely to severely challenge the Army's ability to provide CSS (combat service support) capability to support future warfighting in a disaggregated and complex battlespace. This proliferation of new combat capabilities is without commensurate improvement to CSS in the DCP (Defence Capability Plan) and it would be short-sighted to assume there will not be serious consequences without this appropriate investment (or development) in key areas.[17]

Given the contrast between the natures of the operations examined here, from the large-scale commitment to East Timor to the niche expeditionary deployments in the Middle East, it could be argued the problems identified are too idiosyncratic or too varied for widely applicable conclusions to be drawn. This is not the case. At their heart, these logistic problems come from a common root. As Smith remarks with respect to capability in 2002, logistics development was an unequal partner in the Army, a mere 'enabler' for other areas deemed more important.[18] This is hardly revelatory – just as tactics and strategy have always held more appeal than the idea of logistics in the philosophy of Western warfare, so too are the means of warfighting often held in higher regard than other functions that sustain them.

Addressing the modernisation of logistics capabilities was further complicated by their nature. Typically, logistics functions only reveal their importance when described as a system, and as such, generally receive cursory treatment in 'equipment-dominated capability fora'.[19] As operations unfolded, the Army's logistics force developers undertook a series of reviews that aimed to prevent such an outcome, and allow for effective capability development. In 2002 the Army's Land Warfare Development Group responded to the absence of new logistics projects within the Defence Capability Plan and proposed numerous initiatives to remediate capability gaps as part of the logistic review of the Hardening and Networking Army (HNA) initiative.[20] Joint Project 126 – Joint Theatre Distribution System (JP 126 Ph 1) became the focus of the significant (and expensive) Kellogg-Brown-Root review that quantified many of the requirements for logistic support in maritime operations arising from INTER-FET.[21] In 2005, a second logistic study of HNA was undertaken, resulting in an 'Army Capability Requirement' that prescriptively enunciated logistics requirements (and a further plan for logistic capability delivery) until 2015.[22]

Complementing these capability initiatives, two Force Modernisation Reviews into land logistics were conducted. Each recommended further capability development and force structure realignment. Despite the considerable effort undertaken in capability and force modernisation reviews, these systemic assessments failed to convince the Army's leadership to introduce change. Instead logistic capability continued to be treated idiosyncratically. It was apparently too difficult a problem to resolve systematically given the requirement to properly integrate logistics with other Army initiatives already underway. This approach to solving problems has produced its fair share of victims. For example Land 121, the replacement for the Army's transportation, encountered multiple design changes and other challenges that, when combined with the absence of an endorsed concept for its use, have meant the development and delivery of its vehicles will have spanned five decades.[23]

The Army has a good reason to address the logistic problems revealed by its latest transformation initiative, Plan Beersheba. The readiness model is based upon the rotation of three combat brigades over a three-year period. But its force logistics support elements, described as 'enablers', lack the capacity to match this cycle. In order to meet the requirements of its capstone operational concept, the Concept of Employment of the Reinforced Combat Brigade (CONEMP), and in the wake of an abortive Army Headquarters Force Modernisation Review of logistics, the Commander of Forces Command, Mick Slater, directed further work be undertaken in 2013 into his Command's logistics capabilities. In contorting a logistically limited 'army-in-being' into an operating concept, and despite its best attempts to rebalance logistics capabilities to address functional weaknesses, The resulting logistic contempt has proven to be controversial even as it approaches implementation. Its approach to centralising logistics from units to the combat brigade in the hope of attaining efficiencies is a symptom of logistic hollowness. In the absence of additional resources, it has relied upon adjusting process rather than truly remediating capabilities long known to be vulnerable. Nonetheless, the review has been cathartic for a function often neglected. Fortunately, the Army now has a very clear picture of where its logistic deficiencies and first-order logistic challenges lie.

Consequently, the Army's leadership must respond to these new challenges rather than perpetuating a corporate culture that accepts too much operational risk and thrives on a misguided assumption that the operational sustainment of its forces will come from other quarters. The Army may never have the luxury of obtaining everything it wants, let alone what it often needs – decisions on logistics capability are always bounded by government direction, funding, obligations and a historic tendency to base decisions on a 'peacetime pursuit of efficiency'.[24] But the decision to invest resources available into logistic capabilities remains firmly within the remit of the Army's leadership. There are enough operational lessons from the last 15 years that suggest substantial investment is needed, and prioritisation should be directed towards remediating long-standing deficiencies. Some might view reacting to these problems as a responsibility of joint strategic agencies to resolve, given these agencies are now more empowered than ever to contribute to logistic capability development under a nominally Defence logistic framework.[25] However, there can be no other agency, organisation or service better suited to addressing the Army's unique challenges and needs than the Army itself. Even in a joint environment, the Army is responsible for strategic land power. Every factor contributing directly to its mastery is of immediate concern to the Army.

For their part, the Army's logisticians must be guides in improving this situation and break their typical reluctance to engage openly with the wider Army. Although they inhabit a world that is often seen as inaccessible, overly specialised and inclined towards self-indulgence in professional dialogue, logisticians need to broaden their vision and lift their sight. Too often they exchange genuine engagement with the theory and practice of modern war for spirited defence of a cloistered professionalism defined by appointment, trade or corps. The historian

Duncan Ballantine cautioned against making 'a specialist of the logistician' for exactly this reason. He also stressed that 'logistics is a function of command'.[26] It is the responsibility of *all* commanders and not *some* to promote an environment where logistics concerns can be enunciated and logistics processes can be explained in order that this vital component of the art of warfighting is better understood. In turn, professional logisticians are obliged to initiate and lead adaptation as part of well-informed stewardship, a stewardship that informs a coherent doctrinal and conceptual philosophy with respect to logistic capabilities. Internal arguments and professional disagreements among logisticians are rarely an effective means by which this aspiration can be advanced in any way. As Smith identifies, the failure to deliver the necessary message eloquently and persuasively will leave the logistics requirements of the Army unarticulated and the potential capability 'edge' unexploited.[27]

The Army must therefore treat logistics reverently. It cannot afford to fall into the trap of thinking that all is right by not examining its performance critically.[28] But this critical reflection requires practical action. Although advancements have been made, the Army's modernisation features numerous abortive attempts to remediate logistic problems observed on operations. This is as paradoxical a situation as it is bewildering, as a failure to afford logistics the same priority as other arms in the Army is ultimately self-defeating. Recent Exercise Headline experiments constitute a warning to the Army of the challenges ahead if new capabilities, such as armoured vehicles, are introduced without a commensurate logistic backbone to support their acquisition and operation.[29] The consequences of expeditious 'conceptual' solutions to these problems, or the pretense that technology might render logistics obsolete, will be borne by a future Army at mercy of present-day convenience. Indeed, history routinely shows new technology simply introduces new requirements rather than reducing them.[30] To produce a robust Army, it will not be sufficient to stubbornly think that the Army can make do with the smallest number of supporting troops. The goal of force design, instead, should be using logistics forces and capabilities to produce the greatest possible fighting power it can.[31]

Rethinking the importance of logistics for the Army presents other, more immediate and tangible, rewards. The Army, as part of the ADF, has often been fortunate enough to choose its commitments to recent operations, and has benefitted greatly in being able to plan thoroughly prior to the deployment of forces. This is the primary reason that operational logistic failure is largely avoided. Yet, as INTERFET showed, events often deny this privilege – in those times the Army will need hardy logistic capabilities that bestow freedom of action. As Thomas Kane puts it, logistics becomes the 'arbiter of opportunity'.[32] But in more dire circumstances, logistics considerations influence more than just an army's freedom of action. War is inherently asymmetric and wise opponents rarely target each other's strengths. Every logistic problem that is left as a risk by the Army is a short step from becoming an exploitable vulnerability. If the Army doesn't invest time to properly understand logistic factors that are so fundamental to its combat power, someone with ill intent in mind undoubtedly will.

Establishing priorities

Speaking as Chief of Army in 2004, Lieutenant General Peter Leahy lamented that 'too much of the burden of recent deployments has fallen on too small a portion of the land force, especially the Special Forces and our combat support and combat service support elements'.[33] Despite this realisation, the Army has been typically poor at distilling such observations into actual logistic capability outcomes. History reminds us that logistics cannot be an aside to purportedly more dynamic pursuits. The American historian James A Huston reviewed centuries of American conflicts – rather than the 15 years viewed here – and remarked that 'no distinction in importance can be made between combat functions and logistics functions' and that 'no distinction should be drawn … in establishing priorities' between them.[34] As the experiences captured here have shown, this is an axiom that should be at the forefront of contemporary force structure and modernisation planning in the Army, just as it should have been in the years before its deployment on INTERFET.

As the Army looks to the future beyond Plan Beersheba, it must consider logistics beyond the pretense it is merely an enabler of other, more important capabilities. The Army's leaders must fund logistic modernisation, and resource its force structure rather than continuing the deleterious trend of centralising logistic capability. They must accept that the efficiency dividend from logistic jointery is often a peacetime one, and an outcome that will never completely overcome a lack of resilience in the Army's integral logistics capabilities. Force planners must move from the often-naive assumption that commercialisation and contractors will always offer an effective operational solution to its force structure challenges. As argued, there are clear benefits to the Army if it maintains a readily deployable, robust and capable logistic capability, and there are compelling reasons that further modernisation effort be directed towards it. Without changing its current modernisation imperatives, the Army will be unconsciously taking steps that will constrain its strategic usefulness to the joint force for decades to come.

It is worrying that these problems have been the subject of numerous Australian reviews and reports over the last decade.

This suggests other factors are influencing the desire for change or the lack of it. While the Army has significant funding and resource constraints that limit its operations, there are clear, deep-seeded, cultural impediments that have yet to be overcome. Until the Army overcomes these impediments and real change is implemented, it will continue to gamble with its own preparedness. If it does not embrace change, the Army risks repeating the mistakes of the 1990s. These mistakes manifested in a major operation for which the Army was largely unprepared. Observing the outcomes 15 years ago, Smith saw that logistics – this mere 'enabling capability' – cast a long shadow over political and military options.[35] It is concerning that nearly two decades after INTERFET, the Army continues to describe logistics in these very same terms rather than as the fountain from which it draws its potential to fight.

9

LOGISTICS AND EMERGING TECHNOLOGY

ALLISON SONNEVELD

Since the origins of war logistics, military organisations have sought technological solutions to the problems of its conduct. It is, therefore, surprising the Australian Army has struggled to embrace technology solutions that could improve the efficiency and effectiveness of its operations to its logistic challenges. For example, the Army experienced a supply chain breakdown during the Australian Defence Force's (ADF's) support to the East Timor transition to independence, and has managed unwieldy liquid fuel lines in Iraq and Afghanistan. These handicaps remain 15 years later, despite the commercial availability of Radio Frequency Identification (RFID) and smart power and energy technologies. Plainly there is great scope to implement lessons from these two examples for the benefit of future operations.

Land forces carry out diverse functions under the general ambit of warfighting, and none perhaps are as important as logistics. For the Israeli military historian, Martin van Creveld, logistics makes up nine-tenths of the business of war, and is 'nothing but an endless series of difficulties succeeding each other'.[1]

Although far from new, logistics is vital to successful operations. It can make or break militaries. A hallmark of Alexander the Great's expedition was his ability to supply his forces through difficult lands, where others suffered from severe food and water shortages. Yet he was not infallible. After conquering tribes in the Indus Valley (circa 325BC), Alexander's failure to maintain supply while marching through the Gedrosian Desert cost the lives of 70 per cent of his 85,000-strong company, most of whom were non-combatants, along with all support animals and their stores.[2] The Australian Army, too, has experienced the challenge of logistics throughout its history, whether co-ordinating supply to the Australian Imperial Force across several fronts during the First World War, or restoring water supplies in Vanuatu as part of Operation Pacific Assist 2015.

Technology can be critical to military success. When the Royal Navy's battleships started converting from coal-fired to oil-fired boilers in the early 20th century, the fleet expanded the duration and range of activities that could be carried out without refuelling. It also gave Britain a relative advantage by enhancing its naval power at a time when it faced an arms race with Germany.[3] During this period, the advent of armoured cars and tanks offered land forces more range, protection, and firepower than horse-mounted forces had previously enjoyed. Yet it has also meant that supply lines increased, requiring more complex items, and saw an enormous increase in the need for liquid fuels and spare parts along with food and water.

The Australian Army could be expected to do logistics better than it currently does by using a suite of technological solutions. It is a modern land force of a developed nation that has ranked among the world's 20 largest military spenders per capita since 1999, and in the top ten since 2010.[4] With a sustained tempo of Australian operational commitments since 1999, including the involvement in Afghanistan, which it refers to as 'the longest war',[5] the Army has had ample opportunity to identify and remedy logistical challenges. Yet the Army encountered major supply chain problems throughout Operation Warden, during East Timor's transition to independence, and has continued to rely on burdensome power and energy systems throughout its commitments to Afghanistan and Iraq. If technology is to support the Army's logistical challenges, it will need resourcing, a faster capability development turnaround, and a greater acceptance of risk.

Technology adoption in logistics

In the academic literature, the issue of technology adoption in logistics tends to fall within the domains of business and management studies. Most contributions seek to understand adoption based on specific industries, locations, and technologies. With a vacuum in understandings of practices within military organisations,[6] an examination of the Army's technology use in supply aligns with this practice.

There are not many guidelines at hand that explain technology adoption generally. One of the few studies was conducted by Kirk Patterson, a US Air Force Major and assistant professor at the Air Force Institute of Technology, along with Curtis Grimm and Thomas Corsi of the University of Maryland. The team developed a macro-level model of adoption, in which they hypothesised a series of factors facing organisations and their environments that underpin adoption in the logistics sector – namely, an organisation's size, structure, performance, the relationship between its supply chain strategy and its corporate strategy, the nature of its relationships and transactions with supply chain partners, and environmental uncertainty.[7] As this model was developed as a foundation for further analysis, examining the Army's technology adoption based on the hypotheses of Patterson, Grimm and Corsi is not only in the spirit of existing studies, but also addresses the paucity of attention given to military logistics. It is also suitable given that the Australian Department of Defence increasingly looks to industry for logistics benchmarks.[8]

Organisational factors

Organisations that are large, decentralised, underperforming, and have their supply chain strategies reflected in their corporate strategies are expected to be technology adopters in logistics. This is based on the notions that larger organisations are better positioned to change, invest and carry the risk, more loosely structured organisations have the flexibility to trial new projects, poorly performing organisations seek to overcome their weaknesses, and organisations that have their logistics strategies reflected in their corporate strategies have innovative supply chain practices.[9]

Despite being a small land force relative to its major operating partners, the Australian Army still meets the criteria for a large organisation. The Australian Bureau of Statistics defines large employing businesses as comprising 200 or more employees. Ignoring the technicality that members of the Australian Defence Force (ADF) are not 'employees' but 'members' of the Army under the *Defence Act 1903*, the Army's workforce has grown from 24,164 on 30 June 2000 to 29,010 on 30 June 2014.[10] As is usually the case with land forces, the Army is also the largest of Australia's uniformed services.

Although it is dispersed in the geographical sense, with a large number of bases and establishments around Australia, the Army is a highly centralised organisation that has long been built on a formal hierarchy of a chain of command. The First Principles Review of the Department of Defence that was completed in early 2015 found structure proliferates throughout the department. It found that the Defence senior leadership group had nearly doubled in size since 1998, that some areas in the department have up to 12 layers of management (where best practice is seven), that most managers supervise fewer than five staff, and that some 200 committees operate throughout the organisation.[11] Plan Beersheba, the Army's continuing establishment of comparable multi-role combat brigades, is more a form of restructuring than decentralisation in that it is creating a total force arrangement. This said, noting the concern of Patterson, Grimm and Corsi as to whether organisations can trial new technologies, the Army meets this requirement from its involvement in Defence's Capability and Technology Demonstrator program. This program was established to promote the integration of leading-edge technologies into priority capabilities, including logistics in the sea, land and air domains.[12]

Military performance is more difficult to measure than commercial sector performance, where success can be defined by financial benchmarks. Instead it is tied to capability – is a force able to deploy effectively, can it produce the effect governments require of it? Clearly, much of this information is not available outside national security agencies. Since Australia only has one Army, it cannot easily be compared against other services or other national security organisations. What can be done, in accordance with the hypothesis of Patterson, Grimm and Corsi, is to assess whether the Army is aware of its weaknesses and seeks to overcome them. The Army does endeavour to improve its shortcomings where identified. An example is the championing of efforts to address gender and diversity within the Army by

Lieutenant General David Morrison. Another is Plan Beersheba, which has sought to optimise the Army's provision of land forces, on rotation, with combined arms warfighting skills. However, as the two case studies examined later will show, there is broad scope for improving aspects of the Army's logistics. As the Army clearly has the ability to implement large-scale changes, this raises questions about how logistics is prioritised over other functions.

The Army's logistics is reflected throughout its high-level strategic documentation, though it is perhaps not well articulated. The last three Defence White Papers have stressed that logistics will be reformed, that it will be a niche activity carried out with Defence partners, and that the Army's supply vehicles will be upgraded.[13] Likewise, the Army's key publication, Land Warfare Doctrine 1: The Fundamentals of Land Power, which describes how the Army currently operates, addresses logistics and combat service support (CSS) in passing, while focusing on land power and combat.[14] Army's extant description of how it will operate in the future in Adaptive Campaigning – Army's Future Land Operating Concept simply identifies a need for logistics that supports situational awareness of supply, is protected, and has strong administrative capacity.[15] There is, however, cause for optimism as its draft successor, Joint Integraed Land Operations (JILO), stresses the need to develop a specific CSS capability.

Environmental factors

Logistics providers are also likely to adopt technology solutions if they experience external pressures. This primarily comes from supply chain partners and is premised on the idea that organisations can be encouraged to improve co-ordination with stakeholders, more so if relationships are built on trust and respect. An uncertain environment is also a driver for adoption, on the basis that uncertainty necessitates fast rates of change to respond and maintain competitiveness.[16]

The Army has incentive to co-ordinate its logistics systems with supply partners when on operations. As this mainly involves longstanding coalition and allied forces, these relationships are mature. The US Department of Defense is routinely held up as having logistics excellence[17] and Australia has a long operational history of interaction with its supply chains. This is formalised through international agreements such as the Acquisition and Cross-Servicing Agreement (ACSA) between the Government of Australia and the Government of the United States of America and the Agreement between Australia and the United States Concerning Cooperation in Defense Logistics Support (CDLSA), which facilitate the reciprocal provision of logistics support, supplies and services between militaries. The American, British, Canadian, Australian and New Zealand Armies' Program (ABCA Armies) also co-ordinates logistics projects with aims that include leveraging common logistics information systems to support interoperability.

Uncertainty has long been a standard characteristic of the Army's operating environment, as stated throughout strategic level documents.[18] Uncertainty is also expected to be an ongoing feature of the future land-operating environment. 'Army's Future Land Warfare Report (FLWR) 2014', for example, observes that post Cold War-era military activities have become increasingly unpredictable. The future, it argues, can at best be anticipated by identifying the trajectories of meta-trends.[19]

It is clear that business logistics and military logistics are not the same. They have different bottom lines and scopes. Industry seeks to establish a competitive advantage and profit, whereas militaries seek advantage on battlefield and cost efficiencies in using public money. The commercial sector is often focused on transporting goods to consumers. Yet military logistics aims to protect and support soldiers, so its core functions are broader. The definition used by the North Atlantic Treaty Organisation (NATO), for instance, encompasses 'supply, maintenance, movement and transportation, petroleum support, infrastructure and medical support'.[20]

Since the Army broadly matches the majority of the Patterson, Grimm and Corsi hypotheses, it should be expected to champion technology adoption in logistics. Despite this, there are several technologies that the Army could have taken on board that would have reduced operational risk. Further study is therefore needed to better understand how technology adoption occurs in military organisations. It is worth exploring the logistics systems used during Operation Warden and energy consumption in Iraq and Afghanistan because together they illustrate a broad range of solutions. The first requires a cheaper and incremental technology, whereas the second demands more resources and integration with the land force's equipment.

Technology and logistics in East Timor

An examination of the logistics component of the Army's experiences during Operation Warden, the ADF involvement for the International Force for East Timor (INTERFET) from late 1999 illustrates the challenges that can emerge when military logistics systems do not work well. Australia's logistics support to the East Timor deployments has been described as being 'as easy as it gets', owing to the small size and close location of East Timor to Australia, the absence of ongoing combat that could disrupt supply, and because of the small number of personnel deployed, which initially peaked at 5700, dropped to between 1500 and 2000 the following year.[21]

The Army used three logistics systems during the operation, namely the Standard Defence Supply System (SDSS), Lotus Notes Interim Demand System (LNIDS) and the Cargo Visibility System (CVS). None if these systems were ready to operate when deployed. Most of the deployment's inventory was managed through SDSS, with the exception of explosive ordnance and non-military materiel. At the time, SDSS was not capable of field deployment, and was not widely used. A lack of trained personnel and support documentation, glitches within CVS that linked to SDSS and an incomplete catalogue of items meant that it was easy to corrupt records. LNIDS was used to raise requests outside of standard unit authorisation, such as ordering high-value equipment or managing peaks in staff workloads. While it was faster, more reliable, intuitive, and had better tracking capability, it performed poorly under high volumes of demand. Stores visibility was enabled through CVS software, through which SDSS or LNIDS could then track. It too has been described as unreliable, having questionable data integrity, and only having visibility of items at major storage and movement depots. Barcodes were available to help track items but scanners were not located throughout the entire supply chain. Operators did not always scan items because they lacked time during the fast-paced tempo of operations or because they did not understand the need to do so. As a consequence, item demands were not always finalised through the software, leading to poor reporting functionality.[22]

The problematic nature of SDSS, LNIDS and CVS had serious effects for the operation. LNIDS was often used over SDSS because it was a better system, but it meant that requests had to be to be manually transferred back to SDSS, meaning a waste of time and resources. Poor visibility of items led to request duplications, with as many as 8000 unmet demands on SDSS at one point.[23] It also meant that in order to know what items were within a container, it had to be physically checked.

Exacerbating these issues was Dili's relatively small and primitive port facilities. Items were stockpiled at Darwin and fed to Dili, and then had to be sent immediately to the users. The sheer scale of constant demand at Darwin saw a breakdown in supply. Operators did not have control over what items arrived at Darwin, so they moved whatever arrived first. Six weeks into the operation, soldiers were still sleeping on the ground with no tents and washing their uniforms in tins. It was eight weeks after landing in Dili that 2 RAR received full stores and equipment.[24] A great deal can go wrong on an operation in this kind of timeframe, keeping in mind that entire wars, such as the 1967 Six-Day War and the 1982 Falklands War, have started and concluded in relatively short periods. Although Australia's contribution to INTERFET was successful, future deployments may not encounter the same 'easy' conditions.

Track-and-trace capability using RFID

The East Timor experience underlines the importance of being able to track and trace items electronically and, where possible, with less direct human involvement. While far from being a silver bullet, having this ability could significantly alleviate bottleneck and duplication issues. In the view of an Army officer interviewed while conducting research for this paper,[25] this capability could have avoided much of the East Timor docks problem by removing double, triple and quadruple ordering on LNIDS against a single stores requirement.

Radio Frequency Identification technology (RFID) is an ideal way to support a track-and-trace capability. RFID is a wireless communication technology that can uniquely identify tagged objects, and uses radio frequency or magnetic field variations to communicate. RFID is superior to barcodes because a high number of tags can be scanned at once and they can be attached to almost anything. Unlike barcodes they do not need to align with a scanner to be read and simply pass through a gate. 'Passive' RFID tags are relatively cheap because they are powered by the reading equipment and carry no power source. 'Active' RFID tags in comparison contain batteries that power the chip, but come at a higher cost. RFID technology is widely used for tracking books in libraries, timing people in fun runs, preventing retail theft and for contactless credit card payments.

Defence has used RFID technology intermittently. Active RFID tags were rolled out at the joint level to the Middle East area of operations under JP2077 in 2007. Despite interoperability with major partners, including the United States, Britain and Canada,[26] JP2077 has only provided a warehouse level of visibility and does not encompass tracking at the item level. Far from being made available to all users, implementation lies with business managers to adopt on an as-needed basis. Further, Defence use of RFID has since stepped back from discussions in the public domain.

For the Army, RFID tracking can, and is, being used with CVS to support real-time inventory management. RFID technology is being trialled at the item level, in combination with 2-D barcodes. This is promising, though managing two tracking technologies will double the technical burden on enabling logistics systems to recognise them. These developments are belated but nonetheless good news. But the fact that it has taken seven to 15 years to adopt a technology that has been available for decades should not be overlooked. I will return to this issue after considering a second case for technology adoption.

Technology and logistics
in Afghanistan and Iraq

For modern military operations fuel is a critical priority. This means that the Army's main fuel sources, in comparison to previous energy systems based on coal and wood, are energy dense relative to their volume and weight, and are easy to transport in liquid form. Unfortunately, the Army's liquid fuel reliance has become more burdensome as its equipment, vehicles and weapons have become larger, heavier and more complex. For example, the Army's next generation of military combat vehicles being developed through the LAND 400 project will have improved protection over existing capabilities, along with features such as better firepower, mobility and communication. More armour is crucial at a time of persistent weapons proliferation. Yet it also means that protected military vehicles with be heavier and likely to have greater fuel requirements.

Defence reports that 76.6 per cent of the department's energy consumption in 2012–13 was attributed to operations, a proportion that includes aircraft, ships, and vehicles.[27] Although partly due to the large platforms that the other services use in the sea and air domains, forward-operating bases, which tend to be organised and staffed by the land force, can be significant consumers in their own right. Military camps will often use as much as 70 per cent of their fuel to generate electricity in order to heat or cool water and air and power communication systems. The diesel-powered generators performing these functions are inefficient; one-third of the fuel consumed is turned into electricity and the rest is waste heat.[28] A task force-sized forward-operating base could consume between 9000 and 30,000 litres of fuel per day.[29]

There is clearly substantial scope to reduce the Army's liquid fuel footprint, especially at a time when the ADF Posture Review 2012 found that Australia's increasing reliance on oil imports may not meet ADF needs for large operations or when global fuel supplies experience major stress.[30] The Defence fuel supply chain is long and complicated. It is even harder to manage when forces deploy to distant locations. According to one American estimate in 2011, it would take 18 days to move fuel over 1200 kilometres from Karachi in Pakistan to a remote outpost in Afghanistan to power an air conditioner.[31]

There are security implications as well. The majority of fuel in theatres such as Afghanistan is moved by truck. These are soft targets that are highly vulnerable to enemy attack. Even when provided with considerable protection, significant risks to fuel-carrying trucks remain, as well as to the soldiers and contractors operating them. Political considerations can also affect the timely arrival of fuel. For example, more than 4000 supply trucks were delayed in November 2011 when Pakistan closed its border crossings into Afghanistan in response to American air strikes. Convoys were attacked at least once nearly every day that month.[32] More than 3000 American soldiers or contractors were killed in fuel supply convoys between 2003 and 2007 in Iraq and Afghanistan. In Iraq during 2004 the majority of Purple Hearts awarded were to troops operating along communication lines.[33] Clearly, a reliance on liquid fuels brings with it numerous complications and risks that absorb considerable resources and can affect an operation's success.

A case for alternative energy systems

Unlike developing track-and-trace measures for logistics information systems, there is no one single solution to reducing the Army's reliance on liquid fuels. There are, however, a wide range of innovative technologies that could reduce fuel consumption by targeting electricity generation, demand management, energy storage, renewables, and reducing power usage. Solar panels and mats can provide micro-energy solutions at the soldier level. Small, deployable wind turbines could be integrated into a base's power system. Waste heat can be redirected from electricity generation for other purposes, and smarter systems are under development that can better manage peaks and troughs in electricity consumption. Fuel cell technology continues to offer a means to reduce battery consumption and lighten the load on the soldiers who carry them. Waste can be used for fuel, whether in biomass digesters that produce methane or by incinerating garbage or food waste.[34]

These kinds of technologies could reduce the financial cost of supply, de-stress the fuel supply chain, and reduce the physical risk to fuel convoys. While Army efforts to address these problems are in train, it is still early days and much is yet to be done. For instance, researchers at the Australian National University's Centre for Sustainable Energy Systems have trialled a lightweight and flexible Solar Integrated Power System that has double the power to weight ratio of existing panels and can sustain soldiers' batteries during standard mission conditions.[35] The bigger challenge is that liquid fuels have long been the established energy source for militaries and moving away from this form of reliance will not be a simple one-for-one fuel replacement strategy. Rather, it will require an overarching assessment of how the Army's future kit and equipment might interoperate in the future, and how multiple energy technologies could be integrated into any solution. The need for such an assessment has not yet been recognised in Army's FLWR. Consequently, if the Army is to develop smart-energy solutions, it requires a dedicated and well-resourced research and development program that it does not yet have.

On reflection

An examination of the Army's deployment to East Timor during its transition to independence and an assessment of the Army's energy supply in Afghanistan and Iraq has shown that logistics problems can be partly addressed through cheaper and incremental solutions like RFID or through multiple and more complex measures of varying sophistication that can reduce the liquid fuel burden. But it is not apparent, given the importance of some very obvious lessons, why it has taken well over a decade since Operation Warden for the ADF to explore RFID technology when it has been widely available for decades, or why liquid fuel continues to be the Army's dominant energy source. Are the lessons not that obvious or important? Or are the solutions too complex or expensive?

One answer appears to lie in the difficulties associated with change. The difficulties impeding change include high financial barriers that delay implementation, complex issues that prevent ready understanding or an inefficient and risk-averse modernisation process that discourage change. By comparison, maintaining the status quo is the easy option, especially when the solution is multifaceted, as is the case with energy. Implementing change could initially be costly, complex and controversial, notwithstanding the longer-term benefit of enhanced-operational performance and cost-savings. A technology change program for the Army will also need to compete with funds for very large and expensive sea and air platforms, such as Air Warfare Destroyers or Joint Strike Fighters. From my observation, American land forces have a comparatively greater capacity to resource research and development activities.

A related challenge lies at the joint level. The SDSS, LNIDS and CVS systems are joint products used throughout the three services, meaning that there are a large number of users and stakeholders involved when changes are required and that broad consensus is needed if one service wants to function differently. According to the First Principles Review, Defence's capability development process is lengthy and highly bureaucratic, burdened by the very number stakeholders involved and weakened by a collective lack of commercial experience.[36]

The implications of embracing new technologies naturally need to be understood to ensure that soldiers' lives are not put at risk on the battlefield. Every new piece of equipment needs to be tested rigorously and in a range of settings. While there is a great deal to commend increased use of solar cells, they could produce a signature on the non-visible spectrum that might alert an adversary of their presence. Likewise there are signature issues with RFID technologies that could interfere with interoperability on operations. The Defence Science and Technology Group has examined this problem and finalised a Rapid Technology Assessment Framework for Land Logistics in 2015.[37] This framework can assist analysts and staff officers in selecting emerging technologies for use in land logistics.

Answers can also be found in less obvious and more tangible areas, such as in the Army's characteristic overemphasis on command and combat in comparison to logistics. The Army's 'warrior culture', as described by the former Sex Discrimination

Commissioner Elizabeth Broderick, has dominated functional and non-warfighting areas, such as logistics, and perhaps marginalised their contribution to overall operational performance. As shown earlier, this bias in the Army's functions is also evident throughout its strategic-level publications. However, the inclusion of a dedicated CSS functional concept within the prospective JILO is promising for balance in the Army's modernisation.

The focus here has been on identifying and managing risk – not just the risk of using new technologies but also the risk of their non-use. An army that cannot keep up with, let alone keep ahead of, technological change will struggle to generate land power when it is needed. It might be the case that the Australian Army should consider having a greater acceptance of risk in its modernisation activities and rely more on off-the-shelf solutions, if it means a shorter acquisition process. Another option is to continue passing risk to other stakeholders by relying on contractors and coalition partners to perform logistics functions. If the circumstances of warfare change, however, the Army needs to be aware that it might not be able to buy its way out of a logistical problem and be prepared for difficult questions and even harder answers. Noting that a failure to address logistic issues has plagued military commanders since Alexander the Great, there is no excuse for a poorly supplied and badly equipped army.

In retrospect it is easy to review the Army's operations and, with the benefit of hindsight, point out what went wrong and who or what is ostensibly to blame. Perhaps worse is a situation in which no one learns anything from experience. A genuine attentiveness to lessons and challenges means that even now, with emerging technologies promising to enhance logistics – such as big data, UAV technology or 3-D printing – the Army needs to think hard about how it can build logistics excellence. If nine-tenths of warfare lies in getting logistics right, then there is a clear impetus for the Army to exploit these technologies to reform its logistics systems, and in doing so gain a competitive advantage on the battlefield.

10

THE COSTS AND COMPLEXITIES OF HEALTH SUPPORT

ANTHONY J CHAMBERS

The last 15 years has been a period of high-operational activity for the Australian Army. Since the deployment of the International Force for East Timor (INTERFET) in 1999, the Army has been involved in operations in multiple theatres. It has contributed to peacekeeping missions in East Timor, the Solomon Islands and Bougainville, conducted humanitarian assistance operations in response to natural disasters in Indonesia and Pakistan, and undertaken combat operations as part of coalitions against insurgencies in Afghanistan and Iraq. In all of these very different operations, Army health services have provided significant support to both our deployed forces and to civilian populations. Successfully supporting these operations during this high-activity period has proven to be challenging in a number of unexpected ways.

Health support to regional stabilisation operations

During the period 1999 to 2014, the Army has been the lead nation in stabilisation operations in East Timor, the Solomon Islands and Bougainville. These have been protracted and resource-intensive operations. The deployment to East Timor alone continued for more than a decade. They have also occurred concurrently, placing additional strain on already stretched resources.

The absence of suitable health infrastructure within these areas of operations, as well as the distance from those in mainland Australia, necessitated the deployment of Army field hospitals and surgical teams to support the stabilisation force. In East Timor and Bougainville, where the local health infrastructure had been destroyed during the violence leading up to the arrival of the stabilisation force, the deployed Army health facilities were also required to support the civilian population until those local health facilities could be rebuilt. The Army hospital supporting INTERFET and the United Nations missions in East Timor between 1999 and 2003 performed 702 surgical procedures; 57 per cent were for members of the stabilisation force while 43 per cent were for local civilians.[1] During the stabilisation mission in Bougainville the deployed Army hospital was almost entirely involved in providing healthcare to the local population. Of the 810 surgical procedures performed at this facility, 90 per cent were for local civilians.[2] The provision of essential life- and limb-saving health support to the local population during the rebuilding of the local health infrastructure was a powerful demonstration of the Australian Defence Force (ADF) support to the local community, contributing substantially to the success of these missions and winning the battle for the hearts and minds of the civilian population.

Military health facilities are manned and equipped to provide health support to the deployed force element, largely a population of fit adult males. By their nature they are focused on providing combat health support for potential battle casualties, and their training and equipment reflects this. The reality of providing health support to the civilian population of a developing nation is very different, and this provided distinct challenges to deployed Army health assets. During the deployment to Bougainville, children aged under sixteen years accounted for 13 per cent of admissions to the deployed hospital.[3] Obstetrics and gynaecology emergencies accounted for 19 per cent of all surgical cases at this facility. One of the most common surgical procedures performed at the deployed hospital in East Timor was caesarean section for complications of labour.[4] In this way, providing support to the civilian population presented significant challenges to the deployed medical teams. Instruments, equipment and medications to treat paediatric and obstetric patients needed to be acquired at short notice. Medical specialists deploying to the operation were encouraged to become familiar with common obstetric and gynaecology emergencies and their management prior to arrival in theatre. In the finest traditions of the Army health services, personnel improvised and adapted to meet these challenges, providing effective life- and limb-saving healthcare to the local population recovering from their recent violent upheaval.

Providing healthcare to the significant needs of the local civilian community while also maintaining a constant readiness to support deployed force members required a delicate balancing of competing priorities by commanders of the stabilisation force and the deployed hospital. Co-ordination and communication between military health assets, the stabilisation force, the local community and their representatives, external healthcare providers such as the International Committee of the Red Cross and existing healthcare providers was critical during all phases of these stabilisation missions. Maintaining the relationships between these various stakeholders required considerable diplomacy.

In keeping with the nature of these stabilisation operations, where the threat posed by opposition elements was low, few members of the deployed force sustained combat-related injuries. In East Timor, only 5 per cent of all surgical procedures were for battle casualties. The majority of presentations to this facility were for non-battle injuries and illness. Tropical infectious diseases such as Dengue fever and malaria, which are highly prevalent in these communities, were important health threats to the deployed force despite the use of preventative measures. The low-intensity nature of the peacekeeping operations in East Timor, Bougainville and the Solomon Islands meant that the deployed forces could be supported with limited health assets and resources, and this allowed for the sustainment of this support during these protracted operations. As a result, however, the ability of Army health assets to provide effective care to combat casualties remained largely untested during this period.

Humanitarian assistance and disaster relief

During the period from 1999 to 2014 the ADF was increasingly called upon to deploy in response to natural disasters occurring in the Asia–Pacific region. Army engineering and health assets deployed to Pakistan in response to earthquakes as part of Operation Pakistan Assist 1 and Operation Pakistan Assist 2 in 2005 and 2010, respectively. The signature disaster relief operation of this period was the whole of Australian government response to the Indian Ocean tsunami of December 2004, Operation Sumatra Assist. This remains the largest humanitarian assistance operation ever conducted by the ADF.

A major component of the initial response to this disaster was the deployment of an Army field hospital and engineering reconstruction assets to the city of Banda Aceh, the capital of this most western part of the island of Sumatra and the population centre most affected by the earthquake and resulting tsunami. It is estimated that 167,000 residents of Banda Aceh died in this disaster. Almost all civilian infrastructure in the city was destroyed, including water, sanitation and hospitals. Amid this devastation there were 800,000 civilians left homeless. The Australian Army field hospital deployed to the site of the damaged Zainoel Abidin hospital and was able to provide life- and limb-saving healthcare to those injured in the disaster, and to provide continuing healthcare to the local population for a three-month period while this hospital was rebuilt. In the first four weeks of the deployment of the Army hospital, 173 life- and limb-saving surgical procedures were performed for survivors of the disaster.[5]

The deployment of Army engineering assets to Banda Aceh was critical to the response to the disaster, and arguably saved far more lives than the deployed hospital. Army engineering assets moved into the city early and were able to provide the only large-scale source of potable drinking water to the survivors of the disaster, preventing even more deaths. The engineers then set about reconstructing the damaged water, sanitation and power systems in the city.

The humanitarian assistance mission to Aceh presented unique challenges to the ADF. To offer meaningful assistance to the government of Indonesia in the early aftermath of the disaster required the rapid mobilisation and deployment of personnel and equipment, presenting considerable logistic challenges. Once deployed to the disaster area, it was critical that ADF elements co-ordinated their efforts with those of myriad government and non-government organisations, both from Indonesia and the international community, that were at that stage streaming into Aceh. International stakeholders included the International Committee of the Red Cross and the militaries of the United States, Germany and Pakistan, all of which had provided deployable hospitals – in the form of the hospital ship USNS *Mercy* in the case of the United States. This required effective communication and diplomacy with the government of Indonesia, civilian authorities and the Indonesian military. Establishing a close and effective working relationship with the Indonesian military and civilian authorities was even more important in order to overcome any lingering sensitivities in the relationship between the two nations as a result of Australia's role in East Timor's transition from Indonesian sovereignty to independence after 1999. The fact that the province of Aceh had been the site of a separatist movement and was the home of an armed militia, the Free Aceh Movement, provided an additional measure of complexity to ADF assets responding to the disaster.

Despite these challenges, it is widely considered that the Australia's whole of government response to the tsunami disaster in Sumatra was highly effective, and the deployment of Army health assets as part of the response was a key contribution to this success.

Combat health support in Afghanistan and Iraq

The operations in Iraq and Afghanistan have come to define the last decade for the ADF. In these coalition operations, the Army has been involved in combat and counter-insurgency operations against insurgent forces in a complex environment. This has created a distinct shift in focus away from the low-intensity peacekeeping and humanitarian assistance operations within our region to the higher-intensity and more warlike operations against armed insurgent groups in the Middle East Area of Operations. This shift in focus has had wide-ranging effects on the Army as an organisation, with Army health services being no exception.

The risk to deployed personnel from hostile force action in Iraq and Afghanistan was considerable, leading to the adoption of significant force-protection measures. The use of protected mobility vehicles, improved combat body armour systems, counter-battery radar systems and unmanned aerial vehicle surveillance are just some examples of these measures. In this asymmetric warfare, where anti-coalition forces could rarely achieve superiority of firepower in battle, the adversary's weapon of choice was the improvised explosive device. Crudely fashioned from plastic palm oil containers filled with an explosive material, or utilising reconfigured artillery shells or anti-tank mines, these devices accounted for the majority of casualties and deaths to coalition forces in Iraq and Afghanistan. The devices were particularly devastating to soldiers on foot, and those mounted in soft-skinned vehicles. Stand-off attacks on coalition bases using rockets or mortars were also employed by anti-coalition forces and accounted for further casualties from blast weapons. In total, almost two-thirds of all ADF casualties in Afghanistan and Iraq were caused by blast weapons such as improvised explosive devices, rockets and mortars.

The injuries sustained from exposure to these weapons followed typical patterns.[6] As most of these devices were buried, rocks and dirt would become projectiles, causing 'fragmentation' penetrating injuries. These penetrating wounds would be highly contaminated, requiring extensive surgery to reduce the risk of life- and limb-threatening infection. For troops unfortunate enough to be close to the detonation of the device, traumatic amputation of the lower or upper limbs, sometimes involving multiple limbs, could occur. Traumatic amputation of a limb in this way leads to significant blood loss that is life-threatening if not treated immediately. Traumatic brain injury and injuries to the ears from the blast shockwave was commonly seen. The relative protection offered by the use of combat body armour to the chest, abdomen and back meant that injuries to these sites were less common. Conversely, injuries to the exposed areas of the limbs, pelvis, genitalia, neck and face occurred more commonly and could be devastating.

Providing effective combat health support to deployed forces in Afghanistan and Iraq was challenging given the significant risks posed by hostile force action. The individual training of all deployed personnel in advanced first aid techniques was enhanced to incorporate tactical care of the combat casualty principles developed by the American military. Tourniquets were issued to all deploying troops for use in the first aid treatment of blood loss from limb injuries. At the unit level, medical technicians received additional training in the care of the combat trauma casualty, and treatment scenarios were included within mission rehearsal exercises prior to units deploying.

As the ADF was operating as part of a larger coalition in both Afghanistan and Iraq, Australian casualties received their treatment in coalition health facilities, primarily those of the American military. In both of these theatres, the United States had deployed a sophisticated network of forward surgical teams and larger military hospitals. Casualty evacuation from the battlefield to a coalition surgical facility was achieved rapidly by helicopter assets, allowing life- and limb-saving treatment within the 'golden hour' from the time of wounding. Typically, a severely wounded Australian soldier would undergo life-saving surgery at a forward surgical team ('Role 2E' hospital in the NATO nomenclature) and then be evacuated to larger, more capable 'Role 3' health facilities within Iraq or Afghanistan for further, more definitive treatment. From here they would be transported to the large US military hospital in Landstuhl, Germany, in preparation for their final repatriation to Australia.

The contribution of the ADF to combat health support in Iraq and Afghanistan was limited to the embedding of teams of specialists within existing coalition health facilities. These teams were comprised of surgeons, anaesthetic specialists, intensive-care specialists and specialised nursing staff, and were drawn from the Navy, Army and Air Force. ADF specialist teams served in the United States Air Force hospital in Balad, Iraq, the US Navy 'Role 3' hospital in Kandahar, Afghanistan, and in the Netherlands Defence Force 'Role 2E' hospital in Tarin Kot, Afghanistan.

Managing severely wounded casualties with high-velocity military gunshot wounds and blast injuries from explosive devices on these deployments also presented major challenges to these teams as few Australian specialists had significant exposure to such injuries from their previous military or civilian experience or training. Despite these challenges the deployed Australian specialist teams integrated effectively within these facilities and earned a reputation for providing high-quality care to coalition combat casualties. Their contribution was valued highly, and on two occasions Australian medical teams were awarded American meritorious unit citations in recognition of their service in Iraq.

The experience of managing complex trauma patients during the conflicts in Afghanistan and Iraq has lead to innovations and refinements in military medicine and surgery, largely lead by the health professionals of the American military. The rapid evacuation of casualties from the battlefield and improvements in their care by medics in the field and en route to the military hospital has meant that severely wounded soldiers, who in previous conflicts would not have survived their injuries, were saved. At the US Navy Role 3 Hospital in Kandahar, a wounded soldier had a 98 per cent chance of survival if he had signs of life present on arrival to the emergency room. Survival rates such as this are unprecedented in the history of warfare, and are testament to the combat health support provided by the coalition forces in these conflicts. Improvements in the trauma care of such casualties, including the use of tourniquets in the field to treat blood loss from limb injuries, field dressings for wounds that assist the control of blood loss and improvements in the use of blood transfusions, all contributed to the improved survival rates seen in these modern conflicts. There were also advancements in the life- and limb-saving surgery for these injuries with the development of 'damage control' surgical techniques aimed at saving the patient's life by using rapid surgical manoeuvres to control blood loss.

Challenges and opportunities

From providing health support to the low-intensity but prolonged peacekeeping operations in our region, to deploying health assets in response to major natural disasters, and recently to providing high-end specialist care within coalition hospitals for combat trauma casualties in Afghanistan and Iraq, the last 15 years have been a high-tempo period for Army health services. These varied missions have all had very different health support requirements. Army health services have had to be flexible and adaptive to support these operations successfully. The equipment, medical supplies, skillset and training of health assets deployed in support of peacekeeping operations is vastly different from that required to support combat operations. To support all of these likely mission scenarios, Army health services have effectively had to master a broad range of capabilities, including tropical health and infectious diseases, paediatrics, obstetrics and gynaecology, as well as the treatment of major trauma from combat injuries. Army health units have had to broaden their medical equipment holdings as well as their stocks of consumables to reflect the diversity of these support tasks.

Perhaps even more challenging is the individual and collective training of health personnel to prepare them adequately for these varied missions. Providing the training, and perhaps more importantly the hands-on experience of treating patients, encompassing all of these capabilities, is difficult to achieve. For health personnel from the regular Army, clinical placements within civilian health facilities can provide valuable experience with managing patients with traumatic injuries. Exposure to, and experience with, the treatment of injuries that approximate to those seen in combat is, however, almost impossible to obtain within the Australian healthcare system due to low levels of firearm ownership and related gun violence in this country. By way of contrast, American military health personnel have the advantage of training within civilian trauma hospitals to gain valuable experience in managing these injuries. Gaining experience in managing injuries from blasts and explosions is, of course, almost impossible to obtain in either country prior to deploying to a conflict zone.

Providing effective health support to the numerous operations during this period of high-operational tempo since 1999 has been a continuous challenge to Army health services. The Australian Army is a comparatively small force, and Army health is correspondingly constrained in its manning and resources. For this reason, most Army health personnel have deployed on multiple operations during this period, and this high level of activity has taken its toll on the personnel involved. The requirement to deploy on overseas operations as well as to support exercises and other activities in Australia has meant that health units and their members have had limited opportunities to 'reset' between deployments, and the pressures on these units and individuals has been significant and sustained.

The demands on Army health personnel have created challenges for maintaining this workforce. Army health must compete in the marketplace for appropriately trained nursing, medical and allied health personnel. This is particularly the case for highly specialised medical personnel, such as surgeons, anaesthesia specialists and intensive specialists who are critical to maintaining a deployable surgical capability. For most of the last 15 years, all of Army's medical specialists have been members of the Army Reserve. This lack of permanent force specialists has meant the Army has had to rely on the volunteerism of their Reserve specialists to deploy a surgical capability on operations. The difficulties of recruiting and retaining such specialist medical officers, who can command very high remuneration in civilian practice, has meant that only a relatively small pool of such specialists exists within the ADF. As these specialists are reservists with civilian hospital commitments, deploying these members at short notice is also highly problematic. For all of these reasons, providing high-level specialist support, particularly surgical capability, to multiple operations has been testing. It has meant that the workload for members of the Army's small specialist workforce has been high, with most personnel deploying on multiple occasions.

This period of high operational activity has also provided significant opportunities. The experience obtained during multiple operations has created a more capable force, with higher levels of individual and collective skills. The deployment of forces on combat operations in Iraq and Afghanistan has also lead to an enhanced appreciation for the role of Army health assets across the organisation, and has demonstrated the capability of Army health personnel to manage combat trauma. The opportunities to work with coalition partners from the United States, the United Kingdom and the Netherlands within their deployed health facilities and health support networks has also been an invaluable experience for Army health personnel. The experience in managing combat trauma from high-velocity military small arms as well as blast injuries within these facilities was also an irreplaceable opportunity for Army health personnel, and the corporate knowledge gained will add value to the entire organisation.

The experience and lessons

Demands on the Army's health services have reflected the higher operational tempo that the Australian Army has experienced since 1999. Army health services have provided effective support to deployed troops as well as civilian populations during peacekeeping operations within the region, were critical components of our government's response to major disasters in the region, and have effectively cared for the casualties of combat operations in Iraq and Afghanistan. Providing high-quality health support to these varied missions has tested Army health assets, given the limited resources and restricted manning. Despite these challenges, Army health has effectively supported all of these operations, providing effective support to our deployed troops while they are in harms way, and in this way has been a critical contributor to their success. The experience and lessons from these operations means that Army health has become an even more capable organisation, and is well positioned to meet the challenges of the operations of the future.

PART 4: VIEWS FROM THE MEDIA

Head of Regional Assistance Mission Solomon Islands, diplomat Nick Warner, holding a press conference in Honaria, 2003.

11

THE MILITARY AND THE MEDIA

BRENDAN NICHOLSON

Journalism has been frequently described as 'the first draft of history'. While it is not clear who first uttered those words, their meaning was exemplified in the extraordinary work of Charles Bean, who covered the Gallipoli campaign as a journalist and then edited the 12-volume official history of Australia's involvement in the Great War, writing six of the volumes himself. If journalism is indeed the first draft of recent history, then both the media and the Australian Defence Force (ADF) have failed badly to inform the current and coming generations of the nation's involvement in conflicts in Afghanistan and elsewhere. This failure can be accounted for in a number of ways.

Much of the fighting against the Taliban in Afghanistan has involved Special Forces in a war with very amorphous 'front lines'. There is clearly a need to stop information reaching the enemy that might endanger small detachments of troops or reveal details of the strategy they use that might threaten their safety in future operations. While the ADF's approach to the media has been far from ideal, inaccurate reporting has at times not helped to encourage members of the ADF to speak up or to speak out about organisational inadequacies or system failures. Levels of access to the Australian military during operations have declined dramatically over the past century, to the point where covering a war properly has been extremely difficult for any journalist no matter how energised they have been or how much goodwill they have shown towards the military.

I have a great personal and professional concern about media coverage of the war in Afghanistan. It has become increasingly difficult to gain access to people and places that are needed to do a reporter's job properly. There is a great deal that a journalist cannot, for legitimate reasons, write about. But there is also a high level of risk aversion throughout the Australian military that makes it difficult to report on events, even in a way that poses no threat to ADF personnel on operations. Being embarrassed about an important event that may not have gone according to plan is not a reason to keep it out of the media. In large part, the refusal to speak about the Afghanistan campaign comes from a perception that the nation's political leaders are going to come down hard on any officer or soldier who breaks ranks and says too much about what they and others have done. Speaking to the media without authorisation or speaking to the media with authorisation and being too candid can, and has, ended other-wise promising careers. In my view, the alleged offence is usually well out of proportion to the effective punishment. But it is not just the military to which this observation applies. This malaise has spread throughout government.

Two decades ago, when a state or federal budget was delivered in parliament, a journalist could contact a government depart-ment by telephone and, for instance, ask for the details of new taxes the government had decided to impose. The departmental switchboard would put the journalist through to the staff member who was the subject matter expert and he or she would outline the likely impact of the budget measure in as much detail as the journalist required. Quite possibly they would tell the journalist if they thought the new tax was a good tax or a bad tax. Any 'negative' comments would not put the public servant's job on the line. The treasurer was not going to demand that they be sacked. If the minister wanted the public servant punished, the departmental secretary would thump the minister's desk and tell him or her to back off. Because the political independence of the public service has been seriously eroded, it is now virtually impossible for a journalist to penetrate every department's screen of assorted 'minders' in order to speak with a frank and fearless public servant. If the journalist does happen to speak to such an individual, the official is likely to be fearful of what might happen to his or her career should he or she be willing to say anything, let alone appear critical of a government decision.

Every public organisation has its own coterie of media advisers (some of whom are ex-journalists) whose main job appears to be stalling or, in some cases, preventing journalists from accessing the information they are seeking, and certainly to stop the journalist talking directly to those who know most about the issue at hand. Some of these advisers are very smart and give persuasive and often prudent counsel to those who employ them. But those who come from a public relations background, who have no 'feel' for the media and its legitimate needs, seem to know little about what journalists require, and to which they are entitled when it comes to the activities of government in a free and demo-cratic society. These advisers are there purportedly to deal with the proliferation of media inquiries from the 'old' and the 'new' (online) media. Their presence is defended on the grounds of organisational efficiency and treating all media outlets fairly. But the reality is usually the opposite. They make access to information uniformly difficult so that the media essentially has to plead for information with only the most compliant journalists agreeing to often-draconian access conditions. Increasingly, experienced journalists rely on personal contact with senior people to get the information they need to write a comprehensive story with any credibility. Let me stress, it is not just the Army to which this observation applies. It is equally valid across state and federal bureaucracies and agencies.

It is very much an Australian phenomenon. I have made trips into Iraq on behalf of my newspaper and found I learned much more about current operations from a British paratroop sergeant or a relatively junior American soldier than from a room of senior Australian officers. Australia's allies are likely to be much more forthcoming with views on how they think the war is being fought, how they regard the senior leadership and where the principal operational challenges might lie. Australian personnel are, I suspect, trained from the beginning to be suspicious of the media and to resent journalists. This has the most regrettable consequences in addition to compounding the problem. When a journalist does go to Afghanistan and spends sufficient time with officers and soldiers so that they relax and loosen up, they are often heard to complain, 'We are doing all this amazing stuff here so why aren't you telling people at home about it.' Of course, competent journalists with professional pride are unwilling to produce sanitised versions of any event, let alone a war in which people are dying and young Australians are suffering severe wounds of body, mind or spirit. But the human-interest stories only make sense against the backdrop of reliable reporting of operations and frank assessment of their effectiveness. Parts of Defence seem unable to help the media to assist their efforts to present the positive work being done by uniformed Australians abroad.

By way of example, in early 2015 a group of defence writers was invited by the retiring Chief of Army, Lieutenant General David Morrison, to watch a video depicting the Australians' experience in Afghanistan. It was gut-wrenching stuff, visceral, strong and very well put together. It was produced internally by the Army but was nonetheless a spectacular piece of journalism. The film began with images of an Australian vehicle hit by an improvised explosive device that badly wounded some of those on board. We saw and heard their pain and fear. It had two immediate impacts on the journalist audience. We were impressed by the frankness with which this material was presented but there was a deep frustration too. At the presentation, I sat alongside a colleague who had been in Afghanistan with a photographer when a medivac helicopter brought in a wounded soldier. The photographer did what he was there for – he took photographs. As a result of this entirely predictable action, the pair of them were dressed down and warned that if they tried to publish the pictures they could and would be sent home. They pointed out that expelling them from the country would be a major story in its own right. Eventually an agreement was reached. They could publish the least shocking photographic images. In broad terms, there is a double standard here and a substantial level of risk aversion. While the Australian public no longer accepts long lists of dead soldiers running into the thousands as they did during the two world wars, it does accept that when those in the military are deployed to a war zone some of them may well be killed or wounded.

If a journalist phones the Defence media room they are likely to talk to a very pleasant, well meaning and probably highly educated young person who knows absolutely nothing about the ADF or its operations abroad. Often the information journalists are seeking is completely innocuous. It might be advice on what sort of helicopters Australia operates in Afghanistan or how many wheels are fitted to a Land Rover used by the Special Forces because a newspaper artist who wants to get the detail right is putting together a graphic to accompany a story explaining an incident. Trying to get this sort of mundane information can be excruciatingly difficult and the process is incredibly time consuming in an age of ever-tighter editorial deadlines. If the newspapers get the type of helicopter wrong or the number of wheels is incorrect, someone from the Defence force or a follower of military affairs will telephone the editor's desk the next day to complain about our lack of commitment to accuracy. Readers are close observers of these kinds of details and they do not tolerate mistakes.

The British and the American military establishments also seem to be far more accepting of press criticism, including adverse commentary, from those who are actually deployed. Some of the material carried in *Stars and Stripes* is a good example. The American service newspapers can be very critical of operational command and organisational leadership, and soldiers have been scathing in their assessment of the politicians who sent them and their colleagues into harm's way. It is easy and sometimes convenient to overestimate risk and to err on the side of caution when it comes to reporting armed conflict. Rarely is censorship or burying a story the answer. I recall an episode many years ago where a member of a sports parachuting club was killed. Members of the club committee asked me, as a very young journalist, how they could keep the news out of the media. I explained that they couldn't keep this tragedy from being reported. They were worried that if news of the accident spread throughout the community, the reputation of the sport would be tarnished and no new members would ever join the club. In fact, the converse was true. On the weekend after the accident more people turned up to inquire about joining the club than on any weekend in living memory. Fears that the club would wither were actually misguided and inaccurate, while trying to hide the death of a member would have aroused suspicion and ill will, leading the community to think the club was secretive and that the sport was unsafe.

Defence needs, therefore, to loosen its constraints on the flow of information and shed some of its paranoia about negative reporting. It makes a lot of sense to have someone available to whom journalists can go with questions – a person who actually knows the answers and who can, without placing anyone in danger, judiciously provide them. Of course, it is always going to be easier to get a negative story into the media than a positive one. This is a sad fact of life. We all know that 'man bites dog' is an engaging story because it is an unusual role reversal. 'Dog bites man' is commonplace and therefore uninteresting and, therefore, not much of a news story. And 'no one got bitten by anything today' is generally not a story at all. Journalists will always produce stories about Defence projects that come in late and are over budget because they usually embody lapses of judgement or cases of poor performance. The public interest has not been well served and the public needs to know they have been let down. Not much can be said and will be reported in the media about projects that come in on time and with cost savings. Accordingly, the Air Warfare Destroyer project, now late and costing more, has featured on front pages while the very successful Anzac Frigate program gets only the occasional nod in the media. Organisations doing what they said they would do, that does not constitute news.

My point is not that the Australian Army cannot get strong publicity from solid stories. A skilled journalist can get a large part of the narrative into the paper if the material is available. But they cannot make bricks from straw. They need information and insights that are accurate and reliable. One reason journalists are given by Defence to preclude them from reporting on a particular group of people or events in a certain place is the physical danger involved in producing such a report. Some operational zones are not safe for civilians, let alone civilians who are looking for trouble to write about. Journalists generally do not seek postings to places such as Iraq and Afghanistan unless they are willing to take some risks, not unlike those accepted by Charles Bean during the 1915 Gallipoli campaign or by the photographer Tim Page who sustained four serious wounds (one life-threatening) while covering the Vietnam conflict. Many reporters are perfectly prepared to go 'beyond the wire' to cover the ADF's activities. For their part, news organisations understand that they cannot expect a unit of highly trained and physically fit soldiers to nurse-maid a journalist who is neither acquainted with their duties nor prepared for physically demanding operations. While some journalists are active and vital, there are places were previously untried civilians can be taken without them becoming a burden to the Army. It is an investment the ADF as a whole might find worthwhile.

Australian journalists working for American news organisations have been out on potentially dangerous patrols with American units and have come under fire in the process. Canadian journalists lived on bases in Afghanistan with their nation's troops and regularly travelled with them. Some, like the Irish–Australian journalist Paul McGeough, have essentially gone around the military bureaucracy by hiring private cars in Afghanistan and Iraq, taking the substantial risk of driving across the country without an armed escort. Others, such as former soldier turned photographer Gary Ramage, have been with patrols in firefights and come home with graphic material. Many journalists are willing to spend time in a forward base in a 'hot' area, something that happened all the time during the Vietnam conflict. In effect, they are willing to accept danger and discomfort for the sake of their profession and the importance of fair reporting.

Most people who become journalists believe the public should have access to considerable information about conflicts such as those in Afghanistan and Iraq. They also believe that there should be unfettered discussion and debate about the merits of placing the men and women of the ADF in hazardous, if not dangerous, situations. The public should be conscious of what is being done in their name and why it is being done on their behalf. If ADF members receive orders from their government via the Chief of Defence Force to turn up at 0500 to be sent overseas to fight, we expect that they will follow orders, set their alarms and turn up at 0500 to do as they are directed. They do not argue about whether they should be going or not. We do not want a politically active military community that exercises discretion in relation to the tasks it will and will not undertake.

But on every occasion Australia sends its uniformed person-nel abroad, someone should be having a serious debate about whether or not a dangerous deployment is necessary, whether the mission is moral and how the operation serves the nation's inter-ests. This is the way public accountability should work. What drives most good journalists is the desire to tell a story accurately and well so that the cause of public accountability is properly served. When people are risking their lives in a cause sanctioned by the nation's political leadership, there is a very strong story to be told. Often what is happening on a day-to-day basis needs to be put into a broader context so it will make sense. Additionally, if something bad has happened (or is happening) in Defence or anywhere else in the community, and if someone does not want something reported, journalists have a duty to ensure the event is made public in a story that is accurate and unbiased. Decent journalists who get things wrong will always be willing to put the record straight. Their reputation will suffer among those whose opinions they value if they don't.

A major part of the information flow problem for the Army is political interference or even just the perception within Defence that the 'minister will be upset' with a bad news report or that the minister will be denied a media opportunity if good news is reported too soon. This uncooperative and unproductive mindset goes back in many cases to media advisers and their preoccupation with 'announceables'. If bad news needs to be presented, many politicians will be happy to leave the announcement to senior uniformed leaders who can deal with the fallout. But if there is a nugget, a jewel, a diamond, a piece of really good information to be passed on to the voting public – maybe someone unexpected receiving an esteemed foreign decoration – it will be hard to see a uniform among a forest of politicians. This may appear cynical but it reflects two decades of observing how news is handled in the Defence portfolio.

Sadly, windows into events within Afghanistan have been opened by the more than 40 occasions in which Australian personnel have been killed on active service. There will be a media conference and perhaps an investigating officer's report, although they are always heavily redacted. Sometimes, frustrated family members have applied pressure for a civil inquest and a lot more detail has emerged of what went wrong or whether it was intelligence failures or equipment malfunctions. The other occasion that prompts an abundant flow of real information is when a service member is recognised for bravery in the field. If it is safe to allow information to circulate when someone is praised for their heroism, why is it so difficult for Defence to be more generous with information about routine operations?

The problem has tended to start with a minister who keeps a ludicrously tight grip on information flows, with ministerial staffers insisting that every bit of information coming out of Defence must be cleared by them. This sort of stranglehold is fatal to the development of a detailed and valuable narrative about what Australians are doing and how well they are doing it. Knowing that their story is being told is often all soldiers want to see in the media. But their leaders appear to believe that truth is dangerous. A senior officer who makes a comment to a journalist or who releases information he or she sincerely believes will benefit the men and women under their command risks a poor performance report if the information is even slightly 'off message' with the story the government is telling the public. This has been the fate of capable and experienced officers whose motivation has been serving the national interest and the wellbeing of those within their command. They do not deserve to have their career prospects tarnished by what purports to be politics but is actually little more than personal ambition on the part of a politician or one of their staffers.

Some of the issues surrounding current military deployments are highly complex and the risks posed to troops abroad if wrong decisions are made can be substantial. It has, for instance, been argued that our troops in Iraq should go into battle with the local forces they are training, and that if there had been 50 coalition advisers with the Iraqis when the city of Ramadi was attacked by Islamic extremists, the Iraq soldiers might have stood firm and not let Islamic State terrorists capture the area and its inhabitants. The counter-argument was put that Iraqis might well have fled anyway and we might have lost 50 of our soldiers. People are not stupid and the public can handle an actual debate that deals with the presenting issues. It is also important for those in the military to understand what is happening within the media as they try to engage or grapple with the demand for stories – and why media leaders often have little time to wait for detailed answers to their questions.

A key issue is that the rapid development of the online media has already had an impact on what we have referred to as the 'mainstream' media, or the old media. It has given the old media a shakeup and some competition, which is good. The so-called 'rivers of gold' – the advertising revenues that funded newspaper journalism for decades – have been drained away by websites that are much less expensive to run and are accessible and enticing to the young in particular. Newspapers have all set-up online versions, some with firewalls, but no one has yet come up with a foolproof way to make money by selling news on the internet.

The impact on newspapers of these developments has been catastrophic. Cities that had several evening papers and two or more morning papers have, in many cases, seen all but one newspaper close. Broadly, the internet has enormous reach and it has proven very effective at mobilising people. The Arab Spring and mass demonstrations in Iran have revealed what is possible online. Conversely, much of what is read on many websites is nothing more than commentary of variable quality. Editorial standards are inconsistent but it is telling that these websites often rely on material gathered, at some financial cost to their companies, by journalists in the old media. In effect, newspapers are providing a good deal of electronic content. Online media has accelerated the immediacy of breaking news with television channels regularly featuring news 'flashes' from tweets that something has happened somewhere in the world. A leadership challenge might be on or off or being thought about by someone who thinks they might have overheard a comment in a restaurant by someone who looks like a politician and certainly sounded like one. This development has had a number of impacts, and not all of them are healthy.

The greater urgency brought to journalism by the internet has increased pressure on journalists to be the first to get a story online. This pressure leaves less time for fact checking. To demonstrate this point, in November 2010 on a flight from Singapore to Australia, a Qantas airliner suffered an engine explosion that resulted in pieces of the engine landing on an Indonesian island. Someone tweeted that a Qantas jet had crashed in Indonesia. A mainstream news organisation picked up the tweet and reported it as a fact, effectively killing off a plane full of passengers. In reality, the highly experienced pilot, Richard de Crespigny, and his team returned the crippled Airbus A380 aircraft to Changi Airport, where an emergency landing was successfully made. It is difficult to know how much grief the tweet, and the unprofessional news report that followed it, triggered among relatives and friends waiting for passengers. This incorrect information also resulted in an immediate drop in the Qantas share price.

Defence and national security issues can also be used as political footballs with announcements and warnings trotted out against a backdrop of flags and uniforms. In that environment, the media tries to reveal as much about national security issues as is possible without placing people in danger. It is never easy, however, to get information from those who know what is happening and can talk candidly about the objectives being pursued and the risks being negotiated. Generally, representatives of government agencies, including the ADF and the Department of Defence, are very reluctant to disclose their views, leaving the space to ministers and to some extent their staff to offer their partisan depictions of what is happening and why.

While uncertainty remains about who can say what to whom within Defence, there is also the revolution in communication being wrought by social media. Defence is facing new security challenges in the Twitter age. During past wars censors were able to deal with security risks by using a heavy black pencil, or even scissors, to remove sensitive information from a soldier's letter home. In the days before Skype and Facebook, letters from loved ones took weeks at least, and often many months, to reach soldiers serving overseas. Sometimes a reassuring note saying all was well would arrive after a soldier had been killed in action. For both the writers and the readers, every word was treasured. Those responsible for OPSEC (operations security) had an easy job of it. No longer is this the case. In the hands of a technologically skilled Gen Y, social media – with its smartphones, ubiquitous computers and the promise of instant communication from almost anywhere on the planet – has changed everything irreversibly. It is an enormous benefit to morale that ADF personnel stationed abroad for months at a time can be in constant touch with partners and children but, unless major steps are taken to shutdown networks, social media takes the ability to exercise simple censorship out of the hands of the officer with the scissors.

A former Chief of Defence Force, General David Hurley, said the answer was not attempting to shutdown the internet or even restricting access to it. The solution was acquainting personnel with the dangers of deliberately or unknowingly launching into cyberspace sensitive information that might get them or their mates killed. He concluded that the ADF could not realistically ban the use of social media even if it tried to prohibit its use. The ADF might issue an order that no personal phones, tablets or computers were to be taken into an area, but human nature was such that someone would try to sneak a phone in somewhere. The use of social media on operations boils down to operational requirements. Far from trying to preclude access to social media, Hurley embraced the new technology by signing up to Facebook and Twitter. 'I do not intend Facebook or Twitter messages to replace official communications or the chain of command, but if you are following me online you might just hear it first,' he told his information-hungry audience in the ADF. 'What you see are my messages delivered without media filter and without distortion,' he explained. But even savvy young Gen Y sailors, soldiers or airmen and women might be giving away much more information than they intend or realise when, for instance, they post what they think are simply 'happy snaps' on Instagram. A big problem for forces deployed overseas is that an enemy that uses the internet comprehensively – as the Taliban does – may have the technology to untangle the data on photographs that are geo-tagged, to find out where and when they were taken. This could give away the location of an individual serviceman or woman or their whole unit. It might be done by a foreign intelligence agency and then passed on to insurgents.

Many in the ADF have long had a near-obsessive desire for secrecy and may embrace the communications revolution with less enthusiasm than Hurley. The ADF's reputation has taken a battering when racist or sexist comments by a small number of soldiers have found their way on to Facebook, and from there to headlines in the media. Hurley noted that a yarn among mates that might go unnoticed in the pub could explode into a front-page story when the same information is posted online. It was a massive exercise in risk management, Hurley said:

> Yes, there's the morale and welfare benefit of allowing our servicemen and women to communicate with friends and families back home, but they need to be conscious, having that level of access, of how to protect what they're doing and what their fellow servicemen and women are doing in the battlefield.

So information from the 'battlespace', and from Defence generally, will emerge – eventually.

To avoid the distorting effect of Chinese whispers, the Army needs to be more forthcoming with journalists and to engage with them directly. They are not an adversary to be resisted or an enemy to be defeated. An important consequence of the massive shift from writing in ink on paper to the cyber world is the problem for historians of tracking down and preserving a cross section of the material that goes to and from soldiers in the war zones. In the past, diggers' letters and diaries provided real-time accounts of wartime life. While much more is probably written now, that 'first draft of history' could well vanish as thousands of computer files are deleted or hard discs eventually give up the ghost. At the very least, this is something that the Army should want to avoid if only because it will prevent future generations from learning the lessons of history.

12

BALANCING INFORMATION AND REPUTATION

LEANNE GLENNY

From the initial scramble for seats for journalists on the first sortie into East Timor in 1999, to the media embedding program in Afghanistan in 2011, reporting of war has continued to challenge both the Australian military and media. Over that time, the public reporting landscape has transformed considerably, particularly in relation to new technology and its impact on the business of the mainstream mass media. The reporting of the Australian Army's involvement in wars and peacekeeping operations since the late 1990s has received considerable analysis and commentary by both journalists and media scholars. Many contributions contend that the Australian Defence Force (ADF) has erected defensive positions around its activities, limiting access by the Fourth Estate and denying the democratic right of Australian citizens to be fully aware of the actions of their military.[1] Contrastingly, the military contends that it is bound by political and security concerns,[2] has logistical limitations in supporting the media,[3] and that the media can be (and has been) irresponsible, inaccurate and too focused on negative reporting.[4]

Consequently, it argues that it cannot afford news reporters unfettered access to uniformed personnel or operational deployments. As often the case, the truth often lies between these polarities.

Assessing where 'truth' lies is highly problematic and dependent on the site of the observer and the desired objectives for media coverage. Ideally, the purpose of public reporting of operational activities in a democratic nation is to ensure that citizens are fully informed of the justification, activities and costs of participating in conflict. Yet vested interests cannot be avoided. Differences between this idealistic objective and the practical interests of the media and the military in war reporting create challenges in judging balance, objectivity and appropriateness. While both institutions may claim their actions sit under the mantle of informing the public, each has its own priorities. The media industry is about 'selling' the news whereas the military is striving to build a strong reputation. For the media, success could therefore be determined by the reader, viewer or listener numbers. For the military, success could be determined by its standing within government agencies or its reputation among operating partners and the general public. But neither of these assessments necessarily gives an indication of how well the public has been informed.

For the Australian Army, the ideal purpose of war reporting may well be to keep the citizens informed[5] but this perception is based on the deeper desire to build 'credibility and trust with the Australian public'.[6] Jason Logue emphasises that the embedding of journalists within Army operational units should be about 'sustaining public understanding, not just facilitating media demands'.[7] Yet goals and objectives for media coverage are often framed in terms of the Army's reputation – seeking public support, which in turn provides benefits in areas such as political support, recruitment and the raising of morale for soldiers and their families who believe their efforts are being valued by others.

Developments and activities in media reporting during the most recent conflicts have actually demonstrated that reputation does not need to be built in a manner that is detrimental to information sharing. The reputation of an organisation is built on its performance and communication efforts over a long term, creating an ability to withstand any lapses due to a respect for previous success. In general, the performance of the Australian Army in the most recent conflicts has been admirable, enhancing its existing reputation. Media coverage has generally been positive. Yet, attempts to prevent access to information, places or personnel, have been reported in negative terms, resulting in avoidable damaging perceptions. Detailed and useful accounts have been written about the media's challenges in covering recent operations.[8] Taking a different approach, four lessons that either have been or could be learned by the Australian Army as a consequence of recent operations are the focus here. These lessons concern the opportunity to embrace change in the media landscape, the need to navigate relationships within a tumultuous media industry, the benefits of openness and transparency, and the significance of a strategic view of communication. Finally, I want to show that the dual aims of maintaining strong public support for the ADF and achieving an informed citizenry are completely compatible.

The changing media landscape

The Vietnam conflict is often described as the first television war although challenges in providing film coverage were still quite significant.[9] In the decades since, technologies have continued to impact significantly on the public reporting of war. In reflecting on the 2003 Iraq War, Nicholas O'Shaughnessy observed the 'visualities of war had attained new levels of immediacy and vividness. The public record had never before captured the sense of actually being in a war with such a degree of accuracy before.'[10] Since then, change has continued with the proliferation of new media channels, providing capacity for an even greater distribution of information and new platforms offering forums for debate on complex issues.

These developments are forcing businesses and organisations of all kinds to adapt. The media and military are no different. The traditional mass media is, and will always be, an important channel for the public to receive reports about armed conflict. But traditional media it is no longer the only channel. As Laurie Oakes predicted in the 2011 Andrew Ollie Media Address, 'political journalists will be bypassed more and more' and 'bloggers will start to usurp the role of determining what is news'.[11] The media landscape is no longer limited to the newspapers, radio and television or their online editions. In any event, the public is not necessarily turning to traditional media to source their news and to acquire information. Traditional media is increasingly shunned because alleged connections with political and financial interests make it highly susceptible to bias. In particular, bloggers are challenging journalists and providing 'alternative narratives', featuring authors from diverse personal and professional positions, including activists, NGOs, eyewitnesses, specialists, military officials and individuals, and insurgents.[12]

An integral part of the transformed media landscape is the rise of the citizen journalist, providing information and video footage from a place or an event, direct to social media or news outlets. Cynthia Banham argues that this innovation, and the ability for states to communicate directly with its citizens, 'throws up new perils for the public's ability to properly scrutinise and comprehend their government's wars'.[13] Despite any effort by the military to control information from the front line, sources providing information to the media will continue to be enlarged.

One of the impacts of the proliferation of new technologies has been the demassification or disintegration of the public. Rather than accessing one or two mediums, the public now divides its attention across many channels of information. Online publications such as *Crikey*, *New Matilda* and *The Conversation* may have fewer readers than traditional newspapers but they are drawing on those who look for more detail than the headline stories provide. Articles are also not only written by journalists; instead specialists and commentators, such as defence interest groups and retired military officers, are writing opinion pieces that are often shared, re-tweeted and promoted through social media and prominent websites. Audiences with specific interests turn to Google to fulfil their information needs, often resulting in a range of international perspectives.

From an ADF perspective, this more complex media landscape creates a requirement for greater monitoring of information flow and the management of information demands from increasingly diverse sources. Monitoring traditional media coverage alone is not sufficient in determining public sentiment towards the military. Media stakeholders now extend beyond traditional journalists with a greater diversity of interest groups and individuals also seeking information and engagement with the military and its members. While this could initially appear to be an additional burden for Defence personnel and public affairs structures, it presents new opportunities as well. The ADF's own channels for promoting information about operational activities, through the service newspapers, websites, video channels and social media, become even more significant as a means of influencing various forms of public reporting of conflict. But substantial responsibilities accompany this wide and direct reach. The

Army must ensure that the objective of building reputation is not achieved at the expense of fully informing the public. This duty will always be a highly contentious issue if Banham is right in asserting that democratic states are 'keen to utilise new media technologies for the purposes of entrenching their own power and legitimacy'.[14] Ensuring that the technologies are used for empowering citizens will remain a challenge, but an essential one for an apolitical ADF and Department of Defence in a highly politicised environment.

Changes in the media landscape since 2000 have been little short of transformative. What is now considered 'the media' transcends the traditional mass media that existed at the end of the 20th century. In sum, the Australian Army can embrace the opportunities offered by the new technologies to keep the public informed as well as build its reputation.

Navigating relationships in the media industry

The media industry is also facing significant change, introducing new challenges and opportunities for the military-media relationship.[15] Both threatened and enhanced by technological changes, media outlets are also under significant commercial pressures and at times 'editorial indifference to stories of Australians at war'.[16] The 24-hour news cycle places demands on journalists for increased coverage, additional angles and more breaking stories, often at the expense of depth and analysis. In turn, this reduces the capacity of journalists for 'follow up and independent verification of sources'.[17] Print media journalists are no longer limited to words on paper and photographic images. They are also producing online content that demands up-to-date commentary and engaging video footage. At the same time, the media industry often takes more of a consumer focus in trying to keep readership figures and ratings buoyant. At times, the media has moved away from its traditional role of facilitating political debate and headed towards info-tainment.

The noble idea of the Fourth Estate and its government watch-dog role is actually threatened by the commercial goals of news organisations. With increased pressure to sell the news – making its presentation more engaging, sometimes at the expense of con-tent – populism becomes almost irresistible, influencing both the media agenda and the framing of narratives. Human-interest stories that provoke sympathy are favoured over hard-news sto-ries that provoke debate. News values of conflict, controversy and drama often become the focus in shaping the selection and craft-ing of news stories. When Sharon Hobson claimed in 2007 that 'the prospect of increased risk and potential combat brought the [Canadian] media to Afghanistan in droves',[18] it was these news values that acquired prominence, not the specific desire to fully inform the citizens of their nation about the Canadian Forces activities and achievements. Tom Hyland concurs with the view of fellow journalist David Salter that media support for the ADF, 'lasts only until journalists smell blood – the blood of scandal. If journalists love diggers, they also love stories about dithering high command, cover-ups, friendly-fire catastrophes and pro-curement bungles.'[19]

Kevin Foster argues that it was 'not unreasonable' for the media to justify a greater news value in reports 'of combat and casualties' rather than of 'the digging of a well or the comple-tion of a health centre', as they 'were the stories their readers and viewers were most keen to follow'.[20] In doing so, Foster pits 'combat and casualties' against community reconstruction tasks. Yet, if the Australian public is to be genuinely informed of the full extent of the Army's activities, this focus is just as unbalanced as the ADF's focus on the positive stories that are often derided by journalists as 'fluff'. There is a balance to be struck, as the Award-winning journalist Chris Masters explains:

> If you're a serious journalist and the story in front of you
> is about a reconstruction effort … where they are teaching
> young people how to build houses rather than join the
> Taliban, it is a legitimate story, it is a valid story and it is all
> part of the reconstruction effort. But if journalists are going
> to say 'I'm not interested in that story: I only want to do a
> story where I get shot at so I can win an award', if I was the
> ADF, I would say 'Piss off'.[21]

While not all journalists want to risk being killed or to stare down any hazard in order to win awards, there remains the journalists' tendency to prioritise action accounts or controversial stories. More positive stories of slow and steady progress become interesting only when there is no competing narrative. One example of this kind of story was the extensive mainstream media reporting of the return of Sarbi, the explosive detection dog, 13 months after she had gone missing in Afghanistan.[22]

Logue's report on the impact of media coverage during the 2011 embedding program provides an overview of the news agenda during that period.[23] It lists as 'unfavourable' the coverage of operational deaths, troubles in the wider international campaign, and the court martial of Australian Special Forces soldiers. Favourable coverage, which was considered newsworthy by the mass media, included Anzac Day coverage, the presentation of military awards, and the bravery of an individual soldier in a fatal action. Perpetuation of the Anzac hero storyline, where journalists are generally supportive of the soldiers, emerges in favourable reporting. These are the easiest stories to write because they are sheer description; no analysis is required. Conversely, stories that contain controversy and conflict as the principal news values are usually critical of the military hierarchy and the national government.

With the traditional media's desire for more information and at greater speed than ever before, some material is now being sourced and written by journalists who are not specialists in defence matters. Journalists are spread thinly across multiple 'rounds' or they frequently change responsibilities resulting in a 'decline of the traditional war reporter'.[24] The existing core of well-credentialed journalists with an in-depth knowledge and experience of military matters should be highly valued and supported by the ADF. But there is an increasing number of individual journalists as well as entire media outlets professing a broader range of interests who also pursue war stories, particularly those with high levels of human drama. As a result, reporting of recent wars ranges in depth, quality and content, from the Chris Masters two-part television documentary 'A Careful War'[25] to 'Operation Radio Storm', a visit to the Australian troops in Afghanistan by popular commercial radio personalities in 2008.[26]

The foremost impact of these changes to the media landscape for the Army is the need to provide swift and regular access to newsworthy content, including appropriate visual material, fulfilling a diverse range of needs. Lengthy and involved bureaucratic approval processes have to make way for devolved authority, and standard procedures need to allow for the timely release of information. Military commanders in the field need to be equipped and authorised to judge the appropriateness of releasing material and they must be trusted to do so. These commanders may also need a greater involvement in both briefing and guiding journalists who are less experienced in operational matters than traditional war correspondents. In some cases, this may involve correcting the record when inaccurate or superficial reporting occurs.

Achieving balanced and realistic coverage of both positive messages and the issues the Army finds more problematic informs the public and attends to the Army's reputational needs. A narrative of incompetence and controversy alone is obviously inadequate and inaccurate. At the other end of the spectrum, however, striving for maximum positive news coverage creates the impression that the Army is willing to preserve its reputation through obfuscation and cover-ups. The main lessons here include the need for the military to understand the media's constraints and motivations, and to work within them rather than contesting them. The media agenda cannot, and should not, be managed by the military. It is not the Army's job and it is dangerous for senior officers to even try. Understanding the impacts of the changes and restrictions in the media industry as well can provide a greater ability to navigate the military–media relationship to the benefit of both institutions and overcome the tension between informing the public and building and sustaining reputation.

Building trust and openness

One of the most serious criticisms over the past 15 years of Australian war reporting has emerged from journalists' dissatisfaction with their access to information and the people involved in operations. This appears to have manifested primarily in journalists' disappointment in the lack of embedding opportunities with the Australian military in Afghanistan, or the restrictive practices that accompanied any attempts to embed reporters.[27] Dissatisfied with official briefings, supervised tours and strict limitations on their ability to go 'beyond the wire', journalists have pushed for greater access through improved embedding programs.

The reluctance to share information appears to stem largely from the military's mistrust of the media. The 2011 study by Kevin Foster and Jason Pallant into the opinions of middle-ranking ADF officers revealed strident criticism of both the quality of media coverage and the professional competence of correspondents.[28] The respondents accepted the public's right to know but felt that the Army's public affairs personnel were better placed to meet this need. The majority of those surveyed believed that military 'media people' were more objective than civilian 'media people'. Foster and Pallant concluded that the 'ADF's default position towards the media is suspicion bordering on disdain'.[29] They argued that cultural issues are so deep that a concerted effort would be required to repair the relationship. Furthermore, it may simply be better to 'stop dreaming of a happy marriage and make the best of this rancorous cohabitation'.[30]

For an organisation that prides itself in managing risky situations, the relationship the Army has with the media throughout this period demonstrated a considerable reluctance to take risk when it came to public information. Military resistance to embedding programs appeared to arise from concerns with the security of operational information, the personal security of journalists and the logistical implications of a civilian 'tagging along' for the deploying force. Despite these valid concerns, attempts to hide or avoid the criticisms, or even the appearance of avoiding controversy when nothing controversial has actually happened, can create suspicion and do more damage to the military's reputation than the story itself. Building trust with journalists means sharing the bad with the good, and accepting that not every journalist will get it right every time.

In comparison to the militaries of other nations deployed to Afghanistan, the ADF was very slow to introduce any substantial formal program of access for journalists.[31] When a program was introduced, it featured different levels of access: fully embedded programs for general reporting, documentaries, and regional media, which are all supported logistically by the ADF; an in-country embed program for journalists already in location; and media participation in VIP visits and arts-cultural tours, such as the Forces Entertainment tours or the War Artist Program.[32]

This increasing openness, through revision and extension of the embedding program, did not wreak havoc on the Army's reputation in the media but provided positive, and perhaps unexpected, positive outcomes for the ADF. Jason Logue's report, Herding Cats, gives details of both the positive coverage received as well as the generally positive responses concerning the military–media relationship from both the operational commanders and the journalists.[33] Commanders described embedding as 'an enhancement of the journalist's understanding', 'an absolute requirement', 'an opportunity rather than a burden or a risk'.[34] One commander recorded his belief that the 'greater sophistication and nuance in the reporting on Australia's involvement in Afghanistan in the latter half of 2011 was directly related to the exposure of journalists to the operations in Uruzgan Province through the embed program'.[35]

It is clear that journalists rapidly gain a broader and more nuanced understanding of operations when they embed with a unit. In talking with soldiers at all levels, they achieve a clearer perspective on the reasons for the operation and how it is being conducted. And this is conveyed in the stories they write. An American study that compared 2003 coverage of the Iraq War by embedded journalists with coverage by reporters situated behind the lines showed that 'embedded reporters presented a much more positive view of US military actions and possibilities'[36]. While this is positive from the Army's perspective, there is also potential for the journalists to become too close to their subjects and become less objective in their reporting, favouring the narrative of the military, and perhaps the government.[37]

Chris Master's documentary for ABC television's *Four Corners* program was highly acclaimed and demonstrated the value of openness.[38] In commenting on the program, the retired Chief of Army, Lieutenant General Peter Leahy, argued that the principal lesson learned was 'not to leave the message to the spin merchants … Let the soldiers tell the story'.[39] In contrast, an example of when the failure to provide access to information resulted in a missed opportunity was an instance in which raw footage of an operation in northern Kandahar province in October 2010 was suppressed by the office of the Minister for Defence, although it had been cleared by the local commander.[40] The footage presented a positive image of the soldiers and the operation but when it was finally obtained and broadcast by the ABC's *Hungry Beast* program in 2011, the news angle was not the ability of Australian soldiers but the unnecessary censorship of their operations by government. These two cases, among many others, demonstrate how a greater openness benefits the building of reputation as well as keeping citizens informed. These instances also demonstrate that a willingness among uniformed people to be more open can be usurped by political interests. This remains a continuing challenge for the military and for ministerial staffers who need to be persuaded that being more open and transparent might help rather then hinder the politician they are trying to serve.

Access to information and military personnel at all levels improves the levels of trust between the military and the media. This truism has been demonstrated clearly in recent operations.

Openness does not guarantee complete accuracy or constant positive reports about the Australian military but it does build trust and leads to more favourable outcomes for the both the military and the media. While there is obviously operationally sensitive information that cannot be shared, there are other important stories that can, and should be told, if only for the sake of assuring the Australian people that the taxpayers' investment in national defence is worthwhile. Correction of the record following any misrepresentation or inaccurate reporting has never been easier with the media channels now available to Army commanders, lessening the risk in providing greater transparency.

The strategic value of communication

Similar reputational issues occur in the reporting of non-operational issues involving the Army. While these do not neatly fit into the reporting of war, the separation of the reporting of conflict from reporting of other Army actions cannot be achieved. Reputation extends beyond operations, blurring the line between media coverage of operational and non-operational activities and issues. The stories continue as the soldiers return home. While news articles from operations showcasing bravery and commitment may be favourable to the Army, the current media focus on issues such as post-traumatic stress disorder, veteran homelessness and incarceration is detracting from the overall positive impact. Media stories on broader issues, such as systemic sexual abuse or problems with equipment procurement, all contribute to a holistic image of the capabilities of the Army and the ADF. To achieve the dual aims of informing citizens and building reputation, the military needs a much wider narrative. A more strategic view of communication would provide a much more cohesive perspective.

Many organisations are now viewing communication or public affairs as more than an appendix to their planning and activities. A former US Special Assistant to the Secretary of Defense, argued that, 'the old-fashioned idea that you develop the policy and then pitch it over the transom to the communicator is over. You're continually thinking about communication throughout the course of the policy development process.'[41] Similarly, the Australian military also has the opportunity to consider communication as more than a supplement to operational activities – more than an after-thought. From an outside perspective, communication appears to be more reactive than an attempt to strategically position the Australian military. There is typically no significant mention of strategic communications in successive White Papers or in the most recent First Principles Review.[42] By way of contrast, in Britain there has been a detailed Chatham House report[43] and a 'Joint Doctrine on Strategic Communication: The Defence Contribution'.[44] Both are high-level documents that emphasise the importance of strategic communication in meeting national policy goals. The authors of the Joint Doctrine in particular say that a key driver for this renewed focus was, 'the recent experience of our struggle to forge coherent strategies for our campaigns in Iraq and Afghanistan, and to communicate them to audiences in a compelling way against a backdrop of 24-hour and, increasingly pervasive, social media.'[45]

While general media reporting of Army activities has been positive, support for the Australian involvement in operations has not always been as positive. Strategic communication, as described by US Brigadier-General Mari K Eder, 'acknowledges the need to create communications with forethought, insight and ties to national strategy and US Government policy objectives'.[46] The reporting of Australia's involvement in recent conflicts could potentially be enhanced by a much more expansive and strategic view of communication. Of course, the drive for public support needs to be balanced with the Australian public's fundamental information needs.

Taking the strategic view of the media

Over the past 15 years of war reporting, the Australian Army has managed to maintain a sound reputation and in the most part, keep the citizens informed of its operations. While not all media coverage has been positive or perhaps accurate, overall the Army's activities have generally been reported fairly and with some balance by the media. This can perhaps be attributed to the fact that the Army genuinely has a good story to tell and, for the most part, that is being reflected by the Australian media. There is, however, always room for improvement. An initial scoping of some lessons to be learned from the reporting of recent wars and operations has been examined and more can be done.

The military can embrace the full range of media available to reach the nation's citizens and does not need to depend solely on the mass media. This does not mean that mainstream media can, or should be, avoided. The media still plays a crucial role, but it is also working under new constraints. The military needs to understand the media's limitations and work with them for the greater goal of an informed citizenry. At the same time, trust can be built through openness and mitigation of any negative impacts this may have. Finally, taking a strategic view of communication can assist the ADF find a cohesive and suitable position in a crowded and constantly changing media space.

Reputation management does not need to be seen by the media as incongruous to objective information dissemination. But it will be if the military is not fully open with the public and does not work closely with the media to assist them in achieving their aims as well. Working openly alongside the traditional news media to promulgate information, while also using the ADF's own media channels will provide a consistency of messages, engage the public and allow any misrepresentations to be addressed. Reputation can be built and maintained on honesty and transparency. Clear and accurate reporting of the all actions, whether they impact positively or negatively on the ADF, ensures that the public is duly informed.

13

PUBLIC INTEREST AND DEFENCE INFORMATION

MICHAEL HARRIS

There is a growing acceptance that the right of the people
to know whether a government's deeds match its words, to
know what information the government holds about them,
and to know the information that underlies debate and
informs decision-making, is fundamental to democracy.[1]

The Australian Defence Force (ADF) is often criticised by
the so-called 'chattering class' for its preoccupation with
secrecy and subsequent lack of openness.[2] It is an age-long argument for militaries. In the words of Winston Churchill, 'In wartime, truth is so precious that she should always be attended by a
bodyguard of lies.'[3] However, if the essential elements of a functional, representative and liberal democracy are contended to be
open discussion, the pursuit of truth and the freedom of opinion,[4]
military practice may be axiomatic within the democratic polity.
The contemporary thinking is that the foundations of democracy
in Australia are cracking: trust in government continues to ebb,
trust in the major institutions of society is declining while trust

in social media may soon pass traditional media. There is significant change with how society is interacting and the manner in which the ADF has historically – and more recently – handled official, 'public interest' information, and this may provide useful insight into the health of the government's actions to restore trust with the public.

Military and public information

History tells us that military commanders have long understood the political advantages and risks of having journalists accompany them into the battlespace. Australia's earliest military expedition to Sudan in 1895 included a news reporter from *The Age*.[5] The British military gave the visiting press access to food and fodder, use of the telegraph and an entitlement to campaign medals. In doing so, the news media became an extension of the military. The military hierarchy was to learn quickly that such control of the media was beneficial to political interests. According to Peter Young and Peter Jesser, the lessons drawn from the Sudan conflict found, 'the press could be controlled and its power to influence public opinion could also be exploited. The correspondent was now seen, and used, as an extension of policy in an attempt to win international support.'[6]

Australia's official war correspondent in the Great War, Charles Bean, was equally partisan in his reporting and saw his role as giving 'Australia a knowledge of what the men and officers of the force are doing, and what is really happening in the war as far as they are concerned in it' while at the same time 'not giving information to the enemy' and 'not needlessly distressing their families at home'.[7] But it was the actions of a young newspaperman, Keith Murdoch (the father of global media magnate

Rupert Murdoch) who was to show to the military hierarchy the 'power of the press' during the disastrous Dardanelles campaign. His briefing to the Australian and British military leadership contributed to the decision to withdraw from the peninsula.

Unlike during the Gallipoli campaign, Australia's recent wars have been conducted much more in the public light. If the scrutiny applied for the tragic loss of life and injury during the decade-long campaign against the Taliban in Afghanistan is a gauge of the improvements to the accountability and transparency mechanisms that the ADF now has in place, then the Australian public should be assured that their interests are being well served. Still, the application of the public interest test for this information is neither uniformly applied nor is it consistent. Therefore, a closer examination of this issue is required.

Public interest definition

Is the public interest solely related to accountability and governance systems within the ADF or is it also about the transmission of information about Defence decision-making to the public to keep them informed? Could the public interest mean both and more than this? Defence's capstone doctrine, 'Foundations of Australian Military Doctrine', is unequivocal:

> Operations involving the ADF require both Defence and
> the government to balance the military need for operational
> security with the need for openness and accountability
> in accordance with our democratic political system. In a
> liberal-democratic political system, it is essential to maintain
> an unbreakable link between ADF operations and political
> control. The latter ultimately relies on community support.

Accordingly, ADF operations are carried out with the maximum degree of transparency achievable.[8]

While the pursuit of 'openness, accountability and transparency' requires the exercising of value judgements on whether official information should be publicly released in meeting the 'public interest' test, the doctrine tells Defence that it should strive to be as transparent as possible.

Defining what information constitutes the public interest is a test in itself. It is described as information that serves the public good, the common good, or even as the Australian Constitution describes, the commonweal. One definition says the public interest represents acceptance among members of society of the legitimacy of organised political authority that mediates conflicts of interest within the society[9] or as 'selfish behaviour continues', a determined authority that exists to promote the public interest will be needed to control the effects of such behaviour and to assert the public interest in the face of selfish demands'.[10] Australian National University (ANU) Professor Richard Mulgan proposes that the public interest in Australia is simply defined as the interests of those living in Australia while a more recent definition draws from the United Nations' International Code of Conduct for Public Officials that states 'a position of trust, implying a duty to act in the public interest'.[11] Public interest is a subjective concept and each of these positions requires a decision as to whether an act to keep information secret or for it to be publicly released meets this public interest test. These discussions are inherently political ones to be made.

Public information policy

Defence's sole policy on guiding the handing and release of public interest information, Defence Instruction (General) Administration (DI(G)) 08-1: Public Comment and Dissemination of Official Information by Defence Personnel, is confused and confusing. While recognising that 'internal and external public awareness and understanding of Defence policies and activities are vital to maintain public support for the organisation and its operations', it advises that 'all information proposed for public release is to be coordinated, agreed and authorised ... and carefully managed'.[12] The department's performance in managing the balance between maintaining public awareness while administering the 'clearance process' for public information continues to draw vitriolic responses from the news media. By way of example:

> It's hard to know whether those handling media for the Australian Defence Force are as clueless as they seem or are now openly trying to bait the Australian media ... Both the ADF and the Government should realise that limiting the media's – and by extension the public's – access to the war in Afghanistan does not encourage support, it encourages skepticism and from that grows outright opposition.[13]

> Strenuous efforts by governments and defence officials to restrict the flow of information about our role in the conflict ... Writing on the Lowy Institute's blog in July, an anonymous soldier lamented the failure of politicians and defence chiefs to spell out a detailed, public policy underpinning the campaign. 'That Australians neither understand the war nor why its soldiers' sacrifice is needed in Afghanistan is shameful', he wrote.[14]

Defence had been unaccountable and opaque, missing in the battle for public opinion and had serious issues with how it communicates.[15]

The inadequacies of the department's public information policy was highlighted following the Australian Defence Force Academy's (ADFA's) 'Skype-scandal' and again after offensive and racist comments were made by ADF members on Facebook about Afghan operations. The Defence minister ordered communication agency George Patterson to conduct a review of the department's use of social media and subsequently found the policy document seriously lacking. The Defence Instruction was assessed as being unable to adapt to the rapid evolution of the social media environment with a recommendation to revise the policy 'to ensure clarity of roles and responsibilities in social media, specifically for official Defence social media channels, but also for private communications about Defence activities in social media'.[16] Since the publication of that report little has changed and Defence's ability to reach the public through social media remains infantile.

Lessons learned

So what has the ADF learned in the past decade or so since the troubles in East Timor? In August 1999, the East Timorese pushed for self-determination after almost 25 years of Indonesian rule. Following a referendum, the security situation in East Timor collapsed and the ADF found itself leading a 22-nation coalition as part of the International Force for East Timor (INTERFET). The ADF planning for the provision of Public Affairs support to military operations was not operationalised and had to be quickly assembled from personnel across Australia.

Following the INTERFET experience, a Defence review found the public affairs support was 'inadequate' and was without 'systemic rigour'.[17] According to Lieutenant Colonel Jason Logue:

> the lack of understanding by military planners when developing the force flow for INTERFET played out on the morning of 20 September 1999 when political and strategic direction forced air-load and operational planners to quickly re-prioritise manifests for C130 flights from Darwin to allow the Media Support Unit, 41 journalists and five tonnes of stores to be inserted into Comoro Airfield on the leading edge of the initial 25 waves of aircraft.[18]

The tension of the media queue jumping the assembled soldiers was palpable but the government was adamant – the media needed to show the Australian government in action. By the end of the first day of military operations, a further 120 non-accredited media had made their way to the capital, Dili. By day three, an estimated 250 media were operating in East Timor.[19]

The security environment in Timor remained dangerous. The Australian-led contingent arrived in Dili while the city was still burning, the result of widespread looting and wholesale destruction of property. The news media reoccupied the Hotel Turismo. The ADF Media Support Unit used the hotel as the home base for Defence-sponsored media, complete with its commando minders and Military Public Affairs (MPA) escorts. Just streets away the militia remained at large as the Dutch journalist Sander Thoenes fatally found when he was murdered within eight hours of arriving in Dili. On 25 September 1999 were killed.[20]

Elements of the Indonesian military remained in barracks for several days while the international forces established themselves initially in Dili, then to the western border and finally eastwards. Militia had fled to West Timor but frequently conducted incursions into the border towns of East Timor. A border incident in October 1999 further inflamed tensions. An Australian Army patrol involving a company element from the 2nd Battalion, Royal Australian Regiment, under the command of Major David Kilcullen (now a counter-insurgency advisor), moved to the border hamlet of Motaain, where they came under fire from Indonesian police and military. The patrol also involved television crews from the Nine Network and CNN and reporters from a Portuguese news agency. An MPA team under my command accompanied the patrol. The ADF's video camera was the only operational camera and it recorded both the opening salvo and the subsequent border discussions between a shaken Kilcullen and the Indonesian military, where it was eventually acknowledged that the wrong map was being used as a reference:

> Television footage of the incident shot moments after the exchange of fire showed the senior Indonesian border officer, Colonel Sidjid Yuwyno, a Kopassus officer, consulting Australian officers. He was apparently using a 1933 Dutch map that showed Motaain in West Timor. The Australians were using an Indonesian map that clearly showed the hamlet to be in East Timor. The Indonesian officer later admitted his men had fired first from within East Timor.[21]

The ADF video material armed the INTERFET Commander, Major General Peter Cosgrove, with hard evidence that Australia had not initiated the international incident. Fortunately for Australia the matter was quickly diffused. Without the video gathered by the MPA team, the matter could have radically changed the course of the international mission in East Timor and worsened the fractured relationship with Indonesia.

Post-operational assessments of the ADF's media efforts during INTERFET concluded that its media engagement efforts were mostly adequate at the tactical and operational levels, where there were procedures in place; however, at the strategic level there were no resources to deliver messages to key regional and allied nations,[22] limiting the effectiveness of Australia's public diplomacy strategy in support of the important mission in East Timor. At the front end of this history-making moment, ADF's MPA officers had to rely on their core skills as communication advisors because the operational commanders had little appreciation and only grudging acceptance that the presence of media and MPA were strategically vital.

During the 2003 Iraq War, international media criticism of the American media management policies from the first Gulf War (1990–91) resulted in a reversal of the United States' approach to media embedding. Australia, however, did not have this history on which to reflect. It continued its policy of pacifying the news media through non-engagement. The Australian media were unhappy about the deliberate lack of access. The head of ABC news and current affairs, Max Uechtritz, said, 'By not being with the Australians right now we have a blind spot in our coverage … We'd be very disappointed if, come a conflict, Australians aren't getting first-hand information from Australians about Australians.'[23] The ADF covered its operations in a blanket of absolute secrecy. In the weeks leading up to the invasion of Iraq in March 2003, Australian Special Forces and their support elements entered a communication blackout that lasted almost eight weeks. As news media speculated about the coalition's likely scheme of manouevre, the only information to be released was that gathered by ADF MPA personnel. The media were frustrated and unhappy with the arrangement and only begrudgingly used the content because there was literally no other way of telling the public about the Australian mission. Prophetically, Uechtritz said at the time:

> This is the biggest event in the world at the moment and it could have repercussions for decades and generations to come. When Australia is sending its sons and daughters off to war we have an obligation to give Australians every bit of information we can about their involvement.[24]

According to ADF spokesperson Brigadier Mike Hannan, the decision to not embed Australian media with its Army units was because it was 'impractical'.[25] According to a review of the ADF's media approach to the Iraq War, 'With the advent of instant reporting, ADF believed it could only guarantee this secrecy by denying access to all media.'[26] In understanding how the restricted media access had impacted on Australia's military–media relations, Zoe Hibbert and Peter Simmons interviewed nine Australian journalists who had covered the Iraq conflict and 13 MPA officers. The results of the interviews confirmed the commonly held view of the critics of the Defence approach to handling official information: Defence wished to control the narrative while the media wanted more openness and transparency. According to a parliamentary report on ADF operations in Iraq, the key lesson for the ADF's public affairs operations involved the deployment of an MPA capability that helped, 'maintain community support by providing visibility of ADF operations to both the general public and Defence families. Defence will continue to deploy Public Affairs officers and encourage coverage by civilian journalists for operations where operational circumstances permit.'[27]

Australia's military campaign in Iraq evolved from decisive operations in 2003 to security support to the Australian Head of Mission and then to reconstruction and rehabilitation in 2005 when the Australian Government announced that it was contributing a security element to support a Japanese reconstruction force in Al Muthanna province. The announcement was made against a backdrop of diminishing public support for military operations in Iraq. Since the Special Force Task Group was protected from direct media engagement in 2003 (other than a visit by the Minister for Defence to the Al Asad airbase that had been captured on 11 April 2003), the Al Muthanna Task Group (AMTG) provided the first ground force element that was accessible by Australian and local media. Australian media covered the arrival of the AMTG at a coalition base on the outskirts of As Samawah on the eve of Anzac Day 2005. In the middle of a sandstorm, Australian media were in attendance not only for the informal ceremony of the dawn service but also the important first media engagement with Australian troops who were providing force protection to a Japanese military engineer element. Iraqi media, a satellite operator from Turkey and Australian media intermingled with a sizeable ADF public affairs team and the personnel of the AMTG and British Task Force Eagle. For the following two months, a period of intense media engagement was undertaken as an integrated component of the military plan for maintaining peaceful relations with the local population, managing the international relationships with the Japanese military and British Task Force Command, and meeting the strategic and operational objectives of the ADF.

The public information approach in Iraq by Defence was not without its media critics. In 2007, following an article written for the *Australian Army Journal* about the strategic communication plan executed in support of the first rotation of the AMTG,[28] the Defence reporter for the *Sunday Age*, Tom Allard, critiqued the ADF's public information approach:

information [is] important in modern wars. It shows how, when it comes to the ADF's handling of the media, control is everything. It shows the military has perfected the art of bypassing journalists to deliver its message. And it reveals that the message can be inherently political.[29]

Without strategic direction or oversight, the public information approach taken with the AMTG was to open the aperture on the ADF's actions to ensure there was not in control. Instead, it was strong, local public awareness of the actions of the Australian Task Group. A freelance reporter for Network Seven who lived in As Samawah was one of about a dozen Iraqi journalists who were engaged on an almost daily basis to tell the Australian story to the people of the province. The ADF didn't bypass reporters, it just shifted its focus to the information battlespace in Al Muthanna Province, which was assessed as being critical for mission success.

Allard's article drew a rebuttal from the Director General of Defence Public Affairs, Brigadier Peter Gilmore, who insisted his branch and its people had not strayed into partisan politics:

This is stated policy, that we're not to say or do anything that can be perceived as a political statement. We have to stay apolitical and we're very focused on how we do that. What's important for us is that the good work of the men and women in the Defence Force ... is communicated to the public so that the public understand that Defence people are doing the public proud.[30]

The approach to managing public information release was inherently tactical as discovered when the Commander of the Australian Task Group, Lieutenant Colonel Roger Noble, made the decision to remove bar armour from the Australian Light

Armoured Vehicles (ASLAV). He was concerned that local children who rushed to the roads when military vehicles passed would be accidentally injured or killed by the protruding metal grid that protected the ASLAVs. Oblivious that the tactical decision would lead to negative press coverage in Australia about the waste of money in purchasing the armour, Noble balanced the trade-off between force protection and losing the support of the local population if a child was killed or injured.

Defence has also not been able to maintain consistency in the manner in which it managed public information. When there was intentional non-engagement of Australian media as the ADF withdrew from military operations in Iraq in 2008, the media renewed their criticism of Defence's lack of transparency. The Nine Network was told that they could not be supported due to logistical issues – although Nine said they would make their own way to the Talil Airbase – while the ABC was told it was due to operational security issues. Instead, the ADF distributed its own video package of the event to loud complaints from the media. Trust, as SBS reporter Kate Middleton explained, cuts both ways.[31]

In eventually responding to the need for Australian media to access ADF operations, as the United States and other coalition countries had been doing openly since 2002, the ADF programmed a trial on embedding news media with ADF forces in 2009. The trial was based on the best media embedding practices that were in place with the British, Dutch, Canadian and US militaries and the ADF chose two news agencies to test their processes and procedures, News Limited and the ABC. Ian McPhedran from News Limited had been a vocal critic of Defence's Public Affairs activities when he was deployed as an Australian media 'embed': 'The media wants greater access and ordinary diggers, who are doing extraordinary work in our name in

Afghanistan, are desperate to have their stories recorded in the first draft of history'.[32]

SBS's Kate Middleton has been embedded with the ADF in Afghanistan on several occasions. She believes that embedding:

> allows civilian reporters to be exposed to what they
> (Defence) do and better comprehend – and explain –
> the role of the ADF at war … For the media, it requires
> sacrificing independence for the sake of an inside look at a
> force on operations … It's valuable and frustrating at once
> … In short, the whole embedding process is a risk – and a
> compromise – for both sides.[33]

In a further critique of the Department of Defence's approach to the media and the handling of public information, Monash University academic Kevin Foster found that ADF officers strongly believed in 'the public's right to be informed' but they perhaps believed more strongly that media coverage of the military was 'dismal' because 'correspondents lacked the basic knowledge to do their jobs'.[34] The ADF officers agreed that media coverage of the military would be better if there was greater 'military openness' but military access arrangements for reporters remained sufficient. Foster's research found there was a reasonably uniform belief the 'the media's role in keeping the military accountable to the public was negligible', supporting Fay Anderson's observation of the fractious nature of relations between the military and the media in the ADF.[35]

In the public interest

Defence has previous stated that it is committed to the principle that 'it is always the intent … to disclose information that is in the public interest'.[36] In responding to a parliamentary question raised by the Opposition about the nature of media embedding, the then Chief of the Defence Force, General David Hurley, believed that there had been some improvement in military–media relations.

> We are getting to understand each other better – that would be one way of putting it. The journalists have a job to do and each of them goes in with a perspective that they will either be looking to reinforce or perhaps see things differently. On the whole, it has to be positive because it does get a message out and help an informed debate, if nothing else, about what is happening in Afghanistan.[37]

The ADF currently occupies a unique position in the public consciousness – rated as the most-trusted public institution.[38] Against this backdrop is data that puts the public's confidence in the government to help the people 'live a fulfilling and healthy life' at less than 50 per cent, its lowest level since the 1960s.[39] The media, politicians and policy analysts already routinely complain about the lack of transparency with Defence decision-making. Thanks to the glare of media scrutiny, the resources applied by Defence to the handling and release of official information are under constant review and scrutiny. There is already little appetite within Defence to expand the manpower invested in Public Affairs. Increasing demands are being placed on these specialists, however, who are required to communicate in new and innovative ways to socially networked audiences, respond to the increased demands of Freedom of Information applications, while also meeting the continuing internal and external communication needs of a large, complex bureaucracy.

If the experiences of Wikileaks and Edward Snowden are the norm and not the exception, and the news media continues to fracture and reform itself into smaller, dynamic information portals, Defence and the ADF need to accept that there is a different political and social paradigm operating in which government and its agencies are to conduct their business. The ADF needs to grapple, however, with the policy and governance challenges of transparency and openness in an information environment where secrecy and control of official information no longer offer cast-iron guarantees that decision-making will not be publicly released. Except at the highest echelons, where senior Defence leaders accept that managing public interest information is a critical requirement of leadership, there is little to suggest an awakening elsewhere within Defence. The lessons from more than a decade of high-tempo military operations have not led to updated doctrine or policy, improvements within force-generation and training, streamlined business processes, or resource allocation.

The confronting aspect of the information environment is that the adversary has a better grasp on communicating its actions and adapting to the opportunities posed by digital channels and technology than we do. Changes within the information environment is not a passing fad and Defence should heed the lessons of the past and focus its efforts on incorporating the information aspects of the battlespace to ensure it is able to achieve its mission within a contemporary democratic polity.

PART 5: ON ETHICS AND MORALITY

14

INTERVENTION –
A DUTY TO PROTECT?

STEPHEN COLEMAN

The last quarter of a century has featured a fundamental and worldwide shift in the understanding of where and when and why the defence forces maintained by Western nations can and should be used. Their traditional role has been the protection of territory interests. During Australia's history, the nation's armed forces have fought wars far from the home – in Europe, the Middle East, South-East Asia – to protect Australian territory and the Australian people from threats. Australian forces have also been deployed as part of multinational peacekeeping and nation-building operations in other parts of the world, usually under the auspices of the United Nations, for reasons usually linked to Australian interests. Since 1990, however, there has been a shift in the operational context of some of these missions, which has seen defence forces deployed in very different situations with a significant number of operations being conducted exclusively for humanitarian reasons. The notion of uninvited intervention in the affairs of another state on purely humanitarian grounds, something that has become very common over the last 25 years, is a relatively recent phenomena lacking in historical precedent. This new enthusiasm for humanitarian intervention and its effect on the deployed contract with the state needs further evaluation.

Origin of humanitarian intervention

The end of the Cold War encouraged a change in thinking about how military forces are, and perhaps ought to be, used. Until 1989, military operations, even if they had at least some humanitarian implications, were only mounted in response to threats to territorial security or trade. The 1971 civil war in Bangladesh, for example, descended into genocide and led to millions of refugees crossing the border into India. When India intervened in December 1971, the national security problems caused by having to deal with all of these refugees was cited as the cause of the intervention. The first post-Cold War decade saw a huge change, however, with a significant number of military interventions being mounted in response to purely humanitarian concerns. This included major international operations in Somalia during 1992–1994, and in the Balkans following the breakup of the Yugoslavia federation. Locally, Australia participated in operations in Bougainville, East Timor and the Solomon Islands. These regional operations are less well known internationally but are probably even more important in terms of moulding the Australian view on the use of military power to meet a humanitarian need.

What has brought about this change? The world's collective guilt at the failure to prevent the 1994 Rwandan genocide, as well as the failure to prevent the mass murders committed within the UN Declared 'Safe Area' at Srebrenica in 1995, led to a rethink that challenged fundamental ideas of state sovereignty that had existed more or less unchanged since the Treaties of Westphalia were signed in the mid seventeenth century. Internationally sanctioned armed interventions for purely humanitarian purposes are now considered acceptable and, in some cases, even mandatory. In contrast to military forces being used exclusively to protect national self-interest, there is broad-based readiness to use uniformed personnel to uphold human rights wherever they are threatened and whenever they are ignored. In some cases the impetus for intervention, coupled with general public expectations of governmental responsibility to preserve and protect human rights, has been so strong that nations have been obliged to provide military forces for humanitarian interventions notwithstanding a hesitancy of political will to do so. By way of illustration, it has been argued that it was public pressure that practically forced the Australian Government into calling for intervention in the internal affairs of Indonesia's province of East Timor.[1] As a result, Australia mounted and led an international intervention in East Timor that effectively brought about the establishment of a new state – Timor Leste.

These changing views on the ethical character of international humanitarian military interventions were at least partially responsible for the formation of the ad-hoc International Commission on Intervention and State Sovereignty. That commission was convened in 2000 under the authority of the Canadian Government and co-chaired by former Australian Foreign Minister Gareth Evans. Its purpose was to consider an answer to a question posed by then UN Secretary-General Kofi Annan, a question that summarised the debate between those who valued the norm of state sovereignty over that of humanitarian intervention, and those who valued the idea of humanitarian intervention and protection of human rights more than the long-held principle of state sovereignty. Annan had asked, 'If humanitarian intervention is, indeed, an unacceptable assault on sovereignty, how should we respond to a Rwanda, to a Srebrenica – to gross and systematic violations of human rights that affect every precept of our common humanity?'[2] The commission outlined what it called 'Responsibility to Protect' (R2P). This obligation was accepted at the World Summit held at the UN headquarters in New York in September 2005. The principles of R2P were summarised in paragraphs 138 and 139 of the summit's formal outcomes and were affirmed by the UN Security Council (Resolution 1674), adopted unanimously on 28 April 2006:

> 138. Each individual State has the responsibility to protect
> its populations from genocide, war crimes, ethnic cleansing
> and crimes against humanity. This responsibility entails
> the prevention of such crimes, including their incitement,
> through appropriate and necessary means. We accept
> that responsibility and will act in accordance with it. The
> international community should, as appropriate, encourage
> and help States to exercise this responsibility and support the
> United Nations in establishing an early warning capability.

> 139. The international community, through the United
> Nations, also has the responsibility to use appropriate
> diplomatic, humanitarian and other peaceful means, in
> accordance with Chapters VI and VIII of the Charter,
> to help protect populations from genocide, war crimes,
> ethnic cleansing and crimes against humanity. In this
> context, we are prepared to take collective action, in a
> timely and decisive manner, through the Security Council,
> in accordance with the Charter, including Chapter VII,
> on a case-by-case basis and in cooperation with relevant

regional organizations as appropriate, should peaceful means be inadequate and national authorities manifestly fail to protect their populations from genocide, war crimes, ethnic cleansing and crimes against humanity. We stress the need for the General Assembly to continue consideration of the responsibility to protect populations from genocide, war crimes, ethnic cleansing and crimes against humanity and its implications, bearing in mind the principles of the Charter and international law. We also intend to commit ourselves, as necessary and appropriate, to helping States build capacity to protect their populations from genocide, war crimes, ethnic cleansing and crimes against humanity and to assisting those under stress before crises and conflicts break out.[3]

The changing contemporary role of the military has, therefore, become a lot more complex. This complexity arises in part because of an altered view of the morality of humanitarian interventions. The identification of a responsibility to protect is probably most pertinent to the Army, given land forces are the most obvious national assets to be used to prevent or curtail violations of human rights, including genocide, mass deportation, ethnic cleansing and crimes against humanity, often known collectively as 'crimes of mass atrocity'.

Military personnel and the state

While recruiting campaigns tend to minimise the role of the military in national defence, there is increasing emphasis on sailors, soldiers and airmen and women 'making a difference', and with reference to places and people whose lives have been saved or enhanced by those in uniform. Anyone who joins the military forces of their state, especially the volunteer, has duties to the citizens of that state. Those duties are made plain when new recruits take an oath to protect their citizens from harm and hindrance. The duties that military personnel have to citizens of other states are, however, much less clear. Historically speaking, military personnel engaged in an armed conflict might be thought to have a somewhat limited duty to protect citizens of allied states and, a duty to not intentionally cause harm the civilians of 'enemy' states. But the idea of humanitarian intervention, which are entailed by R2P, mean that military personnel can now be ordered into harm's way in order to protect populations in other states from being victims of crimes of mass atrocity. In some cases, this might lead to operations that diverge from those associated with traditional armed conflicts, such as instances in which military personnel serving as international peacekeepers are deployed in order to protect civilians from attacks perpetrated by their own government.

There are at least two different types of ethical problems raised by these ideas of humanitarian intervention. The first relates to the question of whether governments are actually ethically justified in ordering military personnel to deploy for such an operation, given that no national interests are directly at stake. When people enter into military service they serve under conditions of 'unlimited liability', knowing that they may lose their own life in serving that state.[4] If military personnel are willing to risk their lives in the service of the state, it has been argued that the state has a responsibility to put the lives of military personnel at risk *when and only when* vital national interests are at stake.[5] But in some cases, perhaps in many cases of humanitarian intervention, there are no such vital interests at stake. Thus, members of the military who have committed themselves to defending their state and its vital interests from external threats might well argue that the state is violating the moral contract with military personnel by deploying them to situations in which there is no demonstrable external threat. In effect, is the state entitled to risk the lives of its uniformed personnel in the conduct of humanitarian operations? Should the lives of Australian personnel be imperiled to protect the people of Somalia, Cambodia and East Timor and to build the foundations of a participatory democracy or a market economy in those countries? This is not merely a theoretical consideration. The Australian War Memorial recognises 14 Australians who have died while on peacekeeping operations,[6] a figure that does not include the nine ADF members who died when Navy Sea King helicopter 'Shark 02' crashed in the Indonesian island of Nias on 2 April 2005 during humanitarian relief operations following an earthquake.

To be clear, the issue here is not whether or not the state has the *legal* right to order its military personnel to participate in a humanitarian intervention, but whether it has the *moral* right to do so. Such an argument would not apply if the military personnel involved were able to opt in or out of individual operations. That is, if they had a right of selective conscientious objection.[7] Australia recognises a right of selective conscientious objection but only in relation to conscripted personnel and particular operations. At the time of writing, few, if any, military personnel around the world who volunteered for service are actually given such a choice and one wonders how many would choose to exercise it.

The argument in favour of recognising selective conscientious objection seems to have greater strength in some cases than in others, depending upon the particular state involved, when the military personnel in question entered military service, and whether those people entered into military service voluntarily. Consider, for example, the case of a person entering voluntarily into military service in one of the NATO countries in the late 1990s. It would be difficult for such a person to claim that they had no expectation of being ordered to take part in a humanitarian intervention, given the number and scale of humanitarian operations mounted by members of NATO in the 1990s. The same would be true of a young Australian who joined the Army after the nation had contributed to a series of humanitarian operations in Africa, Asia and the South Pacific. Conversely, someone who began their military service in the United States after the 11 September 2001 terrorist attacks might have a more legitimate claim that they had joined up to defend their state against the threat of further terrorist attacks and thus had no expectation of being involved in a humanitarian intervention. In a similar way, a person who was conscripted into service in order to defend the state, and was then ordered to take part in a humanitarian intervention, might well have grounds for arguing that the state was in breach of the moral contract with its conscripted military personnel.

The second type of ethical problem related to the issue of humanitarian intervention concerns the manner in which such operations ought to be conducted by the personnel involved, given that the aims of such operations are so different from those of traditional military operations. This is a particular problem for modern humanitarian operations launched under the doctrine of R2P, since these operations differ not only from traditional inter-state military conflicts, but also from what might be referred to as 'classic' peacekeeping missions, those that have been mounted under the auspices of the United Nations (and occasionally under other organisations) since 1948. One way of highlighting this significant difference is to examine the contrasting rules of engagement (ROE) that are required to order and regulate such missions.

What scholars refer to as classic peacekeeping operations are those that have been undertaken in situations where some sort of ceasefire or peace agreement has been reached between formerly warring parties and where there is a need for independent monitoring of that agreement. A good example of this type of operation is the UN Truce Supervision Organisation (UNTSO), which was the first official UN peacekeeping operation that saw international troops deployed to the Middle East to monitor the ceasefire that came into force at the end of the Arab–Israeli War in 1948. While the role of UNTSO has changed from time to time as a result of renewed hostilities in the region (notably in 1956, 1967 and 1973) it has remained active ever since, acting as a go-between for the hostile parties in the area, and attempting to ensure that isolated incidents do not escalate into major conflicts. UNTSO has served as a model for many subsequent UN peacekeeping operations. In such operations the role of military force has been deliberately circumspect. Uniformed personnel act as impartial observers and report violations of peace agreements. As observers, their role is not to intervene. In order to preserve their impartiality, their mandate is reactive. They do not exist to prevent problems from arising in the first place. In cases where such peace agreements are violated, these usually involve military personnel from one state either infringing upon the territory of the other state, or opening fire on some of the other state's military personnel.

The strict impartiality of the peacekeepers is vital in these cases, since their reports, which might well assign blame for the violation of the peace agreement, will only be trusted and have credibility if peacekeepers are, and are seen to be, unbiased. Military personnel attached to these operations are empowered by their ROE to use lethal force if deemed necessary to protect themselves. ROE of this kind are necessary given the role of these peacekeepers is simply to observe and report – the very nature of the role means that casualty numbers are likely to be relatively low.[8] But if the role of peacekeepers requires them to act beyond merely reporting violations of peace agreements, as is the case in operations mounted under the doctrine of R2P, then very different ROE are required if the mission is not to end in failure. Regrettably, a number of complex peace operations, particularly those mounted in the 1990s when collective experience of such missions was minimal, have relied on essentially the same ROE as those devised for classic peacekeeping operations. In some cases, the ROE were heavily implicated in the failure of an operation.

In modern humanitarian interventions, where for some missions the aim is not peace*keeping* but peace*making*, the situation faced by deploying military personnel is likely to be very different. The conflict that led to the deployment of these international military forces will almost certainly persist. There might be several different groups involved in the conflict and all may be in dispute with each other to a greater or lesser degree. An armed conflict involving or supporting one or more political factions within a nation may have involved regular military forces and irregular forces, such as locally recruited militias, and even less organised groups. The belligerents might include private individuals who have decided to bear arms to defend their farm or their family. The situation confronting the Peace Monitoring Group deployed to Bougainville in the late 1990s and in the Assistance Mission to the Solomon Islands in 2003 contained many of these complexities with regional militias and local armies engaged in struggles that coalesced around the leadership of charismatic 'Big Men'.

Humanitarian interventions, particularly those being conducted under the doctrine of R2P, are military operations being undertaken for largely moral rather than strategic, political or diplomatic purposes. An operation conducted in order to prevent or stop crimes of mass atrocity is carried out to preserve or protect the human rights of the victims. Its primary intent is not to serve the self-interest of the intervening state or states. Similarly, the main focus of operations seeking to restore law and order in a particular region or country is on intrinsic basic human rights. If the operation's aim is explicitly moral, it is imperative that the operation's conduct be compatible with the end sought. Thus, an operation mounted to protect the rights of civilians needs to be conducted in a manner that does not infringe or violate the rights of those civilians. An operation being mounted to restore law and order needs to respect the rule of law and the conventions of justice, including the rights of people suspected of terrorism or crimes of mass atrocity.

The objectives and the conduct of humanitarian interventions can contrast markedly with the aims and tactics of traditional military operations. They do seem, on first inspection, to be a good fit. Collateral damage, for example, is assumed to be an inevitable and regrettable outcome of traditional military operations between two or more belligerents. Conversely, if an operation is being mounted to protect a particular group of civilians, a minority ethnic group within a state for example, collateral damage in the form of civilian casualties is highly problematic. How can military forces claim to be helping this minority ethnic group while their actions are causing harm?

The challenge for military personnel

Military personnel engaged in these types of humanitarian operations, or perhaps in particular tasks as part of these sorts of operations, are often asked to discharge a role more in keeping with policing than soldiering. Military personnel engaged in traditional peacekeeping operations are expected to be impartial. While this is also true of military personnel involved in humanitarian interventions, the impartiality they are expected to display is of a rather different sort. Police, or at least good police, are impartial in that they treat everyone with equal respect no matter what their nationality or ethnic background. But they are not mere observers. They are permitted and, indeed, are required to become involved in situations where fundamental human rights are being threatened. This sort of impartiality is also expected of military personnel who participate in humanitarian interventions. And yet, this sort of impartiality requires soldiers to act in a very different manner from personnel involved in peacekeeping operations. The foremost challenge in expecting soldiers to act like police is that police are equipped and trained to think and act very differently from military personnel. Soldiers who are expected to act like police will encounter difficulties in complex situations where their military training does not adequately prepare them for the demands made upon them.

Such situations arise in a number of different ways. Military personnel who have been trained for combat are familiar with the principles of discrimination and proportionality, of selecting and engaging the appropriate targets, using an appropriate level of force in engaging those targets and assessing whether or not that collateral damage is reasonable given the value of the target. In humanitarian interventions, however, these principles may be very difficult to apply consistently and effectively. It can be very difficult for military personnel to know who they ought to take action against and what sort of proportionate action is appropriate. These challenges become acute in situations where military personnel are tasked with dealing extensively, or perhaps even exclusively, with non-combatants. While these are situations in which police officers are experienced and develop considerable expertise, they are often beyond the usual range of military activities and the standard training of military personnel.

These types of challenges are more practical than theoretical. If the aim of a humanitarian intervention is to be achieved, those in leadership positions will need to spend time and resources explaining to those they lead exactly what they are trying to achieve and why they are trying to achieve it. This will involve detailed briefings on the local political, cultural, social, economic and religious landscape, and careful explanations of how success will be efficiently secured and then measured. This explanatory contextual work is vital and has been a feature of Army operations since 1999, reflecting the need for officers and soldiers to have nuanced understanding of their operating environment, especially the moral component of their mission.

Grappling with the moral context of a humanitarian intervention will shape operational parameters and help to avoid tactics that are incompatible with the overall aims of the operation. If those deployed to such operations are to believe in the mission's objectives and appreciate why they need to achieve them in a manner that differs from conventional military operations, those exercising political leadership need to provide a compelling narrative to explain and even rationalise the use of military personnel in what are often unfamiliar contexts for uniformed men and women. While politicians will answer to the electorate, military organisations tend to be can-do organisations, ready and willing to take on whatever tasks they are given by government. In some cases this attitude becomes a problem. If, for example, the government asks uniformed leaders whether the military is able to take on roles and accomplish tasks for which they are not specifically trained and specially equipped, such as has been the case in some humanitarian interventions, those leaders ought to be at least willing to recommend against an operation being given to those they lead. As professionals, part of their role is to speak truth to those in power, even in cases where doing so is professionally unpalatable and politically unappealing.

Being vigilant about needs and rights

The Australian Army is an instrument of the Australian state and exists solely to serve that state in a range of circumstances as required. In a rapidly changing world, the Army should prepare for and expect unfamiliar tasks that challenge forward planning and defy strategic advice. Despite occasional accusations of paternalism and neo-colonialism,[9] Australia will continue to influence the affairs of other nations because it is not immune from the consequences of social disintegration or political meltdown in, for example, the Middle East. While Australia must be concerned about what happens in its immediate neighbourhood, there are limits to its capacity to intervene. This means that Australian resources need to be applied efficiently and effectively as part of holistic approach to regional security that obliges the Army to think long and hard about its preparedness for a range of contingencies short of armed conflict.

Humanitarian contingencies also require officers and soldiers to have a particular attitude towards their own service. It will not be obvious to some soldiers that helping desperate Rwandans, Somalis, Timorese or Solomon Islanders might become their responsibility. But they will embrace the task more eagerly if the nation of which they are citizens remains vigilante to humanitarian need and human rights. While most humanitarian catastrophes happen beyond Australia's territorial boundaries, those who suffer from oppression or persecution cannot be regarded as strangers who can be safely avoided or morally ignored. While they are unknown and unnamed, they are nonetheless members of the human race whose plight generates obligations that demand definite and decisive action on the part of governments. This is the basis on which Australia has agreed to participate in a range of humanitarian interventions and why the Australian Army has been deployed throughout the world over the past two decades. Having a regard for human dignity is an accepted principle of Australia's political culture.

Humanitarian intervention is now an accepted mission for the ADF. In such circumstances its personnel are being asked, and are becoming increasing willing, to go into harm's way. When a nation resorts to force to uphold values rather than protect its territory and interests, there is an almost inevitable ethical quality to the action that it undertakes and which implies justness – a justness that is perceptible to those serving. This is one of the most significant changes to the Army's corporate mindset since 1999, even as it remains one of its greatest challenges.

15

THE CHALLENGE OF MORAL INJURY

TOM FRAME

There is much to be said for looking back before looking ahead. How did we get *here*? In looking at the past, what lessons can we learn about ourselves and the journey? In looking towards the future, what challenges are most pressing and pertinent to where we want to go? For the Australian Army, while the necessity of sound strategic advice is unquestioned, the importance of clear and unambiguous command arrangements is undisputed and the provision of well maintained equipment undeniable, the best plans and preparations will be thwarted by individuals if their hearts, minds and bodies are not committed to the mission and its conduct or if their personal performance is impaired by an injury of some kind.

A series of studies have shown that Australian Army personnel have been affected by operational service in a number of ways since the East Timor intervention.[1] Some of these 'affects' are not visible. They are, in fact, unseen. The prevalence and persistence of these affects has led some commentators to talk about 'moral injury' and to ask whether this term best describes the experience of many deployed personnel. While much of the extant literature originates in the United States, could it be that Army personnel are sustaining moral injuries during their service and that the Australian experience is very different to that of our major operating partner?

Moral Injury: new or long-standing?

Of course, there is nothing new in the claim that human beings are affected by armed conflict as either combatants or civilians. Most societies have had a certain regard for those who served in their nation's wars, conscious that what they have seen and heard leaves not only visible scars on their bodies but marks on the spirit. In the modern era, the focus of care after the Great War of 1914–18 was on serious physical wounds, although there was growing recognition that war service deeply affected the inner being of those who had experienced the horrors of mechanised warfare.[2] After the Second World War and the repatriation of many Australians who were prisoners of Germany, Italy and Japan, there was increasing awareness of, and sympathy for, those displaying inner stress and moral turmoil derived from memories that persisted in causing grief and anxiety.[3] There was recognition that such people had indeed been injured, leading observers to ask how these injuries were caused and how they are best addressed. Why had some veterans sustained paralysing inner injuries that altered their personalities and changed their outlook while others could put aside the war years and continue life largely unaffected existentially by their experiences?

With the addition of the term post-traumatic stress disorder (PTSD) to the third edition of the American Psychiatric Association's *Diagnostic and Statistical Manual of Mental Disorders* (DSM-III) in 1980, psychologists applied the term to veterans of the Vietnam conflict who were finding it difficult to reintegrate into civilian society after their war service in Indo-china.[4] Notably, the experience of PTSD was not restricted to military personnel. Those employed in civilian policing and emergency services were susceptible to PTSD alongside anyone who had experienced a traumatic event that they constantly relived and were unable to transcend in their everyday living. Since the onset of the 'global war on terror', there has been close study of the unseen wounds that have been associated with military service in Afghanistan and Iraq with American researchers proposing the term 'moral injury'.[5] They implied it was a subset of PTSD and was manifest principally in a disordered personal values system. More recently, researchers have begun to argue that moral injury might exist apart from PTSD because, they contend, an individual need not experience a traumatic event to be morally injured. Indeed, some experiences would be better described as moral injury given PTSD is not necessarily associated with any affront to moral principles or social conventions. The view gaining currency is that PTSD is being applied unhelpfully to all unseen wounds and this tendency is obscuring the particular force and effect of moral injury that is emerging as a distinct experience needing to be addressed (rather than treated) as a social phenomena.[6] But the notion of moral injury is not new.

Moral injury appears to have been associated with the Australian experience of military service since the Anglo–Boer War of 1899–1902, when some volunteers began to doubt the justness of the British Imperial cause in South Africa and were troubled by tactics that inevitably caused harm to innocent women and children. Although the term moral injury has not been used until the last decade, the contents of letters and diaries, plays and poetry, stories and autobiographies from every conflict over the past century reveal a similar personal malaise. There are representations of moral injury in accounts of ancient battles and in classic fables as well. Moral injury isn't new but its features reflect the culture and the character of the society from which, and into which, individuals are deployed. But the possibility and the severity of moral injury is likely greater now than a century ago because of cultural context and social conventions. To demonstrate this point, let me make some observations of the differing contexts in which Australians served during the two world wars and those serving today.

Between 1914 and 1918, and 1939 and 1945:

- the great majority of uniformed personnel were hostilities-only citizen–soldiers who answered a call to defend the nation at a time of great peril; they were not career professionals recruited in peacetime to pursue Australia's national interests as interpreted by political authority
- Australians fought to defend the Australian people and their property from aggression directed at the continent, the nation's offshore possessions and overseas trade; the purpose of most post-1945 campaigns has been achieving a balance in international power relations, preserving regional stability, and preventing crimes against humanity far from Australian shores
- the world wars touched the entire population, the domestic economy and affected everyday life for civilians who were not spared its ravages; post-1990 deployments have involved a fraction of the population and have had no tangible influence on the financial markets or how Australians live their lives
- there was popular support for the cause of both world wars and no political debate over the necessity of sending Australians abroad; recent deployments have been accompanied by intense political debate and widespread community unease that has affected recruitment and retention.

Since 1945, both the nation and its people have changed dramatically with fewer Australians having any appreciation of uniformed service or any acquaintance with its challenges and complexities. Because deployments are experienced by individuals with particular expectations and aspirations, and are interpreted within specific social, religious and political contexts, the moral effects of operational service will be shaped by the character of those being deployed and the culture they have imbibed. While moral injury is an enduring element of operational service, how it is experienced and explained, articulated and addressed, will constantly change.

PTSD and moral injury

Plainly, then, moral injury is not synonymous with PTSD. The incidence of moral injury is not predicated on a traumatic experience. A traumatic event may cause moral injury but a person can be morally injured – an injury manifested in personal guilt and shame or indifference to human pain and suffering – without the causal event being traumatic. Moral injury does not flow from external stress but from internal reflection. It has to do with what a person makes of what they see, hear, smell, touch and taste. Two people can experience the same thing: one will be unaffected while the other will be injured. The difference is how they interpreted their experience in terms of the value structures ordering and regulating their inner being.

While operational service might impose an inordinate number of physical and mental demands and be the cause of intense stress, moral injury arises from existential dissonance associated with comparing idealised conceptions to concrete realities. There is sharp disagreement between how things should be and how they actually are. In reflecting upon a challenging experience, a morally injured individual realises they were not the moral person they previously believed themselves to be (or hoped they were). This realisation causes discomfort and even distress. A morally injured person concludes that the world is ethically ambiguous and morally inconsistent, and that ethical confidence and moral order are ultimately elusive or non-existent. Because the world lacks a reliable and resilient moral framework, it is difficult to discern whether social relations have any overarching point and purpose.

The morally injured person can be debilitated by their injuries in a number of ways. He or she could abandon notions of right and wrong, good and bad as they come to inhabit a world in which legality defines morality. A moral injury could render a person completely hostile to all forms of authority and suspicious of every institution exercising any kind of power. The morally injured could be paralysed by remitting guilt and unrelieved shame with no creative or constructive forms of confession and absolution. Another outcome of moral injury is ambivalence towards wrongdoing and corruption and a casual attitude to injustice and oppression.

Responding to moral injury

There are a number of responses to moral injury. Each begins with meaning making. It is not surprising that many veterans want to tell their story and why the wearing of medals is significant — they bestow a right to speak and an entitlement to be heard. Biography and autobiography are among the most popular genres of military history, especially those explaining how an individual managed to retain civility amid barbarism. The greatest challenge is incorporating moral confusion and existential chaos into a coherent personal story. Most moral injuries are absorbed into personal narrative. The individual is able to deal constructively with what they have seen and heard. Often some experiences are overlooked, ignored or denied while others are recast, reinterpreted or reconciled in the light of a more mature moral outlook. But some moral injuries are so acute that the individual needs assistance in constructing a new personal story that intentionally includes their operational service. For instance, a combatant who has inadvertently killed an innocent civilian could be so affected by remorse and regret that their self-image is marked by loathing and despair. They may not have seen the body of the person they killed or know their name for them to sustain a moral injury. It is a moral assessment of their actions that dominates their inner being and makes them captive to self-guilt and liable to self-condemnation. Alternatively, if an individual shows wanton disregard for human life and kills an innocent person, the shame and disgrace they ought to feel needs to be incorporated into a personal narrative that offers redemption and provides recovery. If the individual feels no regret or remorse, they have probably achieved the transition from soldier to mercenary.

The overall aim in addressing, rather than 'treating', moral injury is integrating the morally injurious experience into a revised sense of self. This may require the individual to renegotiate their view of themselves, their service and the state. A sense of betrayal – that one has been betrayed by themself, the service or the state – may be a contributing factor but is not necessary for moral injury. The most pressing issue is how an individual can live with themselves, continue in the service and remain a citizen of the state when their moral outlook has been thrown into turmoil and they lack confidence in the orientation of their moral compass. An inability to respond to this challenge will mark an individual's approach to ideals, leadership and politics, and affect their identity and destiny.

Moral injury is clearly not even a particular strand of PTSD. Broad-based multidisciplinary inquiry is revealing that it is a concept with its own content – that of moral principles and ethical precepts.[7] Every action and attitude has a context with implicit and explicit values that allow judgements to be made about the quality of the action or attitude. Human life is not experienced in a moral vacuum. The values and virtues that are foundational to human wellbeing are *not* derived from behavioural science, which is descriptive and not prescriptive, but from diverse sources that include philosophical discourse and theological conversation.

American perspectives dominate public perceptions of the effects of recent conflicts on returning personnel, and this has a distorting consequence. The over-expansive claims of some writers in the United States is distracting specialist research into the actual experiences of non-American personnel who do not share that nation's cultural neuroses. Americans led the campaigns in Kuwait, Afghanistan and Iraq. They fought these wars in their own particular way, using massive force and overwhelming firepower – with occasional resorts to 'extraordinary rendition', 'enhanced interrogation' and dehumanising detention. These campaigns produced a great many more veterans than its operating partners – perhaps by a factor of 50 – and provided an enormous pool of returned personnel for research projects. The Australian contribution to, and experience of these campaigns was very different. Those differences have not received the attention they deserve among the very small number of local studies. In fact, the vast majority of literature on PTSD is derived from the United States and deals predominantly with American veterans. There is no doubt that research into PTSD has led to treatments that have been enormously helpful to trauma-affected returning personnel. But to describe every unseen wound as a form or variant of PTSD is seriously mistaken.

The thought that deploying personnel might incur some form of moral injury is unsurprising. In fact, it is rather obvious. The thought that someone might be unaffected by killing other human beings and destroying their property, that someone would be indifferent to a personal encounter with civil chaos and endemic poverty, such as in Somalia, political violence and political 'gangsterism', such as in Cambodia, is actually more surprising. In fact, it is rather worrying. The idea that observing the outcomes of genocide and ethic cleansing might not distort a person's faith in humanity is almost impossible to believe. But a person can be affected by these experiences without suffering from a mental disorder in need of treatment. Our society expects them to be affected. The interpretation of their experiences and their integration into a personal narrative has become critical to our understanding and appreciation of moral injury. It may be, for instance, that the effects of their experiences become the foundations not just for personal maturing but a fuller and more candid account of what it means to be human in the 21st century. We need to consider the possibility that some returning personnel may have a better-developed sense of what is important in life and why, than those who send them or welcome them home.

Moral injury and social relations

Of critical importance is the relationship between the uniformed person and the state, the society, the service and themselves. This makes the experience of military people considerably different to that the civilian police, customs and border protection officers, and emergency services members. From the little we currently know about moral injury, it would appear that those who have incurred a moral injury express a sense of alienation from the people, the organisations, the communities and even the values that once afforded them a sense of identity, and destiny, and which provided stability in everyday living. The morally injured often have an impaired relationship with the state (represented by political authority), with the service (represented by the command structure), with the society (represented by the media) and with self (represented by idealised values). It is within this series of relationships, relationships that previously conveyed a sense of worth and purpose, that the morally injured person asks questions about why they were sent to undertake tasks that were poorly understood, that left indelible marks, and that were hardly imagined among people who barely seemed to care.

If there is one element that is common to the definitions offered, and one thing that distinguishes military personnel, it is the relationship between moral injury and meaning making: what am I to make of what has been done to me and what I myself have done? Every attempt at meaning making begins with the reason for a deployment. Was it necessary and why was I there? Attention naturally turns to the state and the service. The Army is, in a sense, the country's possession but it is the servant of the government – the ruling political party – which sees the Army as an instrument of public policy in pursuit of the national interest. The political leadership discerns this national interest against a set of criteria that are often not disclosed. The notion that the Army simply exists to defend the nation is an inadequate and flawed understanding of the place of the military in most Western societies. It is a servant of government to be used as the government chooses within legislative constraints and limitations. This reality, when understood and personally experienced, can have a deflating effect on uniformed men and women, especially if they feel their deployment is more about party politics than national security. The 1982 Falklands War was, some argued, more about improving the political fortunes of the British Prime Minister Margaret Thatcher than reasserting British sovereignty over a far-flung and insignificant colonial possession.

Of course, nations seldom have just one reason for sending their uniformed personnel on operations. A combination of factors and influences bear upon such decisions. Deploying the Army might further diplomatic, economic, legal and humanitarian objectives. Each can be a valid reason for using a nation's armed services, depending upon the context, of course. But it is sometimes difficult for governments to explain why force is needed and why men and women in uniform are required. They may want to protect intelligence sources, to preserve diplomatic goodwill, to obscure longer-term priorities, to overcome legal complexities or to avoid political opposition. This does not mean that governments are always deceiving their constituents, but they are sometimes constrained from being entirely open or candid about why the 'military option' is being pursued. While some would contend that half-truths are half-lies (an observation that is often too glib), the point being made here is simply that governments have confidences they must preserve. To disclose everything about a nation's interests can be imprudent and even reckless.

Decisions to deploy soldiers are, therefore, always subject to political rhetoric. Elected leaders who make such decisions know every action will have domestic political consequences and international diplomatic ramifications. The complaint is not that governments always tell lies and can never be trusted to tell the truth but that the interactions between nations are so complex, and the conduct of diplomacy so complicated, that most governments say too little rather than too much about why they are doing what they are doing. Governments tend to under-explain rather than over-explain their intentions, and understate rather than over-state their objectives in relation to international affairs. While those unfamiliar with the conduct of government will lament their failure to take the people into its confidence and to be frank about what it wants to do and why, there are valid reasons for being circumspect about using the Army.

In the middle of this complexity are the uniformed men and women who have pledged to obey the lawful directions of those in authority. As servants of the government they are not entitled to refuse lawful directions, notwithstanding their own convictions and beliefs. They must fulfil the government's directions unless those directions are inconsistent with domestic law, military law, international law or the general laws of armed conflict. It does not matter that they think the nation's involvement in an armed conflict is politically motivated or poorly conceived or that participation in a peacekeeping mission is diplomatically driven or practically useless. They must do as they are directed without comment or complaint.

In my observations of uniformed people over 30 years, the vast majority do not think very long or very hard about the missions they are given. They trust senior commanders to 'do the right thing' and tend to give the incumbent government the 'benefit of any doubt' in relation to the legality, practicality and morality of their mission. Some readily confess they have no interest in forming views on government decisions because, they feel, the rhetoric is impenetrable and their first responsibility is to comply. They have decided to be politically disengaged and will do what they have been told to do and leave dissent to others. For the greatest part, most Western governments are content to have their uniformed men and women politically disengaged because Western politicians have seen what political engagement with the military looks like in Egypt, Thailand, Panama and elsewhere. The docility of most Western military establishments might prevent political interference and preclude political intervention but it might also mean that uniformed officers are more inclined to be silent when they should speak.

While it is often said that soldiers live for their country but die for their mates, the fact remains that every deployed person confronted with the prospect of injury or death has, at some level, made an assessment of the point and purpose of their mission and decided they are willing to accept the prospect of pain and suffering. Whereas they could remain neutral and impassive about their service during peacetime training, they cannot avoid taking a stand when they are deployed. They need to have a view about the value of their mission and the manner in which it is being conducted because no amount of money or promise of medals will compensate them for permanent disability or death.

Long after deploying there will be assessments and judgements of the mission's objectives and achievements. In noting that Australians are still talking about the Gallipoli campaign and whether it could ever have been successful, and the Vietnam conflict and whether it was a war worth winning, every deployment will be the subject of conversation and perhaps some controversy for decades. The invasions of Afghanistan and Iraq will no doubt be subject to the same continuing conversation, especially given the persistence of sectarian violence in Afghanistan and the rise of Islamic State in northern Iraq. Were the loss of Australian lives a worthy sacrifice or a tragic waste? Opinions will vary.

Like all operations involving the Australian Army, those deploying will settle on their personal assessment of the objectives – whether they were clear, concise and compelling – and their judgement of the achievements – whether they were worthy of the their time, talent and trouble. If the mission was poorly conceived and badly managed, if the goals were essentially symbolic and the outcomes effectively superficial, those deployed are likely to feel they were manipulated and mistreated. They might become angry with those who deployed them and bitter towards those who led them. These emotions will be highly inflamed and deeply internalised if they have experienced or witnessed the worst expressions of corrupted human nature: hatred, malice and spite in the forms of physical cruelty and sadistic violence. Does the introduction of a political system, such as participatory democracy, redeem the deaths of innocent children, women and men? Is the death of a colleague a sacrifice or a waste when the objectives of the mission were so vague or imprecise that success was never a possibility? In the absence of convincing answers, deployed personnel may well be directing, probably unjustifiably, their feelings of anger, mistreatment and betrayal at their commanders.

Recent operations have revealed that a deployed person does not need to see 'guts and gore' to be deeply wounded when they believe they have been manipulated or mistreated by those they trusted; they do not need to observe first-hand atrocities like genocide or ethic cleansing to have their sense of right and wrong disrupted and their conscience badly injured. Meeting those who have committed such acts, and encountering their victims, is sometimes enough to lead a person to decide that the world is evil and humanity is corrupt, and lose trust and abandon hope. They might conclude such a world is not worth defending; such a species is not worth protecting. Conversely, they could persuade themselves that the world is the venue for a cosmic struggle between good and evil, in which the cause of good was specially entrusted to them and the persistence of evil is evidence they failed. If only they had done more. If only they had been more diligent. For others, a different kind of realisation dawns: the people I am told to protect are neither my family nor my friends. I do not know their names and their faces are unfamiliar. This is not my country and will never be my home. Why should I die for them and for this place? One of the reasons that moral injury may be more prevalent in the modern era is that deployments are a long way from home and it is difficult to see the connection between these activities and the defence of one's own family and home. Indeed, some deployed personnel may see themselves as nothing more than state-sponsored mercenaries being paid to fight a war that has little to do with them or what they value in life.

Ideas and insights about right and wrong are the products of political, social, cultural and spiritual reflections. They may be inconsistent and incoherent when taken together but are sufficiently organised and operative to lead a person to make judgements about whether something accords or conflicts with what they deem to be moral or immoral acts. If a person is directed to act in a manner that conflicts with their sense of right and wrong, if they find themselves compelled to act in the face of wrong-doing but do nothing or if they acted with the best of intentions but find their actions led to the worst of outcomes, it is very likely that the individual's sense of self will be adversely affected. Why? Because the principles that gave point and purpose, and meaning and direction to their life, have been denied or violated in such a manner and to such a degree that they are alienated from themselves and estranged from the world. The person finds they are now living with a stranger in an alien environment. Such a person needs to be reconciled with themselves and relocated in the world. They need a new story that makes sense of what they have done and a fresh account of the world and their place within it. That story and that account might be drawn from art, drama and literature or from history, philosophy and theology. Helping the morally injured to narrate their own life appears to be the foremost emerging challenge.

Moral injury: A way ahead

There are three areas of future research into the incidence of moral injury since 1999 that ought to be of interest to the Army. The first is establishing the contours of the Australian experience of moral injury – both its nature and extent – and comparing that experience to those of the nation's major operating partners, such as Britain, New Zealand, Canada, the Netherlands and the United States. It is possible that such research will confirm existing suspicions: that country of origin and dominant culture has a direct bearing on the experience of moral injury.

The second area is exploring the relationship between the individual officer and soldier and the state and the society. In the context of uncertain loyalties and unstated expectations, the relationship between the state and the society needs to be reformulated in a document that sets out duties and responsibilities, obligations and entitlements given that moral injury resides within personal narrative. There is good reason to be fearful that Army personnel could see their service and themselves in mercenary terms. The fact that a number of uniformed people have become 'civilian security contractors', resembling a group formerly known as mercenaries, shows such fears are not unreasonable.

The third area of research is the structure and content of post-deployment reintegration into family and the community, including public commemorative activity. For more than a century, annual commemoration has arguably been the foremost public 'interpretation' of the Australian experience of armed conflict. Until relatively recently, Anzac and Remembrance observances presumed community familiarity with concepts, such as contrition, repentance, forgiveness and absolution, to help distinguish commemoration from celebration. But as Australian public culture has drifted away from religious affiliation and been supplanted by a deliberately secular strain of humanism, the structure of commemorative services has changed, the object of such gatherings has been altered and the language has lost much of its previous texture. These activities have also moved from the private sphere to government control, which has shaped their tone and tenor in ways that need to be examined.

Exploring moral injury and the possibility that it better describes the deployed experience than PTSD will help to build resilience among Army personnel – and that is no bad thing. But beneath concern for operational efficiency and effectiveness there must be a genuine commitment to the wellbeing of serving men and women. They are human beings and deserve respect. This commitment is usually summed up in the phrase 'duty of care', although it seems a contradictory notion. Someone sincerely cares as a personal choice not because they are duty-bound to do so. The principal humanitarian question for anyone in a command position is this: do those being led have intrinsic value as people, a value that is honoured, or are they simply another asset to move around the battlespace? If the latter, we might conclude that soldiers are effectively being stripped of their humanity, not by adversaries but by Australians. And if this is so, you do wonder what all of this fighting is for.

PART 6: FINAL ASSESSMENTS

16

THE ARMY AND GOVERNMENT OBJECTIVES

JOHN BLAXLAND

So, how did we do? That is, how well did the Australian Army perform over the past two decades? What were its strengths and deficiencies and are there any areas where further reform is required? In answering this, a historical perspective, covering the 'op-tempo' lull of the late Cold War years, what have been referred to 'operations of choice' of the early post-Cold War years, the regional operations of the later 1990s and the post 9/11 Middle East operations, needs to be considered. This includes looking at the conceptual development in the Australian Army and the Australian Defence Force (ADF) in the last dozen or so years, and any lessons and remaining capability shortcomings that need to be addressed in the near future.

Government expectation determinants

The best place to start is identifying those things that determine the government's expectations of the army. Arguably, the first determinant is proximity or necessity, the second alliance management and the third risk tolerance. There are a number of variables at work influencing each of these determinants. Plainly, the closer the operational setting is to Australian shores the larger the force contribution the government will be prepared to make and the greater its tolerance for risk and the possibility of casualties. During 1999, for instance, the government was prepared to accept up to 500 casualties in East Timor. Given its declared support for East Timorese independence, the government was willing to accept the human cost associated with its policy. Similarly, the nearer to the Australian continent the greater the intellectual investment in an operation will be as well. For operations close to shore it is especially important for the ADF to get it right. The ADF's senior leadership needs to contemplate the likely outcomes of using military power and the particular kinds of power that need to be used. The greater the intellectual investment the greater the need for cultural, linguistic and religious understanding. Australia cannot afford to get it wrong in East Timor, Bougainville, the Solomon Islands or elsewhere in the South Pacific because no one is going to tow them away if they descend into chaos or lawlessness. Australia has to get it right. It could not walk away from East Timor in 1999 or 2006 as it can from deployments to Qatar or the United Arabs Emirates and be immune from the consequences of doing so. Added to this, the closer to shore, the greater is the expectation of allies for Australian primacy in any military operation.

In Australia's neighbourhood, be it Bougainville, the Solomon Islands, East Timor or elsewhere, the United States, ASEAN and Southwest Pacific countries are likely to look to Australia and ask, 'What are you going to do?' There is an expectation of regional leadership. Conversely, the further from Australia, the less these factors are at work. This is essentially what Australia's military history of recent decades demonstrates.

The op-tempo lull: 1972 to 1987

There was a lull in operational tempo after the Vietnam conflict that continued for most of the 1970s and 1980s. Sir Arthur Tange, as the Permanent Secretary of the Department of Defence, oversaw the merging of five government departments into a unified Department of Defence. The period witnessed the emergence of the civil–military diarchy, echoing the relationship that had existed between Sir Frederick Shedden as Departmental Secretary and General Sir Thomas Blamey as Commander of Australian Military Forces during the Second World War. The emergence of the Army's functional commands – Field Force (later Land) Command, Training Command and Logistics Command – replaced the territorial-based districts that had preceded this arrangement. The functional command structure was complemented by the establishment of the 1st Division with three functional brigades: 1st Brigade (mechanised), 3 Brigade (light) and 6 Brigade (motorised) with a parachute capability to secure an air point of entry. But the Army, like the RAN and RAAF, largely resisted a joint service approach to operations, reflecting the lack joint experience in the Korean War and the Vietnam conflict, where single service contributions worked more closely with their American or British counterparts than with each other.

Adjusting to the 'defence of Australia'

After the February 1978 bombing of Sydney's Hilton Hotel which was part of a plot to assassinate the Indian Prime Minister Morarji Desai, the government approved the creation of the Tactical Assault Group inside the Special Forces. The mood was changing; a new role for the ADF was taking shape.

Some important conceptual work also took place with the release of the 1986 Dibb Review and the 1987 Defence White Paper, which saw Australia move well away from the 'forward defence' posture of previous decades. Strategic guidance for the ADF focused on the 'defence of Australia' (DOA) from aggressors in the sea–air gap to the north of the continent. There are a number of critics of what the DOA construct did to the Army.[1] But it is important to step back from an Army-centric perspective and note that this was a benign period in Australia's strategic circumstances. It was, in effect, a bit of a breather that allowed for substantial government reinvestment in all three services. For the Army, a numerical decline from 29,000 to 24,000 full-time personnel was offset by investment in the relocation of 1 Brigade to Darwin, the reinvigoration of the regional force surveillance units and the increased operational focus for the Operational Deployment Force based primarily around units within 3 Brigade in Townsville.

Some may have been critical of the infrastructure investment with 'bare bases' established across northern Australia, the creation of Northern Command (NORCOM), the Army Presence in the North (APIN) program and the reinvigoration of the regional force surveillance units.[2] The bottom line is, however, that these initiatives helped create the foundations for the force that was sent to East Timor (INTERFET) in September 1999. Australia could not have undertaken that operation and assumed its leadership without that investment throughout the later 1980s and 1990s.

There are those who would say that during the period of DOA the Army's combat capability, particularly the three combat brigades, were hollowed out and that Paul Dibb's handiwork was responsible for the Army's declining fortunes.[3] But it is important to place this period in context. During the 1950s the Australian

Regular Army had only two combat-capable infantry battalions and a training battalion. The DOA construct actually worked in the Army's favour. The scenarios for which the Army planned stretched credulity but continental defence proved useful as a functional construct to retain what the Army needed at the time.

But the Army could not operate on its own in the light of the strategic guidance it was being given. It needed support from the Navy and the Air Force. The first Chief of the Defence Force (CDF), General Sir Phillip Bennett, understood the importance of 'jointery' and set about generating a small Headquarters ADF staff. This period saw the creation of maritime, air and land commands and the creation of the Australian Defence Force Academy (ADFA) – a significant institution for the evolution of shared identity and jointery within the ADF. Under Bennett (1984–87) and his successor General Peter Gration (1987–93), the ADF responded constructively to DOA imperatives for increased self-reliance. The government stressed self-reliance and the Army and the ADF adjusted accordingly, given the financial constraints, with the Army largely marking time because of the direction of resources by government to other priorities.

In 1987, with the launch of Operation Morris Dance, the DOA construct faced its first real challenge. Lieutenant Colonel Sitiveni Rabuka led a military coup overthrowing Fiji's elected Prime Minister Timoci Bavadra. The Australian Prime Minister Bob Hawke considered all options to help Bavadra and to restore democracy in Fiji. The then CDF, General Gration, advised the government that the ADF could not mount an effective rescue operation for Bavandra's government. He also counselled the government against assuming the ADF could do much more than operate in an entirely permissive environment – that is, possibly conduct evacuation operations of Australian nationals with the permission of the Fiji authorities. Hawke agreed and ADF met the government's scaled-down expectations. Notwithstanding this experience, there was no change to force structure and the DOA paradigm remained. Operation Morris Dance made almost no difference to strategic priorities or the shape of the ADF.

Post-Cold War operations
of choice and reform

With the fall of the Berlin Wall in 1989 and the dissolution of the Soviet Union in 1991, the international community embraced an interventionist role in the world's troubled spots. This saw Australia join international peacekeeping operations in Namibia, Somalia, Rwanda, Cambodia, the Western Sahara and elsewhere. The ADF's members were now 'ambassador/soldier/teacher/peacekeeper'. While these activities softened attitudes to military power and generated goodwill towards the ADF, they did not make any substantive difference in terms of the strategic direction for the Army or the ADF. The Army met government defined requirements but there was no expectation of a change in strategic priorities or in government expectations. This was despite the imperative for a change in emphasis in force structure priorities away from strict adherence to DOA. After all, the Army was doing much more than defend the continent; it was giving the government a range of foreign policy options.

During these 'operations of choice', successive chiefs of Army genuinely tried to make the best of a difficult lot. Lieutenant General John Grey, for instance, facing cutbacks foreshadowed in the 1993 Force Structure Review, focused attention on 'ethos and values'. What else could he do in such financially constrained circumstances? Lieutenant General John Sanderson recognised DOA longevity and created the Land Warfare Studies Centre and the Land Warfare Development Centre. He initiated 'Army 21', ostensibly to comply with DOA guidance. Although it proved, with hindsight, to be a conceptual dead end it justified certain capability requirements including tanks and Bushmaster armoured vehicles. This was partly because the publication of the 1997 Defence White Paper ('Australian Strategic Policy 1997 [ASP 97]') ended DOA as the exclusive force determinant. Suddenly, with the goal posts shifted and a regional crisis looming, Army 21 was seen as redundant.

Lieutenant General Frank Hickling discerned the change in strategic direction that ASP 97 suggested and developed the idea of a 'concept-led, capability-based' Army. He embraced the maritime concept of strategy, which his predecessors were constrained against doing under the DOA construct. He then created the Future Land Warfare Branch, established the Centre for Army Lessons and the Combat Training Centre and initiated the publication of a new *Fundamentals of Land Warfare*. The Army owes a significant debt to Hickling.

Operations of less choice and reform

In the meantime, there was a need for 'operations of less choice'. These were operations in the immediate neighbourhood for which there was a genuine obligation for Australia to play a leading role. This included peace monitoring in Bougainville, drought relief in Irian Jaya and humanitarian assistance and disaster relief after a tsunami struck Papua New Guinea's north coast. The participation of ADF niche elements served to fulfil significant foreign and defence policy priority requirements. In doing so, the ADF and the Army met government expectations and bolstered regional security and stability, helping also to hone the force. As it happened, this was crucial preparation for what was about to happen in East Timor – an event that few predicted 12 months earlier.

The defence analyst Hugh White once described the East Timor intervention as a 'strategic blunder'. It was unintentional and unplanned. Prime Minister John Howard had written to Indonesian President Habibie suggesting a Matignon Accord-like arrangement to see the troubled province of East Timor gain a measure of local autonomy and in so doing settle the independence impulses of the East Timorese community. Habibie resisted Howard's proposal and chose instead to hold a popular vote on autonomy. The implication of Habibie's approach was that the rejection of the offer would see Timor emerge as an independent nation. Following the overwhelming rejection of Indonesian sovereignty by the East Timorese people, the nascent nation descended into chaos and violence. Prime Minister Howard sought American support to restore order and to given expression to the autonomy vote. The United States, being preoccupied with the war in Kosovo and concerned to preserve good relations with Indonesia, felt constrained against playing a prominent role and encouraged Australia to take the lead, seeing this as something that Australia would be able to manage – and they were right. The ADF could do it, albeit with supplementation from allies and coalition partners, notably the United States providing critical trunk communications, logistics, intelligence and transport support to enable forces to deploy and be sustained adequately in East Timor. This was particularly important given that the ADF capabilities were stretched deploying and sustaining Australia's own force contribution to the intervention.

The intervention's remarkable tactical success generated significant impetus for reform across the ADF generally and rejuvenation of the Army in particular. The experience demonstrated the importance of both jointery and collaboration. It also showed the utility of the ties with Australia's (ABCA) partners – New Zealand, America, Britain and Canada – all of which participated in the operation. It was a truly remarkably display of the importance of these ties.

The operation also demonstrated unequivocally the significance of regional security ties. Malaysia and Singapore, partners in the Five Power Defence Arrangements (FPDA), readily participated. Being immediate neighbours of Indonesia and concerned about the long-term fallout in terms of relations, they were naturally reluctant to be the first ASEAN member to commit to INTERFET. Thailand, with whom Australia does not have a formal defence arrangement, saw Australia as a responsible regional power and one with a long friendship dating back to the creation of the Southeast Asia Treaty Organisation (SEATO) in the mid 1950s, and the commitment of RAAF fighters to the defence of Thailand during the Vietnam conflict. They recognised that Australia had been a constant friend, that Australia contributed to neighbourly relations and that it was important for Thailand to be seen supporting Australia in this period of crisis. The Thais agreed to provide the deputy force commander and a battalion-sized joint task force alongside a similar force from the Philippines. Once the path had been trod, other ASEAN countries were prepared to participate alongside Australia.

Operations of choice far away

Shortly after INTERFET handed control to the United Nations Transitional Authority in East Timor (UNTAET), Australia again became involved in operations of choice far from its shores.

In Afghanistan and Iraq, Australian forces performed essentially niche roles. Unlike the Vietnam conflict, where Australia committed a brigade-sized combined arms task force (with naval and air elements as well), the contributions in Iraq and Afghanistan were much smaller and more carefully calibrated. For a number of reasons Australia chose not to follow the path it took in Vietnam of deploying a self-sustained all-arms and services brigade-sized task force. One of the most compelling was an aversion to casualties. This sentiment was reinforced by the fact that Middle East operations were much further from Australia than Vietnam.

Containing the risks while managing alliance expectations became a paramount concern. But this carefully stage-managed approach to the conduct of operations remote from Australian shores generated nagging worries. As the then Chief of Army, Lieutenant General Peter Leahy, observed, for instance, there are few myths and legends arising from this period largely because of the tight media constraints imposed by government.[4] Those hefty media constraints reflected the tightly defined operational and strategic objectives the force contributions were intended to meet. Such niche force packages were in turn reliant on the critical support of significant enabling capabilities provided by coalition partners in the field. But with constrained force contributions reliant on support from partners, the Australian Army may have been learning some incomplete lessons from this experience because of the niche nature of the force contribution.

Regional inter-agency operations

In the meantime and much closer to home, the ADF was involved in a series of inter-agency border operations. The Army had to work much more closely with the Navy and the Air Force, plus coalition partners, as well as with police, customs and quarantine services and an array of aid organisations. This was particularly the case with the Regional Assistance Mission to Solomon Islands (RAMSI), where there was an unprecedented degree of inter-agency co-operation. This affected the way the Army thought about how it needed to conduct operations and triggered some conceptual development aimed at refining the Army's approach to inter-agency operations in Australia's neighbourhood. Operation Sumatra Assist was another campaign that challenged the conventional thinking about what the ADF should be doing, where and with whom. Prior to the Boxing Day 2004 Indian Ocean tsunami that devastated parts on Sumatra, it was inconceivable that the ADF would deploy to the contested conflict zone of Aceh in Indonesia, where a separatist group known as Gerakan Aceh Merdeka (GAM) had fought against the central Indonesian authorities.

When an internal crisis erupted in Dili during May 2006, the ADF cobbled together another force to deploy to East Timor. Few, if any in the policy and intelligence domains in Canberra saw the crisis developing because they were almost all focused on events in the Middle East. Like kids playing primary school soccer, the field had been left vacant at one end while the ball was elsewhere.

Conceptual developments

These events prompted a number of conceptual developments. The Combat Training Centre was established at the end of the 1990s and received a live instrumentation system in 2006. The Directorate of Special Forces was expanded into Special Operations Command in December 2002, following the 2000 Sydney

Olympic Games and operational experiences in Afghanistan during 2001 and 2002.

The notion of 'complex warfighting' emerged in 2004, arising from the work of David Kilcullen.[5] He masterfully distilled the essence of the 'Australian way of war' at the start of the new century. His thinking struck a chord with Australian military practitioners. At home, it was not controversial. Abroad, it was considered groundbreaking, which it was in the sense that it articulated clearly and cogently what many had been thinking but not writing. Kilcullen distilled what soldiers saw as common sense. He described the complexity of warfare and depicted conflict as a human activity. In certain respects it was Clausewitzian, but it was much more than that. It was uncontroversial in Australian Army circles because it resonated with operational experience. Kilcullen articulated what Australian Army personnel believed about contemporary warfare.

There were other responses to the changing circumstances, notably the shift in government emphasis away from a strict adherence to DOA. One example was the emerging concept of military operations in the littoral environment (MOLE). This was the kernel for the creation of the amphibious capability centred around the Navy's landing helicopter dock (LHD) ships.

The Hardened and Networked Army (HNA) initiative was another development that captured the essence of working with unprecedented precision in integrated, small and agile teams.[6] A new generation of main battle tanks was introduced. In addition, the conceptual work behind the Army Learning Environment initiative undertaken in 2005 was handed over to Training Command in 2007. The Centre for Army Lessons had also started producing effective results, disseminating tactical lessons from recent operational rotations and helping to integrate these insights into the Army's thinking for the benefit of those who followed in subsequent rotations to Afghanistan and Iraq. Clearly, progress was being made. It was incremental, to be sure, but it involved constructive progressive steps to further hone the force.

Further conceptual development took place with the 2007 release of the Adaptive Campaigning document, followed by periodic updates.[7] It represented an articulation of an approach to campaigning in terms that were plain and simple and, therefore, easily digestible and memorable for soldiers tasked with complex and often ambiguous operational tasks. Reflecting on this innovation, the former CDF General Peter Gration observed that 'there was nothing new here'. In one sense he was right in that the concepts articulated represented broadly understood and widely practised actions. But the simplified prose and clear articulation of Adaptive Campaigning proved helpful for those tactical and operational commanders tasked with increasingly complex, complicated and constrained post 9/11 era operations.

The five factors outlined in Adaptive Campaigning addressed the complexities associated with operations, including joint land combat, populations support, indigenous capacity building, population protection and information actions.[8] This simple list helped commanders grapple with the following five factors that were adding to the complexity of the task they faced, namely: increased lethality of weapons, the emptying of the battlespace (due to increased range, lethality and precision of weapons), the difficulty in identifying clearly discernible actors, improvements to the ISTAR (intelligence, surveillance, target acquisition and reconnaissance) capability, and operations 'among the people', where the adversary retreated into complex urban terrain to avoid detection by advanced and more precise weapon systems.

Another conceptual initiative was the Enhanced Land Force. Some 2600 soldiers were added to the Army's strength following the spike in the operational tempo during 2006 when Australian troops were deployed on short-notice missions to places such as Lebanon, Fiji, Tonga and Papua New Guinea, in addition to the more substantial forces deployed to Iraq and Afghanistan. 5/7 RAR became two battalions (5 RAR and 7 RAR) and 8/9 RAR was raised again. What these additional troops represented was the delivery to government of a concept-led capability-based force, following the principle Lieutenant General Hickling had advocated a decade earlier. But this was a 'boutique' force. This was not the Second AIF of 1939–1945 with its 14 divisions. This is a regular force of three brigades and a Special Forces component. It is important to keep the actual size of the Army in perspective.

The Future Joint Operational Concept, known as multi-dimensional manoeuvre, was another innovation prompted by the changing operating environment. The concept had its detractors but the idea of 'knowing, reaching, acting and transitioning' organisationally helpful if only as a means of explaining military functions to government. While constructive in its intention, some important questions needed to be asked. How much did this approach really help to conceptualise the need for further reform? Did it actually over-simplify the issues? Was it doing more harm than good? There are few clear answers but these issues needed to be grasped and not simply in reductionist terms. The nuances had to be considered.

Constructive work was also done on core behaviours to reinforce the Army's commitment to life-long learning. This was timely given some of the scandals that emerged. Attention to culture and ethos demonstrated that the Army would respond conscientiously to public expectations that it would maintain the highest ethical standards. Internet connectivity has generated numerous challenges relating to operational security and the distribution of offensive and sensitive material via the web. Plainly, there were some in uniform who were either unaware or indifferent to the conduct that was demanded of them. As with most scandals, the misconduct of a few did not tarnish the image of the Army as a whole because steps were taken to punish and educate.

While attending to its reform agenda, the expansion of Headquarters Australian Theatre in 2006 and 2007 facilitated the creation of a more mature Headquarters Joint Operations Command, based initially in Sydney and then moved to Bungendore, east of Canberra. This new structure absorbed some functions from the Army's Land Command as well as certain responsibilities previously assumed by Navy's Fleet (later Maritime) Command and the RAAF's Air Command. The links with the Deployable Joint Force Headquarters in Brisbane were formalised as well. The greater joint inter-agency and multilateral focus of the Army was driven largely by the surge in operational requirements. This led to the Army seeing itself as being part of a bigger team, with a spectrum of agencies working together, needing to be co-ordinated and their tasks and functions de-conflicted to ensure each organisation was working harmoniously towards the common or agreed purpose. This process engendered closer collaboration among all three services.

The Adaptive Army initiative was introduced to help cope with the increased operational tempo. As part of the mix, Army's Training Command was absorbed by Land Command to become Forces Command. The Army's training continuum, incorporating the component stages of individual and collective training, was refined as part of that process. The foundation warfighting capability was highlighted to ensure the Army's fighting edge remained honed. Specialists were brigaded with the ISTAR and 'command support' elements and grouped together to form 6 Brigade, 16 Aviation Brigade and 17 Brigade, containing force support logistics elements. But this brigading of specialist assets pointed to the lack of redundancy in the component niche capabilities. The capabilities in 6, 16 and 17 brigades are not 'nice to have' enablers. In modern complex warfighting, they are indispensable. This shortfall became all the more apparent during a prolonged period of operational intensity and the rotational training plan that formed the core of Plan Beersheba. The rotational plan saw the three combat brigades (1 Brigade in Darwin, 3 Brigade in Townsville and 7 Brigade in Brisbane) undertake a 36-month cycle with three 12-month phases known as 'readying, ready and reset'. This was a departure from the specialised brigade-sized task forces concept that Lieutenant General Sir Frank Hassett had introduced in the mid 1970s. This rearrangement allowed for operational pauses and for the planned refreshing of the troops. In contrast, the counterpart specialist brigades were required to press on regardless, supporting each of the three combat brigades continuously.

At the same time, while focusing on foundational warfighting was eminently sensible, there was also the need for 'Phase 0' operations – that is, peacetime regional engagement activities to engage constructively with regional security partners to bolster their skills, raise mutual awareness and foster important bilateral and multilateral relationships. This is critical for the Army and its re-engagement with regional security partners – particularly as those relationships have been allowed to atrophy since 2001.

The Future Special Operations Concept that envisaged the Special Forces preparing for a future with no peace or war, just constant conflict, was promulgated in 2011. Special Operations Command (SOCOMD) was portrayed as the 'hedge force' and as the vanguard of the conventional land forces that could and would follow as and when required. Caution is called for against an over-reliance on this model. It is great for operations of choice, like those in which the Army has been involved in recent years, but in existential wars this level of reliance on Special Forces is a dangerous path. Much can be gained from reflecting on Australia's Special Forces experience during the Second World War, including the forces in the Allied Intelligence Bureau, like Special Operations Australia and Z Special Force. There were some spectacular successes, such as the MV *Krait* raid on Singapore Harbour, but there were some spectacular failures as well and people died needlessly. In the long run, their efforts did not do much to shorten the war. In the end, at least until the advent of the atomic bomb in 1945, the enemy had to be defeated comprehensively in battle. Certainly in the New Guinea campaign this involved hard slog conventional campaigning against a determined enemy. It was ugly and bloody.

Lessons and shortcomings

In the years since the East Timor intervention, it is clear that the demanding operational tempo was been a key driver of military reform. A series of institutional mechanisms have emerged to sustain reform despite the slowing of the operational tempo in 2015. These mechanisms include the Centre for Army Lessons, the Combat Training Centre and the Army Training Continuum.

The Middle East Area of Operations has seen the ADF make niche contributions to what can essentially be described from an Australian policy-maker's perspective as 'wars of choice'. Indeed, these contributions have been instrumental in honing the force. As a result, the Army of 2015 has become a far more sharp-edged force than was the Australian Army of 1999. The Special Forces have been the government's force of choice – and for good reason: they have a smaller footprint, they have a strong tendency to a lower casualty rate and have very high standards of operational security. For a politically cautious government contemplating a war of choice far away, it makes eminent sense to commit those who are least likely to generate casualties and, in turn, damaging domestic fallout over their actions. But this overall approach has led to the temptation to draw some false general lessons from the experience. Gilt-edged national support contingents with high fidelity 'reachback' to national agencies and their technical resources have been provided to the smallest of deployed task groups. This is high-quality and highly valued support for the operations deployed. But is it replicable on a larger scale, closer to Australia's shores in wars of less choice or even existential challenges? Probably not, and there is a need to be careful not to learn the wrong lessons from this experience.

Beyond the prospect of learning the wrong lessons, there is a danger that the ADF's focus on operations in the Middle East has come to the point where it now exposes the vulnerabilities becoming evident in its ability to engage constructively and confidently in the South-East Asian and Southwest Pacific regions. The ADF no longer knows these countries as well as they were known prior to 11 September 2001. The decade and a half-long commitment of multiple force rotations to the Middle East has come at the expense of the ADF's mastery of regional understanding, particularly in terms of relationships, language and cultural skills. These skills had been the focus of attention in the 1990s. But the tempo of operations outside of Australia's immediate neighbourhood since then has seen the focus shift and the skills atrophy. The lack of depth in regional relations has been noticed across the region. The Defence Co-operation Program, with its highly valued scholarships, has remained largely in maintenance mode while the region has undergone a quiet revolution as the great power equilibrium has shifted. As a result, the ADF has accentuated its deficit in regional language and cultural-engagement skills. The focus the ADF once had of its people learning Bahasa or Pidgin has faded.

Field training exercises with regional counterpart armies have been supported with half-hearted measures. Ships intended to be assigned to regional exercises but encountering mechanical difficulties have led to exercises being cancelled rather than replaced because of operational tempo constraints. Regional defence diplomacy has been undercooked. The price of this benign neglect of the neighbours and friends is hardly noticeable at first but its effect is cumulative. The ADF knows the region less and it is less known than it was in the lead-up to the East Timor intervention. For too long, the conceptual and creative intellectual space of the Army and the ADF has been taken up by the Middle East Area of Operations, leaving little room for investment with regional partners. This is disconcerting and it is a trend that needs to be reversed.

Defenders of the status quo would argue that the Army and the ADF can 'walk and chew gum': in other words it can sustain the operational tempo in the Middle East indefinitely while maintaining effective regional defence engagement. Maybe, but only just. And at what cost to the ADF's grasp on regional security concerns and local priorities? The ADF needs to think long and hard about the regional implications of striving so hard and for so long to participate and be seen to participate on operations in the Middle East.

One development in recent years that offers a significant opportunity to recalibrate the ADF's approach to regional engagement is the commissioning of the two LHDs. Not unlike its experience with the C-17 transport aircraft, once the ADF acquired the LHDs a whole range of opportunities presented themselves as to how, when and where they could be used to provide assistance to those in need, helping to bolster regional security and stability. Similarly with the LHDs, a remarkable range of opportunities will present themselves for the ADF to explore. Consequently, there are some significant opportunities for bridge building with partner forces in Australia's neighbourhood. This can be on a bilateral or multilateral basis. Medical personnel, engineers, logisticians and combat soldiers could be boarded in one of the RAN's amphibious ships and tasked to share in the completion of a constructive task in the neighbourhood. Clearly some preparatory arrangements would have to be put in place before a site could be agreed upon, but such an arrangement could have incalculable positive spin-offs for Australia's relations with its neighbours. There is a need to show genuine goodwill, to befriend our neighbours anew in order to show them that Australia is not an absentee security partners.

Capabilities for operations of necessity and of choice

Reflecting on the capabilities the government now expects from the ADF, it is worth categorising the requirements in terms of operations of choice and operations of necessity. Once upon a time, operations in the Middle East were not optional. Australia, as part of the British Empire, depended on Britain's success and on free passage of cargoes through the Suez Canal as its vital trading link to its primary export markets. That is no longer the case. In the 'Asian Century', operations of choice tend to be the ones far from Australia's shores, whereas operations of necessity tend to be closer to home. Operations of choice tend to be against an adversary that is not a peer competitor, whereas operations of necessity could well be against a near or peer competitor with precision guided munitions, high-level ISTAR and air support. This is naturally not the environment in which the ADF likes to operate.

For operations of choice, the force assigned is usually a niche contribution cobbled together with gilt-edged national support from ADF resources nationwide. In contrast, for operations of necessity, in all probability the ADF contribution will be a substantial combat force with a rounded 'all-arms' suite of capabilities but probably with more limited access for combat sub-units to the national technical support that one-off deployed task groups have come to expect. For operations of choice, the ADF has come to anticipate few if any casualties, whereas for operations of necessity commanders and their political masters will have to be prepared to absorb casualties on a large scale. In East Timor in 1999, for instance, the Australian Government acknowledged that it had a higher pain tolerance and anticipated considerable casualties. Similarly, operations of necessity may well be 'cyber heavy', with significant electronic attack on the ADF's networked systems.

Finally, operations of choice are sustainable under Plan Beersheba, but operations of necessity will demand a far great contribution than Australia's boutique Army could muster in the short term. In fact, while Plan Beersheba offers the Army a robust framework for sustained capability management in a period of high-operational tempo, there remain considerable vulnerabilities, particularly concerning the one-shot capabilities found in the three specialist brigades. Plan Beersheba provides for a suitable number of infantry-based combat units. That is fine as far as it goes. Infantry generals are happy and satisfied with that but most have not spent much of their careers experiencing the pain felt by those serving in 6, 16 and 17 brigades. While several of the generals understand that well, unfortunately some do not. This is a key area of vulnerability for the Army today.

Challenges for a boutique army

The Australian Army is a respected boutique army. What it does, it can do very well. Yet, it has limited ability to sustain conflict at the higher end of the spectrum and replace casualties particularly if the prospect of facing increased and more complex operations of necessity nearer to Australia. Australia needs some specialist redundancy. Such a situation is no longer satisfactory, if it ever was. Today the Army needs to build in some critical redundancy. The 6, 16 and 17 brigades are too important to be maintained as one-shot capabilities.

Cultural understanding is vital. The Army needs to focus on greater understanding of the region's languages, history, religion and cultures. This may be optional for wars of choice remote from Australia's shores. But in Australia's neighbourhood it is vitally important. Operations cannot be launched without having a detailed understanding beforehand if they are to be effective and achieve assigned objectives.

In this era of cyber war, the command support regiments needs to be bolstered and integrated with the national signals intelligence architecture. The days of reliance on Cold War-era electronic warfare capabilities is over. Cyber war challenges can be expected to affect not only the capital cities and the infrastructure of the worldwide web, but also combat operations and the capabilities of deployed forces. The command support regiments have to be able to leverage off the capabilities of national assets in a way that has not been imagined before. There is a need also to establish a coalition IT network that is Australian owned and operated to facilitate coalition partners plugging into the Australian command and control and communications architecture deployed for use on operations. In INTERFET an interim capability was cobbled together. It met the need – just. In future, if

Australia is serious about being able to lead a coalition force, this kind of capability will have to be available from the outset. The ADF needs one that is ready, on the shelf, to be used on a plug-and-play basis.

In wars of necessity, the ADF will have to be prepared to face greater precision and lethality from the adversary. Australian forces will not simply be facing an old-fashioned rocket like an RPG-7; they will be facing an RPG-21. The ADF needs to understand the implications of war among the people in Australia's region, be it in high- or low-intensity operations, and public opinion needs to be brought along as well. The Army cannot operate without the goodwill of the people.

Reflections

The ADF should beware of falling for half-baked ideas and quick-fix solutions. After the commencement of deployment to Uruzgan, one senior officer observed that the 'mission was accomplished: Australia got into NATO and the Dutch were brought into Uruzgan'. Really? Is that as good as it gets? What this observation reveals is the need for ADF commanders and advisers not to expect their political masters to think through the strategic implications for them. They have domestic politics in mind. The ADF needs to offer holistic, solid advice that thinks through the implications of decisions beyond tomorrow and next week, perhaps to ten years' time – especially if contemplating the use of force in Australia's neighbourhood. ADF commanders must engage their political masters with those strategic implications uppermost in mind. There is not time for complacency.

POSTSCRIPT

ALBERT PALAZZO

All military organisations fulfil a unique and critical function for the governments that maintain them. Alone among all the instruments of modern statecraft, the military exists to exercise state-sanctioned violence (or the threat of violence) in the pursuit of political objectives. While a government may direct its military to undertake other types of operations, such as humanitarian and disaster-relief missions, these are tasks of opportunity and not the reason why states go to the great expense of maintaining defence forces. That reason has always been to wage war.

Preparation for and conduct of war is arguably the most important endeavour a state can undertake, since the existence of security is a prerequisite for the conduct of all other activities. A country beset by a hostile threat environment will find undertaking even the most minor tasks demanding if not impossible. This applies to states at any level, whether they are an organised political body in the Westphalian sense, a chiefdom, a tribe or even a non-state actor. For people to live as they wish, to meet their needs and to plan for a future, they must have confidence in their security and the safety of citizens and property.

War has consequences for far more than just those who wage it; it can affect the lives, prosperity and opportunities of an entire polity, and future generations are hostages to the consequences of victory or defeat. In this sense war matters and, because its ramifications include the destruction of entire civilisations, it matters more than almost any other activity humans choose to pursue. For example, it was the Carthaginian defeat at the Battle of Zama in 202BC that secured the supremacy of Rome in the Mediterranean. For the people of Carthage their army's defeat was a turning point that led to their decline and eventual destruction.

War has also been a significant shaper of human development. Its ability to deliver stark outcomes means that war can close or open options for societal advancement or cultural decay. By way of illustration, a few cases demonstrate the centrality of war as a major force in the evolution of the human condition. In 480BC the Greeks defeated the Persians at Salamis and in doing so secured the continued survival and development of Western civilisation, including principles of diplomacy and jurisprudence that continue to mark the conduct of everyday affairs. The Spanish colonisation of Central America was a consequence of Hernán Cortéz's defeat of the Aztec Empire and led to widespread death and suffering together with the subjugation of an entire people for generations. The Allied victory over the Axis powers in the Second World War prevented the creation of a world dominated by Fascist ideology and preserved one more conducive to Australia, under the tenets of which its people continue to prosper. While some wars do not have such far-reaching effects and many are actually inconclusive, the potential of wars to determine and shape the course of human existence is not in doubt.

Because war matters, how it is conducted has a significance equal to why it is conducted. Military organisations have an obligation to the host state, to other citizens and to themselves to study what they have done on the battlefield in order to distil the lessons and to inculcate knowledge gained often at a painful and significant cost in lives and treasure. The chapters comprising this collection reflect this obligation to examine and think upon past actions. They offer the reader insights into many of the operations in which the Australian Army has participated since 1999, written by an eclectic mix of politicians, academics, defence thinkers, journalists and military practitioners.

Yet the reader may not be aware that the conference at which the chapters in this book were first delivered is a part of the first and, to date, only institutional-level inquiry conducted into the many operations the Army undertook during the period 1999 to 2015. In 2014, the Chief of Army Senior Advisory Committee (CASAC) directed the Army's Head of Modernisation and Strategic Planning to conduct an Institutional Lessons Study with a focus on operational commitments since 1999.[1] The direction had two parts, an internal study conducted by the Army and the external conference that carried the name 'On Ops'. This was a noteworthy initiative because, other than a few classified internal studies with very limited circulation, the Army had not previously invested significant effort in learning the 'big lessons' of its recent past by placing its experiences into an historical context and then incorporating its hard-won lessons into its future concepts of warfighting. Perhaps of more concern, the Army lacked an institutionalised mechanism to conduct the internal institutional review. This meant staff had to create one in 2014.

For a military organisation priding itself on professionalism, this was uncharacteristic. The Army does not usually neglect a core responsibility. It was not for a lack of understanding of the importance of learning that the Army had not commenced an earlier study of its operations since the 1999 East Timor intervention. Its publications frequently mention the need to adapt to changing circumstances and for the Army to do so more quickly than its adversaries. A core policy document, The Fundamentals of Land Power, notes that the Army is committed to continuous self-development and that it has 'sought to evolve its capstone warfighting doctrine to take into account changes in international affairs, technology, government policy and changes in Australian society.'[2] The foreword to its modernisation handbook declares that 'there is nothing unusual about change' and that the Army has been adapting to new circumstances for more than a century.[3]

That being said, while Army publications emphasise the constant need to 'change and modernise' there has been no comparable emphasis on learning. Change, some elements of the Army seem to believe, can be implemented without a firm understanding of the past, without distilling meaning and relevance from the events that shaped the present, and without recourse to self-criticism and institutional awareness. Instead, the Army is inclined to follow a safe and sanitised methodology of change implementation that minimises confrontation with uncomfortable realities while providing a semblance of forward progress. But can any change that is not based on a solid foundation of robust scrutiny and dogged self-assessment actually offer an effective methodology for improvement? Clearly, the answer is no. But this was the fallacy that the Army unwittingly embraced during a period of high-operational tempo, when the need to learn lessons and adapt to its adversaries was arguably at its greatest.

In an environment marked by cognitive dissonance, why did the Army choose to co-host a conference with UNSW Canberra and to sponsor this volume? Next, and perhaps more importantly, why did the Australian Army choose this particular method of self-examination — that is, to open itself to external examination in a public forum rather than taking the safer path of directed internal study, conducted by its own members, remote from public scrutiny and distant from the usual information controls encountered in Defence?

To illuminate the rationale for CASAC's change in policy regarding learning from the past, we need to explore why the Army waited so long to initiate an institutional lessons study. Heightened activity offers a simple if unsatisfying explanation. Commencing in 1999, the Army embarked on a period of continuous, intensive overseas operations that stretched its ability to fulfil the government's demands for military action. But to accept this excuse — and it is only an excuse — one must also accept that the Army was unable to find the handful of experienced military thinkers required to conduct an institutional lessons program. In a force of approximately 29,000 full-time uniform personnel, an inability to find the right number of the right people seems hard to believe. Moreover, the Army's leaders would have been aware that lessons must be learned immediately if the organisation is to benefit from its experience while the learning is still fresh. Being busy does not negate this necessity. In fact, it makes the observation of lessons even more pressing as there is more to learn, a greater need to adapt, and more urgency in applying the new insights. It is only through rapid adaptation that a military organisation can keep pace with an adversary who is also evolving. Plainly, both combatants seek an advantage over the other. To defer lesson learning risks losing the contest for ideas.

Two other explanations offer more satisfying reasons for the Army's long delay in embarking on a high-level lessons study. The first is the Army's operational bias. Faced with the need to get on with the immediate job, the Army was unable to address the requirements of its institutional future simultaneously. Moreover, in 1999 no one could have predicted that the tempo of operations would become so intense and last for so long. Instead it would have been natural to assume a ready return to peace, which would have afforded the opportunity for reflection. Unfortunately, this period of peace did not eventuate and the organisation remained focused on sustaining existing operations and preparing for other government demands.

The second explanation is the Army's cultural bias. The Army tends to prefer 'doers over thinkers'. It prioritises getting on with the immediate job in hand over deep and brutally honest analysis about its strengths and weaknesses, identification of desired outcomes and end states, consideration of potential second- and third-order effects, and challenges to an operation's defining assumptions. It should not be surprising, therefore, that until very recently the Australian Army did not have a formalised and rigorous organisation or mechanism for the study of its operational past. As I have already noted, in order to conduct a directed internal study the Army had first to design the process that the newly tasked personnel were to follow because there was no existing structure or standing policy. It should come as no surprise that the resulting report fell short of the mark and did not achieve its ambitions. It was a useful learning exercise in itself, however, that will help to better prepare the Army for the conduct of such studies in the future.

In the Australian context, this favouring of acting over thinking reflects a national malaise that the Army shares. This is concerning because it discounts the key role played by intellectuals in the advancement of society's interests. As a number of commentators have pointed out, Australia under invests in education and research and places a low value on intellectual pursuits.[4] From within Army, serving soldiers have made similar observations of an institutional discomfort with cognition and criticism.[5] James Brown's book, *Anzac's Long Shadow*, offered a damning account of an organisation that has made remarkably few original contributions to the realm of military ideas.[6] My own research on this subject led me to conclude that on the whole Australians 'favour the happy larrikin over the deep thinker'.[7] This is no less true of the Army.

In its defence, the Army does have organisations dedicated to capturing lessons leading to their interpretation and exploitation. The Centre for Army Lessons (CAL) is one organisation that attempts to extract wisdom and insight from the Army's own experience. Its focus is limited, however, to the tactical level of war. From this perspective it excels and serves the Army with great effect. It aims to capture the experiences of soldiers serving on operations and distil them into observations and insights that the Army can feed into its training and pre-deployment preparation cycles. It maintains a large database of tactical lessons and its periodic publication, *Smart Soldier*, is distributed throughout the Army. CAL's aim is to better prepare troops for what they may face on operations. By contrast, the Army does not have any organisation that examines the lessons that can be derived from the other levels of war, the administration of armed conflict or the effectiveness of the Army at the institutional level. All its lesson learning has been at the lowest tier.

Perhaps it is possible to excuse a lack of attentiveness to lessons other than the tactical. Because the Army has been on continuous operations since 1999, the first priority of institutional reflection has been on helping those placed in harm's way. But there is another possible explanation for the Army's focus on tactical lessons. It is one that holds, if correct, potentially serious implications for the nation's continued success in war. The Australian Army is most comfortable with tactics. It rarely acts independently at the operational level of war and its performance at the strategic level is heavily conditioned by the goals of its senior coalition partner. Logistics, too, are largely overlooked by a force that remains heavily dependent on others for support in the field. The reality is that commencing with the South African War of 1899–1902 and continuing to the current conflicts in Iraq and Afghanistan, the Australian Army has always fought as a junior partner in a coalition that has been led by a great power. Not operating on its own or for its own objectives has conditioned the Army to focus on the one aspect of war at which it can achieve mastery: the tactical. On the few occasions when Australia has been the main contributor to an operation, such as during the East Timor intervention, these missions have been at a level somewhat less than war. We might perhaps conclude that it is the fate of all junior coalition partners to make tactical excellence their main focus. But such a focus is a cause for concern if Australia ever has to fight on its own. The extraordinary complexity of war requires mastery of the whole activity and not just the preferred parts.

While it is possible to explain the absence of a thorough review of lessons (other than tactical) as an unfortunate oversight since 1999, it is clear that other compelling factors were at work. Culture is a strong influence on institutional decision-making, often an invisible one. The Army's reticence about intellectualism and its preference for activity over thinking have inhibited thoughtful and candid examination of its recent past. The Institutional Lessons Study was a first step and, like all first steps, it is tentative and uncertain. It is too early to say if the Army is changing its attitude towards intellectual pursuits but cultural change has been a major initiative for some time and new mood is emerging. The Pathway to Change initiative seeks to promote attitudinal shifts across many aspects of Defence culture.[8] While anti-intellectualism was not one of the focus points expressly identified by Pathways to Change, there are modest signs within the Army that thinking and critical analysis are gaining a degree of traction and respectability. Other initiatives are underway. For example, the Army has adopted a Research and Development Plan, and senior leaders have been increasingly willing to speak of the need for the Army to improve its human capital and creative thinking.[9]

The chapters in this volume reveal an institution that is making up for lost time. The task is by no means complete. The authors could have chosen different themes to examine and, plainly, some operations did not receive sufficient consideration. While future initiatives may close some of these gaps, there is no guarantee that the nascent signs of a cultural shift more favourably inclined to thinking will continue. Cultural change is a notoriously difficult undertaking and one that cannot be rushed. It must be nurtured over the long-term if change is to continue and a new culture become permanent. The conference at which these chapters were first presented should be seen as one step in an organisational effort to become better at learning from the past and implementing changes that lead to a more capable land force. Hopefully, there will be many others.

Let me stress that this book is anything but an exercise in information management or creative censorship. The decision to conduct the conference as an open forum, involving external expertise, was taken when CASAC initiated the Institutional Lesson Study. No one suggested a different format for a number of reasons. First, the committee managing the study had already authorised an internal review. More importantly, the Army wanted external input into its lesson learning process. This was recognition that the Australian community could make a positive, if not critical, contribution to the Army's awareness and development. It was also an acknowledgement that large and sprawling organisations like the Australian Army unintentionally initiate barriers that create blind spots, which preclude critical examination. This is not merely a reflection of misguided institutional loyalty. Instead, those within an organisation can struggle to think laterally or critically on the faults or weak spots of the group to which they belong out of either narrowness of vision or fear of reprisal. Often it takes someone who has not 'grown up' within the organisation, someone free of institutional bias and not shaped by the existing culture, to be able to identify the most pressing lessons that need to be learned and the learning from which the most profound change can come.

The conference participants were neither coached nor scripted. The Army wanted to engage in an honest dialogue with the public and was not interested in platitudes. Its leaders knew that it would receive some direct comments and these were exactly what it sought, irrespective of whether they were agreed or disputed, praised or criticised. The conference represented an opportunity to begin a conversation with the public, and to engage with those on whose behalf the Army pursues its mission. This volume is meant to deepen that engagement. Hopefully this collection will receive wide circulation and attract attention across the Australian community and beyond.

Let me offer one final observation on the intent behind the Army's Institutional Lessons Study, of which the conference and this volume form a part. While the chapters in this volume are important and offer the reader and the Army much to consider, in a large organisation like the Australian Army the process of learning must be more than just an episodic act that occurs when a senior leader notices that a critical task has been overlooked. Rather it needs to be institutionalised to become a catalyst for continuous change. In the context of being given a direction by government, the Army's long-term objective should be to reach the point where the mission's concept of operations reflects the need to identify lessons across the entire spectrum of war. The operational planning staff should include personnel tasked to conduct a lessons learning study and their work should commence before the first deployment of troops. The operation's budget should include provision for this kind of study as well. The desire to record, learn and process lessons should be automatic and not require the passage of years or the accumulated weight of inefficiency to compel action.

Organisations like CAL already exist for the analysis of tactics. The challenge for the Army is to establish standing mechanisms to address lessons at the operational, strategic, administrative and institutional levels of war. The end state is a treatment of war in its entirety. This needs to be the goal. Once in place, the learning of lessons at all levels can continue without hindrance or hiatus.

A welcome of progress is underway. Within the Modernisation and Strategic Planning Division, a standing Army Lessons Seminar has been established with a general officer presiding. There is clear recognition that another 15 years cannot be allowed to pass before the study of lessons continues. The Army Lessons Seminar will convene on an annual basis and attract insights and wisdom from across the Army. It is designed to 'close the loop' on the lesson learning cycle. This is a good beginning. The Army remains committed to reaching out to the nation's subject matter experts and bringing their intellect to bear on problem solving and the imagination of a better future.[10] The 'On Ops' Conference was part of a larger movement within Army designed to raise the level of the organisation's intellectual engagement and its ability to identify lessons that can be absorbed in order to improve the force's capabilities for the future. This must continue.

NOTES

ACSACS series

1   See <www.aif.adfa.edu.au> and <www.vietnam.unsw.adfa.edu.au>.

Lessons and learning

1   AR Millett, W Murray and KH Watman, *The Effectiveness of Military Organizations,* Ohio, 1989, pp. 26–27.

The emerging strategic environment

1   Military personnel are still serving in Iraq and Afghanistan, but in announcing the withdrawal from Afghanistan in December 2014 the government has tried to draw a line under the period.

2   Gough Whitlam, quoted in TB Millar, *Australian in Peace and War: External Relations Since 1788* (second edition), Australian National University Press, Sydney 1991, p. 334.

3   Department of Defence, 'Australian Defence', White Paper presented to Parliament by the Minister for Defence the Honourable DJ Killen MP, November 1976, Australian Government Publishing Service, Canberra 1976, p. 10.

4   Department of Defence, 'The Defence of Australia 1987', White Paper presented to Parliament by the Minister for Defence the Honourable KC Beazley MP, Australian Government Publishing Service, Canberra, 1987.

5   Department of Defence, 'The Defence of Australia 1987', p. 8.

6   P Young, 'The perils of pleasing Washington', *The Australian,* 23 December 1987.

7   Department of Foreign Affairs and Trade, 'In the National Interest, Australian's Foreign and Trade Policy', Canberra, 1997 p. 58.

8   Department of Defence, 'Australia's Strategic Policy', Canberra, 1997, pp. 8, 29, 32–33, 48.

9   J Cotton, 'The East Timor Commitment and Its Consequences' in J Cotton and J Ravenhill (eds), *The National Interest in a Global Era,* Oxford University Press, Melbourne, 2001, p. 226.

10   Department of Defence, 'Defence 2000: Our Future Defence Force', Defence Publishing Service, Canberra, 2000.

11   H White, 'Security, Defence and Terrorism' in J Cotton and J Ravenhill (eds), *Trading on Alliance Security: Australia in World Affairs 2012–2005,* Oxford University Press, Melbourne, 2007, p. 173.

12   J Howard, *Lazarus Rising: A Personal and Political Autobiography,* HarperCollins, Sydney, 201, p. 455.

13 A Palazzo, 'Assessing the War in Iraq', United Service, no. 63, December 2012,
 p. 16.
14 Department of Defence, 'Defending Australia in the Asia Pacific Century: Force 2030',
 Commonwealth of Australia, 2003.

Lessons from East Timor

1 Centre for Army Lessons (CAL) database, 'Operation Warden/Stabilise – East Timor
 Lessons and Insights Database', Event ID: 1/CSS/02-19 & 1/CSS/04-02; '3 Brigade
 Post Operation Report (POR) Operation WARDEN – 20 Sep 1999 to 15 Feb 2000',
 in author's possession, 1 March 2000, p. 9.
2 B Breen, *Mission Accomplished, East Timor: the ADF participation in INTERFET*, Allen
 & Unwin, Sydney, 2000, p. 41.
3 Australian National Audit Office, 'Management of Australian Defence Force
 Deployments to East Timor', The Auditor-General Audit Report No. 38, Canberra,
 2002, p. 110; CAL database, Event ID: 1/CSS/02-19.
4 Breen, *Mission Accomplished, East Timor*, p. 144.
5 CAL database, Event ID: 1/CSS/04-03.
6 Annex E to 'INTERFET POR', dated February 2000, in author's possession.
7 Breen, *Mission Accomplished, East Timor*, pp. 41, 145.
8 CAL database, Event ID: 1/CSS/08-06.
9 Annex E to 'INTERFET POR'.
10 Breen, *Mission Accomplished, East Timor*, p. 144–45.
11 E Downey and V Grant, *10 Force Support Battalion: 'The Force Behind the Force'*, 10
 Force Support Battalion, Townsville, 2000, p. 3; CAL database, Event ID: 1/CSS/02-
 19 & 1/CSS/02-12.
12 CAL database, Event ID: 1/AIR/014.
13 Brief for 10 QWG Int Op Warden Int Lessons Learned, author's possession.
14 '3 RAR Post Operation Report (POR): Operations SPITFIRE and WARDEN –
 27 Aug 1999 to 22 Feb 2000', in author's possession, p. 6.
15 '3 Brigade Post Operation Report (POR) Operation WARDEN', 1 Match 2000,
 in author's possession, p. 10.
16 Annex E to 'INTERFET POR'.
17 Annex E to 'INTERFET POR'.
18 Downey and Grant, *10 Force Support Battalion*, p. 5; CAL database, Event ID: 1/
 CSS/08-06 and 1/CSS/08-01.
19 'Logistic Support Group Supporting Plans Instruction 1/99, 12 November 1999',
 in author's possession; Downey and Grant, *10 Force Support Battalion*, p. 3.
20 CAL database, Event ID: 1/CSS/08-04.
21 Australian National Audit Office (ANAO), *Management of Australian Defence Force
 Deployments to East Timor*, pp. 62, 67.
22 ANAO, *Management of Australian Defence Force Deployments to East Timor*, pp. 64-5.
23 Breen, *Mission Accomplished, East Timor*, p. 172.
24 ANAO, *Management of Australian Defence Force Deployments to East Timor*, p. 79.
25 '3 RAR Post Operation Report (POR): Operations SPITFIRE and WARDEN'; CAL
 database, Event ID: 1/CSS/02-19; ANAO, *Management of Australian Defence Force
 Deployments to East Timor*, p. 12.
26 ANAO, *Management of Australian Defence Force Deployments to East Timor*, pp. 57-8.
27 CAL database, 'Operation Warden/Stabilise – East Timor Lessons and Insights', Event
 ID: 1/INT/69.
28 CAL database, 'Operation Warden/Stabilise – East Timor Lessons and Insights', Event
 ID: 1/INT/39 and I/INT/35.

29 CAL database, 'Operation Warden/Stabilise – East Timor Lessons and Insights', Event ID: 1/INT/71.

30 Commodore JR Stapleton AM RAN, 'Operation Warden NCC Lessons Learned', and SPC-A: 'Operation Stabilise Reference Material 1999–2000', box 1, file Miscellaneous Material.

31 CAL database, 'Operation Warden/Stabilise – East Timor Lessons and Insights', Event ID: 1/AIR/022.

32 Stapleton, 'Operation Warden NCC Lessons Learned'.

33 B Breen, *Struggling for Self-reliance: Four Case Studies of Australian Regional Force Projection in the Late 1980s and the 1990s*, Australian National University E-Press and Strategic and Defence Studies Centre, Canberra, 2008. See also I Martin, *Self-Determination in East Timor: The United Nations, the Ballot and International Intervention*, Internatonal Peace Academy Occasion Paper Series, p. 94; J Martinkus, *A Dirty Little War*, Randon House, 2001; D Greenless and R Garran, *Deliverance: The Inside Story of East Timor's Fight for Freedom*, Allen & Unwin, especially chapter 11.

34 CAL database, Event ID: 1/DMTD1/05.

35 '3 RAR Post Operation Report (POR): Operations SPITFIRE and WARDEN', p. 5.

36 CAL database, 'Operation Warden/Stabilise, BOS & Subject Area Summaries, Civil and Military Affairs'.

37 'Operation Langar: The UN Mandated Peace Enforcement Mission in East Timor, A Tactical Lessons Study, 1 July 2000', author's possession, p. 8.

Islander perspectives:
Bougainville and the Solomon Islands

1 *Bel Isi* is Pidgin for a 'quiet heart', 'calm' or 'peace'.

2 Meaning, 'helping a friend'.

3 RRE Bowd, *Doves Over the Pacific: In Pursuit of Peace and Stability in Bougainville*, Australian Military History Publications, Sydney, 2007, p. 5.

4 National Statistical Office (NSO) PNG, '2011 National Population and Housing Census of PNG – Final Figures', Waigani, 2013, p. 36.

5 Solomon Islands NSO, 'Report on 2009 Population and Housing Censes, Volume 1', Honiara, 2011, p. 1.

6 Ethnologue website <www.ethnologue.com/show_country.asp?name=SB> states the Solomon Islands has 75 languages (71 living/four extinct); Bowd, *Doves Over the Pacific*, p. 7, states Bougainville has 25 languages.

7 Bowd, *Doves Over the Pacific*, p. 18.

8 Joint Standing Committee on Foreign Affairs, Defence and Trade (JSCFADT), 'Bougainville: The Peace Process and Beyond', 27 September 1999, p. 6. The exact figure is unknown, however, estimates range between 8000 and 20,000 people out of a population of around 160,000 civilians, either from the fighting or from disease and deprivation.

9 For Lincoln Agreement, see <peacemaker.un.org/sites/peacemaker.un.org/files/ PG_980123_LincolnAgreement.pdf>.

10 Lincoln Agreement, Article 3.

11 Lincoln Agreement, Article 6.

12 EP Wolfers, 'International Peace Missions in Bougainville, Papua New Guinea, 1990–2005, Host State Perspectives', Regional Forum on Reinventing Government Exchange and Transfer of Innovations for Transparent Governance and State Capacity, Nadi, 20–22 February 2006, pp. 32–33.

13 Australian War Memorial, PNG [Bougainville] (PMG), 1998–2003', see <www.awm.
    gov.au/conflict/CN500099>.

14 WR Jackson, 'Commander PMG Bougainville Post Operation Report – Operation Bel
    Isi II Period 15 Jun – 15 Oct 02', p. 2.

15 Bougainville Peace Agreement, Article 330.

16 Bougainville Peace Agreement, Annex A.

17 United Nations, *Yearbook of the United Nations 2003*, vol. 57, United Nations, New
    York, 2005, p. 394.

18 United Nations, *Yearbook of the United Nations 2003*, p. 394.

19 United Nations, *Yearbook of the United Nations 2003*, p. 395.

20 United Nations, *United Nations Judicial Yearbook 2005*, United Nations, New York,
    2009, p. 159.

21 Bowd, *Doves Over the Pacific*, p. 141.

22 B Breen, 'Presentation to Rotations Deploying to Bougainville at the Lachlan Wilson
    Centre, Lavarack Barracks', Townsville (undated); P Reddy, 'Reconciliation in
    Bougainville: Civil War, Peacekeeping and Restorative Justice', *Contemporary Justice
    Review*, vol. 11, no. 2, June 2008, pp. 118 and 122.

23 Interview between the author and Colonel B Cox, 16 June 2015.

24 J Braithwaite, H Charlesworth, P Reddy and L Dunn, *Reconciliation and Architectures
    of Commitment: Sequencing peace in Bougainville*, ANU E-Press, Canberra, 2010,
    p. 55.

25 Jackson, 'Commander PMG Bougainville Post Operation Report – Operation Bel Isi
    II Period 15 Jun – 15 Oct 02', p. 15.

26 Jackson, 'Commander PMG Bougainville Post Operation Report', p. 19.

27 LCAUST, 'Operation Bel Isi II Post Operation Report dated 29 November 2003',
    pp. 6–7.

28 Braithwaite, et al., *Reconciliation and Architectures of Commitment*, p. 55.

29 Jackson, 'Commander PMG Bougainville Post Operation Report', pp. 10-16.

30 Breen, 'Presentation to Rotations Deploying to Bougainville', p. 6.

31 Interview between the author and Colonel B Cox, 16 June 2015.

32 See also Braithwaite et al., *Reconciliation and Architectures of Commitment*, p. 54.

33 JSCFADT, 'Bougainville: The Peace Process and Beyond', p. 106.

34 Jackson, 'Commander PMG Bougainville Post Operation Report', pp. 19.

35 Authors observation supported by: LCAUST, 'Operation Bel Isi II Post Operation
    Report', p. 21 and interview between the author and Colonel B Cox, 16 June 2015.

36 CTF 635, 'Post Operation Report – OP Anode, 24 Jul – 18 Nov 03 of 21 January
    2004', p. 1.

37 Department of Defence, 'Australian-led Combined Task Force concludes role with
    RAMSI', <www.defence.gov.au/defencenews/stories/2013/jul/0703.htm>.

38 CTF 635, 'Post Operation Report', p. 1.

39 Department of Defence, 'Operation Anode', <www.defence.gov.au/Operations/
    PastOperations/SolomonIslands>.

40 T Anderson, 'The Limits of RAMSI', Report prepared for AID/WATCH, AID/
    WATCH, Sydney, April 2008, p. 7.

41 RAMSI, 'Peoples Survey' conducted by ANU Enterprise (or by its division, ANUedge)
    in collaboration with the ANU (2006–2011) and the University of the South Pacific
    (2013), <www.ramsi.org/media/peoples-survey>.

42 J Braithwaite, S Dinnen, M Allen, V Braithwaite and H Charlesworth, *Pillars and
    Shadows: Statebuilding as Peacebuilding in Solomon Islands*, ANU E-Press, Canberra,
    2010, p. 136.

43 CTF 635, 'Post Operation Report', pp. 11–12.

44	This was certainly the case in my experience. See Braithwaite et al., *Pillars and Shadows*, p. 61.

45	Braithwaite et al., *Pillars and Shadows*, p. 136.

46	Braithwaite et al., *Pillars and Shadows*, p. 52.

47	R Muggah and P Alpers, 'Reconsidering Small Arms in the Solomon Islands' (findings excerpt from a policy briefing commissioned for the Small Arms Survey, Geneva, for internal circulation by stakeholders, agencies and diplomatic missions, Honiara, 1 August 2003), p. 3.

48	Muggah and Alpers, 'Reconsidering Small Arms in the Solomon Islands', p. 3.

49	Muggah and Alpers, 'Reconsidering Small Arms in the Solomon Islands', p. 1.

50	CTF 635, 'Post Operation Report', pp. 2, 12; DFAT, 'Operation Helpem Fren: Rebuilding the Nation of Solomon Islands', speech by N Warner, 23 March 2004, <dfat.gov.au/news/speeches/Pages/operation-helpem-fren-rebuilding-the-nation-of-solomon-islands.aspx>.

51	CTF 635, 'Post Operation Report', p. 12.

52	CTF 635, 'Post Operation Report', pp. 12–13; J Frewen, 'Communication as a Tactic', *Defence Magazine*, July 2005, p. 44.

53	CTF 635, 'Post Operation Report', pp. 11–12.

54	CTF 635, 'Post Operation Report', p. 14.

55	CTF 635, 'Post Operation Report', p. 2.

56	Anderson, 'The Limits of RAMSI', p. 10.

Afghanistan, Iraq and the war on terror

1	GW Bush speech, 20th Anniversary of the National Endowment for Democracy, <www.ned.org/remarks-by-president-george-w-bush-at-the-20th-anniversary>.

2	BBC, 'Afghanistan Election: Millions Vote in Presidential Poll,' *BBC News*, 5 April 2014.

3	Sayed Abbas Kazemi, 'Afghanistan Up with 6 Ranks in Press Freedom Index,' *Tolo News*, 13 February 2015, <www.tolonews.com/en/afghanistan/18190-afghanistan-up-with-6-ranks-in-press-freedom-index>.

4	See A Saikal, *Zone of Crisis: Afghanistan, Pakistan, Iran and Iraq*, IB Tauris, London, 2014, esp. pp. 23–51.

5	See United States Institute of Peace, 'Forging Afghanistan's National Unity Government', Peacebrief 183, January 2015, <www.usip.org/sites/default/files/PB183-Forging-Afghanistans-National-Unity-Government.pdf>.

6	BBC, *BBC News*, 29 July 2015.

7	Dawn, 22 September 2015, <www.dawn.com/new/1208594>.

8	Admiral M Mullen, Chairman of the Joint Chiefs of Staff, called the Haqqani group a 'veritable arm of the ISI' before a US Senate Panel, *The New York Times*, 22 September 2011.

9	See Saikal, *Zone of Crisis*, chapter 5.

10	A Khedery, 'Why we stuck with Maliki – and lost Iraq', *The Washington Post*, 3 July 2015, <www.washingtonpost.com/opinions/why-we-stuck-with-maliki-and-lost-iraq/2014/07/03/0dd6a8a4-11e3-a606-946fd632f9fl_story.html>.

11	E Groll, 'Is the Rise of ISIS Really Such a Mystery?', *Foreign Policy*, 24 July 2015, <foreignpolicy.com/2015/07/24/is-the-rise-of-isis-really-such-a-mystery/>.

12	N MacFarquhar, 'Saddam Hussein, Defiant Dictator Who Ruled Iraq With Violence and Fear, Dies,' *The New York Times*, 30 December 2006, <www.nytimes.com/2006/12/30/world/middleeast/30saddam.html?pagewanted=all&_r=0>.

13	H al-Qarawee, 'Saudi Arabia, Iran Vie for Influence in Iraq,' *Al-Monitor*, 17 September 2013, <www.al-monitor.com/pulse/originals/2013/09/saudi-iran-vie-influence-iraq.

html>; F Wehrey, et al., *Saudi-Iranian Relations Since the Fall of Saddam: Rivalry, Cooperation, and Implications for US Policy*, Rand Corporation, 2009, pp. 60–67.

14   M Madi, 'Haider al-Abadi: A new era for Iraq?', *BBC News*, 9 September 2014, <www. bbc.com/news/world-middle-east-28748366>.

15   N Bisserbe and F Schwartz, 'Iraqi Prime Minister Seeks More Support in Fighting Islamic State', *The Wall Street Journal*, 2 June 2015, <www.wsj.com/articles/iraqi-prime-minister-haider-al-abadi-urges-more-international-support-in-fighting-islamic-state-1433250707>; O Al-Jawoshy and T Arango, 'Premier Haider al-Abadi, Facing Protests, Proposes Iraqi Government Overhaul', *The New York Times*, 9 August 2015, <www.nytimes.com/2015/08/10/world/middleeast/iraqs-premier-facing-protests-proposes-government-overhaul.html>.

16   KR Himes, *Drones and the Ethics of Targeted Killing*, Rowman & Littlefield Publishers, 2015; P Baker and J Hirschfeld Davis, 'Amid Errors, Obama Publicly Wrestles With Drones' Limits', *The New York Times*, 24 April 2015, <www.nytimes.com/2015/04/25/us/politics/hostage-deaths-show-risk-of-drone-strikes.html>.

17   D Welna, 'After A Year Of Bombing ISIS, US Campaign Shows Just Limited Gains', NPR, 7 August 2015, <www.npr.org/sections/parallels/2015/08/07/430151358/after-a-year-of-bombing-isis-u-s-campaign-shows-just-limited-gains>.

18   RM Gates, *Duty: Memoirs of a Secretary at War*, Alfred A Knopf, New York, 2014, p. 336.

19   Declan Walsh, 'The US had 'a frighteningly simplistic' view of Afghanistan says McChrystal', *The Guardian*, 7 October 2011.

20   A Kalinovsky, *A Long Goodbye: The Soviet Withdrawal From Afghanistan*, Harvard University Press, 2011.

21   *The Washington Times*, 15 April 2014.

22   Khedery, *A Long Goodbye*.

23   KSharro, 'Defeating ISIS: The Board Game: Who Can Devise the Most Convoluted Way to Wipe Out the Islamic State?', *The Atlantic*, 31 July 2015, <www.theatlantic.com/international/archive/2015/07/strategy-isis-defeat-board-games/400034/>.

Improvements and challenges for Army's ISR enterprise

1   See M Thompson and A Davies, 'ADF Capability Review: Australian Army', Australian Strategic Policy Institute, Policy Analysis No. 25, 2008; Commonwealth of Australia, 'Management of Australian Defence Force Deployments to East Timor', The Auditor General, Australian National Audit Office, Audit Report no. 38, 2002; MO'Neil, 'Time to Move on in the Defence Policy Debate', *Australian Journal of International Affairs*, vol. 60, no. 3, 2006, pp. 358–63.

2   DA Charters, 'Canadian Military Intelligence in Afghanistan', *International Journal of Intelligence and Counter Intelligence*, vol. 25, no. 3, p. 477.

3   US Army CSA White Paper, 'Adapting our Aim: A Balanced Army for a Balanced Strategy, 07 Apr 09', p. 1.

4   N Carter, *The Future of the British Army: How the Army Must Change to Serve Britain in a Volatile World*, Chatham House, Royal Institute of International Affairs, 17 February 2015, p. 4.

5   Kilcullen identifies the enduring features of the modern operating environment as population, urbanisation and 'littoralisation' – D Kilcullen, 'The Australian Army in the Urban Networked Littoral', Army Research Paper, no. 2, 2014, p. 8.

6   See Army Headquarters, 'Future Land Warfare Report 2014', Commonwealth of Australia, Canberra, 2014; United States Army, 'The US Army Operating Concept: Win in a Complex World', TRADOC Pamphlet 525-3-1, 2014.

7   Highlighting the threat posed by the cyber domain, a virus known as 'Stuxnet' was

able to manipulate systems within Iran's highly guarded Natanz uranium enrichment plant in 2009, resulting in the destruction of a fifth of the centrifuges; see K Zetter, *Countdown to Zero Day: Stuxnet and the Launch of the World's First Digital Weapon*, Crown Books, 2014. For a broader discussion see US Army CSA White Paper, 'Adapting our Aim: A Balanced Army for a Balanced Strategy, 07 April 2009', p. 1.

8   Carter, *The Future of the British Army*, p. 4.

9   M Mandeles, *The Future of War: Organisations as Weapons*, Potomac Books, 2005, p. 122; US Congress, 'Congressional House Record', vol. 151, part 10, 2005.

10   These definitions are adapted from UK JDP 2-00.

11   JW Charlton, *Digitized Chaos: Is Our Military Decision Making Process Ready for the Information Age?*, School of Advanced Military Studies, Fort Leavenworth, Kansas, 1997.

12   See JD Cross, 'Decisive Battle and the Global War on Terror', School of Advanced Military Studies, Fort Leavenworth, Kansas, 2005.

13   See TJ Rutherford, 'Everyone's Accountable: An Examination of How Non-State Armed Groups Interact With International Humanitarian Law', Australian National University, Canberra, 2004; National Research Council, *International Conflict Resolution After the Cold War*, Committee on International Conflict Resolution, PC Stern and D Druckman (eds), National Academy Press, Washington DC, 2000, pp. 1–2.

14   TJ Rutherford, 'Rise of the Warrior Geek: The Impact of Remote Systems on Future Personnel Needs', *ADF Journal*, no. 195, 2014, p. 21.

15   See G Moore, 'Cramming More Components onto Integrated Circuits', *Electronics*, vol. 38, no. 8, 1965; I Toumi, 'The Lives and Death of Moore's Law', *First Monday*, vol. 7, no. 11, 2002; GC Chow, 'Technological Change and the Demand for Computers', *American Economic Review*, vol. 57, no. 5, 1967, pp. 1117–130.

16   HR McMaster, 'On War: Lessons to be Learned', *Survival: Global Politics and Strategy*, 25 March 2008, pp. 22 and 26.

17   RD Hooker and JJ Collins (eds), *Lessons Encountered: Learning from the Long War*, National Defense University Press, Washington DC, 2015, pp. 11–12.

18   I Porche III, B Wilson, E Johnson, S Tierney and E Saltzman, *Data Flood: Helping the Navy Address the Rising Tide of Sensor Information*, RAND Corporation, 2014, p. 14.

19   A McAfee and E Brynjolfsson, 'Big Data: The Management Revolution', *Harvard Business Review*, October 2012, p. 62.

20   L Holmes, 'The Sad, Beautiful Fact That We're All Going to Miss Almost Everything', <www.npr.org/sections/monkeysee/2011/04/21/135508305/the-sad-beautiful-fact-that-were-all-going-to-miss-almost-everything>.

21   Defence White Paper 2013, p. 79.

22   M Evans, 'The Tyranny of Dissonance: Australia's Strategic Culture and Way of War, 1901–2005', Land Warfare Studies Centre, Study Paper no. 306; R Medcalf, 'Towards a New Australian Security', 2015, <www.realcleardefense.com/articles/2015/03/16/towards_a_new_australian_security-107765-2.html>.

23   J Blaxland, *The Australian Army from Whitlam to Howard*, Cambridge University Press, Melbourne, 2013, p. 48.

24   MT Flynn, M Pottinger and PD Batchelor, *Fixing Intel: A Blueprint for Making Intelligence Relevant in Afghanistan*, Center for a New American Security, January 2010, p. 7.

25   Hooker and Collins, *Lessons Encountered*, p. 11.

26   Hooker and Collins, *Lessons Encountered*, p. 12.

27   US Marine Corps, 'Intelligence, Surveillance and Reconnaissance Enterprise Plan, 2015–2020', 2014, p. 4.

28   Defence White Paper 2013, p. 79.

29   This phrase has been used to refer to the US Marine Corps ISR Enterprise's focus on providing continuity of intelligence operations. The US Department of Army G-2 uses a similar 'No cold starts, no Military Intelligence solder at rest' phrase, see US Marine Corps, 'Intelligence, Surveillance and Reconnaissance Enterprise Plan', p. 11.

30   C Andrew, *Defend the Realm: The Authorised History of MI5*, Knopf, Borzoi Books, 2009, p. 684.

31   Joint Doctrine Publication 2-00, *Understanding and Intelligence Support to Joint Operations* (third edition), Development, Concepts and Doctrine Centre, UK Ministry of Defence, August 2011, pp. 1–5 (para 108).

32   Marine Corps Warfighting Publication 2-1, *Intelligence Operations*, Department of the Navy, Headquarters US Marine Corps, Washington DC, 10 September 2003, p. 49; Australian Army, 'Combat Brigade Standard Operating Procedures', Army Knowledge Group, Forces Command, 2015, p. 2.1–3.

33   Department of Defence, 'Australia's Strategic Policy', Commonwealth of Australia, 1997.

34   Army's first Unmanned Aerial System (UAS) unit, the 20th Surveillance and Target Acquisition Regiment, was established in 2006.

35   ADDP 2.0, *Intelligence*, Department of Defence, Canberra, 2009, chapter 1, para 1.5.

36   First Principles Review, 'Creating One Defence', p. 48.

37   M Howard, 'The Use and Abuse of Military History' in M Howard (ed.), *The Causes of War and Other Essays*, Harvard University Press, Cambridge MA, 1983, pp. 194–95.

38   First Principles Review, 'Creating One Defence', p. 47.

Logistics and the failure to modernise

1   S Smith, *A Handmaiden's Tale: An Alternative View of Logistic Lessons Learned from INTERFET*, Australian Defence Studies Centre, UNSW, Canberra, 2001, p. 5.

2   Australian National Audit Office (ANAO), 'Management of Australian Defence Force Deployments to East Timor', Audit Report no. 38, Department of Defence, Canberra, 2002, p. 63.

3   ANAO, 'Management of Australian Defence Force Deployments to East Timor', pp. 52, 88.

4   B Breen, *Struggling for Self-reliance: Four Case Studies of Australian Regional Force Projection in the Late 1980s and the 1990s*, ANU e-press, Australia, 2008, pp. 156

5   A Palazzo, *The Australian Army: a History of its Organisation 1901–2001*, Oxford University Press, Melbourne, 2001, p. 349.

6   D Horner, 'Deploying and Sustaining INTERFET in East Timor in 1999' in Australian Army History Unit, *Raise, Training and Sustain: Delivering Land Combat Power*, Canberra, 2009, <www.army.gov.au/~/.../2009_Chief_of_Armys_Conference_Report.pdf>.

7   P Cosgrove cited in Smith, *A Handmaiden's Tale*, p. 7.

8   Chiefs of Staff Committee cited in ANAO, Management of Australian Defence Force Deployments to East Timor, p. 57.

9   M Slater, 'An interview with Brigadier Mick Slater, Commander JTF 631', *Australian Army Journal*, vol. 3, no. 2, 2006, p. 11 <www.army.gov.au/~/media/Content/Our%20future/Publications/AAJ/2000s/2006/AAJ_2006_2.pdf>.

10   M Slater, 'An interview with Brigadier Mick Slater', p. 11.

11   J Grath, 'The Other End of the Spear: The Tooth-to-Tail Ratio (T3R) in Modern Military Operations', Occasional Paper no. 23, Combat Studies Institute Press, 2007, p. 85.

12   G Waters and J Blackburn, 'Australian Defence Logistics: The Need to Enable and

Equip Logistics Transformation', Kokoda Paper no. 19, Kokoda Foundation, 2014.

13   P Leahy, 'Towards the Hardened and Networked Army', *Australian Army Journal*, vol. 2, no. 1, 2004, p. 29.

14   Palazzo, *The Australian Army*, p. 361.

15   M Granger, 'Supplying An Expeditionary Force: Three Case Studies in Afghanistan', US Army War College, 2003, <www.dtic.mil/dtic/tr/fulltext/u2/a415877.pdf>, p. 47.

16   M van Creveld, *Supplying War* (second edition), Cambridge University Press, 2004, p. 231.

17   Australian Army, 'Army Capability Requirement – Combat Service Support 2015', Department of Defence, Australia (available on the Defence Protected Network or on request), 2005, p. ii.

18   Smith, *A Handmaiden's Tale*, p 16.

19   Smith, *A Handmaiden's Tale*, p. 11.

20   Land Warfare Development Group, Army Capability Requirement CSS 2012, Australian Army, Department of Defence, 2002 (available on the Defence Protected Network).

21   Kellogg Brown & Root Inc., 'Logistics Over the Short Focused Study: Milestone 2.2.4', Department of Defence, 2002 (available on the Defence Protected Network).

22   Australian Army, 'Army Capability Requirement'.

23   A Davies, 'Keep on truckin', *The Strategist*, ASPI, 2015, <www.aspistrategist.org.au/keep-on-truckin/> [accessed 8 July 2015].

24   D Horner, *Making the Australian Defence Force*, Australian Centenary of Defence, vol. 4, Oxford University Press, Melbourne, 2004, p. 279.

25   See Department of Defence, 'Creating one Defence (Defence First Principles Review)', Commonwealth of Australia, 2015.

26   D Ballantine, cited in D Cowen, *The Deadly Life of Logistics*, University of Minneapolis Press, 2014, p. 30.

27   Smith, *A Handmaiden's Tale*, p. 16.

28   V Prebelic, 'Theoretical aspects of military logistics', *Defence and Security Analysis*, vol. 22, no. 2, Routledge, 2006, p. 178.

29   'Exercise Headline 2014', Quicklook report (classified and available on the Defence Protected Network).

30   T Kane, *Military Logistics and Strategic Performance*, Frank Cass, 2001, p. 149.

31   van Creveld, *Supplying War*, p. 235.

32   Kane, *Military Logistics and Strategic Performance*, p. 9.

33   Defence Watch Seminar February 2004, 'Army Capability Requirement – Combat Service Support 2015'.

34   J Huston, *The Sinews of War: Army Logistics 1775–1953*, US Government Printing Office, 1966, p. 656.

35   Smith, *A Handmaiden's Tale*, p. 16.

Logistics and emerging technology

1   M van Creveld, *Supplying War: Logistics from Wallenstein to Patton*, Cambridge University Press, Cambridge, 1977 (1990 reprint), p. 231.

2   P Green, *Alexander of Macedon, 356–323BC: A Historical Biography*, University of California Press, California, 2012, p. 435.

3   D Yergin, *The Prize: The Epic Quest for Oil, Money, and Power*, Simon & Schuster, New York, 1991, pp. 150–64.

4   Stockholm International Peace Research Institute, Military expenditure database, 2014, <milexdata.sipri.org>.

5   Australian Army, 'The Longest War: The Australian Army in Afghanistan', 2015, <army.gov.au/the-longest-war>.

6   KD Yoho, S Rietjens and PH Tatham, 'Defence Logistics: An Important Research
     Field in Need of Researchers', *International Journal of Physical Distribution & Logistics
     Management*, vol. 43, no. 2, 2013, pp. 80–96.

7   KA Patterson, CM Grimm and TM Corsi, 'Adopting New Technologies for Supply
     Chain Management', *Transportation Research Part E*, vol. 39, 2003, pp. 95–121.

8   Joint Logistics Command, 'Future Logistics Concept 2035', 2014, p. 3.

9   Patterson, Grimm and Corsi, 'Adopting New Technologies', pp. 98–101.

10   Excluding public servants and reservists. See Department of Defence, 'Defence Annual
     Report, 1999–2000: Section 4 – Supplementary Information', Canberra, 2000, p. 288,
     <www.defence.gov.au/AnnualReports/99-00/section4.pdf>; Department of Defence,
     'Defence Annual Report, 2013–2014', Chapter 2 'Departmental Overview', Canberra,
     2014, p. 16, <www.defence.gov.au/annualreports/13-14/DAR_1314_V1.pdf>.

11   Department of Defence, 'First Principles Review', 2015, p. 13, <www.defence.gov.au/
     annualreports/13-14/DAR_1314_V1.pdf>.

12   Defence Science and Technology Group, 'Defence Priority Areas', <http://www.dsto.
     defence.gov.au/partner-with-us/demonstrate-your-technology/defence-priority-areas>.

13   Department of Defence, 'Defence 2000: Our Future Defence Force', 2000, Canberra,
     pp. xiv, 49–50, 84, 96, <www.defence.gov.au/publications/wpaper2000.pdf>;
     Department of Defence, 'Defending Australia in the Asia Pacific Century: Force 2030',
     2009, Canberra, pp. 76, 123–4, <www.defence.gov.au/CDG/Documents/defence_
     white_paper_2009.pdf>; Department of Defence, 'Defence White Paper, 2013',
     Canberra, pp. 23, 32, <www.defence.gov.au/whitepaper/2013/docs/wp_2013_web.
     pdf>.

14   A basic word search of the doctrine produces 47 results for the word 'combat',
     67 for 'land power', four for 'combat service support' and nine for the wildcard
     'logistic'. Australian Army, 'Land Warfare Doctrine 1: The Fundamentals of Land
     Power', Canberra, 2014, p. 50, <www.army.gov.au/~/media/Army/Our%20future/
     Publications/Key/LWD1/LWD-1_B5_190914.pdf>.

15   Australian Army, 'Adaptive Campaigning – Army's Future Land Operating Concept',
     Canberra, 2009, pp. 64, 67, 69, <www.army.gov.au/~/media/Army/Our%20future/
     Publications/Key/ACFLOC_2012%20main.pdf>.

16   Patterson, Grimm and Corsi, 'Adopting new technologies', pp. 101–103.

17   SR Waddell, *United States Army Logistics: From the American Revolution to 9/11*, ABC-
     CLIO, California, 2010, p. 1.

18   Australian Army, 2009, p. 22; Department of Defence, 'Joint Operations for the 21st
     Century', Canberra, 2007, p. 1 < www.defence.gov.au/publications/docs/FJOC.pdf>;
     Department of Defence, 2013.

19   Australian Army, 'Future Land Warfare Report', Canberra, 2014, p. 3, <www.army.gov.
     au/~/media/Army/Our%20future/Publications/Key/FLWR_Web_B5_Final.pdf>.

20   North Atlantic Treaty Organization, 'Logistics', 2012, <www.nato.int/cps/en/natohq/
     topics_61741.htm>.

21   J Wilkinson, cited in Australian National Audit Office, 'Management of Australian
     Defence Force deployments to East Timor', Audit Report No. 38, 2002, p. 52,
     <www.anao.gov.au/uploads/documents/2001-02_Audit_Report_38.pdf>; Australian
     Army, 'East Timor peacekeeping mission to conclude', December 2012, <www.
     army.gov.au/Our-work/News-and-media/News-and-media-2012/News-and-media-
     December-2012/East-Timor-peacekeeping-mission-to-conclude>.

22   Australian National Audit Office, 'Management of Australian Defence Force
     deployments to East Timor', pp. 63–68.

23   Australian National Audit Office, 'Management of Australian Defence Force
     deployments to East Timor', pp. 63–68.

24   B Breen, *Struggling for Self Reliance: Four Case Studies of Australia's Regional Force Projection in the Late 1980s and 1990s*, Australian National University, 2008, Chapter 11, Section 7, <press.anu.edu.au/sdsc/sfsr/mobile_devices/ch11s07.html>.

25   Interview with Lieutenant Colonel Robert de Rooy, 11 June 2015.

26   Department of Defence, 'Media release: Australian Defence Force deploys RFID "track and trace" capability to the Middle East', 10 April 2007.

27   Department of Defence, 'Defence Estate Energy Strategy 2014–2019', p. 6, <www.defence.gov.au/estatemanagement/governance/Policy/Environment/EnergyEfficiency/Docs/DefenceEstateEnergyStrategyV2May14.pdf>.

28   North Atlantic Treaty Organization, 'Smart Energy', <www.natolibguides.info/smartenergy>.

29   North Atlantic Treaty Organization, 'Energy Working Group – Phase 2 – Report', 2012, p. 4, <www.natolibguides.info/ld.php?content_id=1675609>.

30   A Hawke and R Smith, 'Australian Defence Force Posture Review', Australian Government, 30 March 2012, p. 49, <www.defence.gov.au/Publications/Reviews/ADFPosture/Docs/Report.pdf>.

31   'Among the costs of war: billions a year in A.C.?', *NPR*, 25 June 2011, <www.npr.org/2011/06/25/137414737/among-the-costs-of-war-20b-in-air-conditioning>.

32   Allied Command Transformation, North Atlantic Treaty Organization, 'Energy Security: Tough Lessons of Afghanistan', 29 March 2012, <www.act.nato.int/article-7>; R Crilly and B Farmer, 'Pakistan Permanently Closes Borders to NATO After Air Strike', *Telegraph*, 28 November 2011, <www.telegraph.co.uk/news/worldnews/asia/pakistan/8919960/Pakistan-permanently-closes-borders-to-Nato-after-air-strike.html>.

33   A Condon, 'Urban Combat Service Support Operations: Observations and Insights from Iraq', *Australian Army Journal*, vol. 3, no. 3, 2006, p. 158; S Hargreaves, 'Ambushes prompt military to cut energy use', *CNNMoney*, 16 August 2011, p. 4 – both cited in D Clark, 'Only the strong survive – CSS in the disaggregated battlespace', *Australian Army Journal*, vol. 11, no. 1, 2014, p. 23, <www.army.gov.au/~/media/Army/Our%20future/Publications/AAJ/2010s/2014/AAJ_2014_1.pdf>.

34   North Atlantic Treaty Organization, 'Energy Working Group'.

35   I McPhedran, 'ANU Solar Technology Replacing Army Troops' Heavy Batteries', *news.com.au*, 28 August 2014, <www.news.com.au/technology/environment/anu-solar-technology-replacing-army-troops-heavy-batteries/story-fnjww1so-1227039039117>.

36   Department of Defence, First Principles Review, pp. 33–34.

37   As part of the First Principles Review implementation, the Defence Science and Technology Organisation was renamed the Defence Science and Technology Group on 1 July 2015. Defence Science and Technology Organisation, 'Rapid Technology Assessment Framework for Land Logistics', Fishermans Bend, March 2015, <oai.dtic.mil/oai/oai?verb=getRecord&metadataPrefix=html&identifier=ADA618588>.

The costs and complexities of health support

1   AJ Chambers and JA Crozier, 'Australian Defence Force Surgical Support to Peacekeeping Operations in East Timor', *ANZ Journal of Surgery*, vol. 74, no. 7, 2004, pp. 577–80.

2   AJ Chambers, 'Surgical Procedures Performed by the Combined Health Element of the Bougainville Peace Monitoring Group', *ADF Health – Journal of the Australian Defence Force Health Services*, vol. 3, no. 1, 2003, pp. 2–4.

3   Chambers, 'Surgical Procedures Performed by the Combined Health Element of the Bougainville Peace Monitoring Group', pp. 2–4.

4   Chambers and Crozier, 'Australian Defence Force Surgical Support to Peacekeeping Operations in East Timor', pp. 577–80.

5   AJ Chambers, MJ Campion, BG Courtenay, JA Crozier and CH New, 'Operation Sumatra Assist: Surgery for Survivors of the Tsunami Disaster in Indonesia', *ANZ Journal of Surgery*, vol. 76, no. 1, 2006, pp. 39–42.

6   AJ Chambers, P Liston, MC Reade, BG Courtenay, A Higgs and JV Rosenfeld, 'Surgery for Blast Injuries: Experience of an Australian Surgical Team in Afghanistan', *ANZ Journal of Surgery*, vol. 81, no. 3, 2011, pp. 110–13.

Balancing information and reputation

1   K Foster, *Don't Mention the War: The Australian Defence Force, the Media and the Afghan Conflict*, Monash University Publishing, Clayton, 2013; F Anderson and R Trembath, *Witnesses to War: The History of Australian Conflict Reporting*, Melbourne University Publishing, Carlton, 2011.

2   Z Hibbert and A Starr, 'Conflict Communication Management: Why Australians Didn't See their Troops in Iraq', *Media International Australia*, no. 113, 2004, pp. 66–74.

3   Z Hibbert and P Simmons, 'War Reporting and Australian Defence Public Relations: An Exchange', *PRism*, vol. 4, issue 2, 2006.

4   K Foster and J Pallant, 'Familiarity Breeds Contempt?: What the Australian Defence Force Thinks of Its Coverage in the Australian Media, and Why', *Media International Australia*, issue 147, 2013, pp. 22–38.

5   For discussion of public interest information see chapter by Michael Harris.

6   J Logue, 'Herding Cats: The Evolution of the ADF's Media Embedding Program in Operational Areas', Land Warfare Studies Centre Working Paper 141, Commonwealth of Australia, 2013, p. vii.

7   J Logue, 'Herding Cats'.

8   See, for example, Foster, *Don't Mention the War*; Anderson et al., *Witness to War*.

9   Anderson et al., *Witness to War*, pp. 230–32.

10   NJ O'Shaughnessy, *Politics and Propaganda: Weapons of Mass Seduction*, Manchester University Press, Manchester, 2004, p. 212.

11   L Oakes, '2011 Andrew Olle Media Lecture – Laurie Oakes', 702 ABC Sydney, 21 October 2011, <www.abc.net.au/local/stories/2011/10/21/3345509.htm>.

12   D Bennett, 'Exploring the Impact of an Evolving War and Terror Blogosphere on Traditional Media Coverage of Conflict', *Media, War and Conflict*, vol. 6, no. 1, 2013, pp. 37–53.

13   C Banham, 'Legitimising War in a Changing Media Landscape', *Australian Journal of International Affairs*, vol. 67, no. 5, 2013, p. 612.

14   Banham, 'Legitimising War', pp. 617–18.

15   Media, Entertainment, and Arts Alliance, 2010, 'Life in the Clickstream: The future of Journalism', <www.alliance.org.au/documents/foj_report_final.pdf>.

16   P Mirchandani, 'Old Stories – New Media' in K Foster (ed.), *The Information Battlefield: Representing Australians at War*, Australian Scholarly Publishing, North Melbourne, 2011, p. 133.

17   A Phillips, 'Old Sources: New Bottles' in N Fenton (ed.), *New Media, Old News: Journalism and Democracy in the Digital Age*, Sage, London, 2010, p. 90.

18   S Hobson, *The Information Gap: Why the Canadian Public Doesn't Know More About Its Military*, Canadian Defence and Foreign Affairs Institute, Calgary, 2007, p. 12.

19   T Hyland, 'The Media Never Lose' in Foster (ed.), *The Information Battlefield*, p. 41.

20   Foster, *Don't Mention the War*, p. 55.

21   C Masters, cited in Anderson et al., *Witness to War*, p. 367.

22   See, for example, S Meacham, 'Welcome Home, Sarbi, Trusty Dog of War', *Sydney Morning Herald*, 11 January 2011, p. 7.

23   Logue, 'Herding Cats', pp. 24–26.

24   Banham, 'Legitimising War', p. 606.

25   C Masters, 'A Careful War', ABC TV *Four Corners*, 5 and 12 July 2010.

26   H Blake, and A Lee, 'Operation Radio Storm', *Hamish and Andy*, 2008, <www.hamishandandy.com/2008/operation-radio-storm/>.

27   Anderson et al., *Witness to War*.

28   Foster and Pallant, 'Familiarity breeds contempt?, pp. 22–38.

29   Foster and Pallant, 'Familiarity breeds contempt?', p. 35.

30   Foster and Pallant, 'Familiarity breeds contempt?', p. 36.

31   Foster, *Don't Mention the War*, 2013.

32   Logue, 'Herding Cats'.

33   Logue, 'Herding Cats'.

34   Logue, 'Herding Cats'.

35   Smith cited in Logue, 'Herding Cats'.

36   JA Kuypers and SD Cooper, 'A Comparative Framing Analysis of Embedded and Behind-the-Lines Reporting of the 2013 Iraq War', < mds.marshall.edu/cgi/viewcontent.cgi?article=1000&context=communications_faculty>, p. 8.

37   Banham, 'Legitimising War', p. 608; O'Shaughnessy, *Politics and Propaganda*, p. 212

38   Masters, 'The Careful War', 2010.

39   P Leahy, 'The Government, the Military and the Media: Hurry, Hit the Reset Button' in Foster (ed), *The Information Battlefield*, p. 16.

40   'RawVision: The ABC Has Obtained Unauthorised Footage of a Successful Operation of the Australian Forces in Afghanistan', ABC News Victoria (online), 23rd March 2011, <search.informit.com.au/documentSummary;dn=TEV20111204449;res=TVNEWS>.

41   MK Eder, 'Toward Strategic Communication', *Military Review*, Jul–Aug 2007, <oai.dtic.mil/oai/oai?verb=getRecord&metadataPrefix=html&identifier=ADA575198>.

42   Department of Defence, 'First Principles Review: Creating One Defence', Australian Government, 2015, <www.defence.gov.au/publications/reviews/firstprinciples/Docs/FirstPrinciplesReviewB.pdf>.

43   P Cornish, J Lindley-French, and C Yorke, *Strategic Communications and National Strategy*, Chatham House, The Royal Institute of International Affair, London, 2011, <www.chathamhouse.org/sites/files/chathamhouse/public/Research/International%20Security/r0911stratcomms.pdf>.

44   Head of Doctrine Air and Space (Development, Concepts and Doctrine), 'Strategic Communication: The Defence Contribution', Joint Doctrine Note 1/12, Ministry of Defence, London, 2012, <www.gov.uk/government/uploads/systems/uploads/attachment_data/file/33710/2012012jdn112_Strategic_CommsU.pdf>.

45   Head of Doctrine Air and Space (Development, Concepts and Doctrine), 'Strategic Communication: The Defence Contribution', p. iii.

46   Eder, 'Toward Strategic Communication'. p. 70.

Public interest and Defence information

1   Senator J Faulkner, 'Open and Transparent Government: The Way Forward, Australia's Right to Know', Freedom of Speech Conference, 24 March 2009 <www.senatorjohnfaulkner.com.au/file.php?file=/news/ROLJYZXTFL/index.html>.

2   See Z Hibbert and P Simmons, 'War Reporting and Australian Defence Public Relations: An Exchange', Open Source, 2005, <www.prismjournal.org/fileadmin/Praxis/Files/Journal_Files/Evaluation_Issue/Hibbert_Simmons_Article.pdf>.

3   W Churchill, BrainyQuote.com, Xplore Inc, 2015, <www.brainyquote.com/quotes/
     quotes/w/winstonchu111291.html>.

4   JS Mill, *On Liberty*, Harvard Classics, volume 25, Collier and Son, London, 1860.

5   F Anderson and R Trembath, *Witness to War: the History of Australian Conflict
     Reporting*, Melbourne University Press, Melbourne, 2011.

6   P Young and P Jesser, *The Media and the Military: From the Crimea to Desert Strike*,
     MacMillan Press, Hampshire, 1997.

7   P Dennis and J Grey (eds), *The Military, the Media and Information Warfare*, Australian
     Military History Publications, 2009.

8   Department of Defence, *Foundations of Australian Military Doctrine* (third edition),
     Australian Defence Doctrine Publication, 2012.

9   G Schubert, *The Public Interest: A Critique of the Theory of a Political Concept*, Free Press
     of Glencoe, Illinois, 1960.

10   R Flathman, *The Public Interest: An Essay Concerning the Normative Discourse of Politics*,
     Wiley and Sons, New York, 1966.

11   UN General Assembly Resolution 51/59, 'Action against corruption', <unpan1.un.org/
     intradoc/groups/public/documents/un/unpan010930.pdf>.

12   A Palazzo, 'The ADF in public debate', *The Interpreter*, 16 August, 2012, <www.
     lowyinterpreter.org/?d=D%20-%20The%20ADF%20in%20public%20debate>.

13   L Shanahan, 'Much Glorious Afghan Victory Has Been Won by ADF', *The Punch*,
     2009.

14   T Hyland, 'Let's Debate Afghanistan, But Give Us the Facts First', *Sydney Morning
     Herald*, 29 August 2010 <www.smh.com.au/federal-politics/political-opinion/lets-
     debate-afghanistan-but-give-us-the-facts-first-20100829-13wsg.html>.

15   J Brown, *Hungry Beast*, ABC TV, 17 November 2009, <andrewzammit.
     org/2013/07/12/videos-about-australias-role-in-afghanistan/>.

16   George Patterson Y&R, 'Review of Social Media and Defence', 2011.

17   Australian National Audit Office (ANAO), 'Management of Australian Defence Force
     Deployments to East Timor', 2002.

18   J Logue, 'Herding Cats: The Evolution of the ADF's Media Embedding Program in
     Operational Areas', Land Warfare Studies Centre Working Paper 141, 2013.

19   ANAO, 'Management of Australian Defence Force Deployments to East Timor'.

20   Anderson and Trembath, *Witness to War*.

21   M Dodd, 'Border Troops' Act of Villiany', *Sydney Morning Herald*, 12 October 1999,
     <www.library.ohiou.edu/indopubs/1999/10/11/0170.html>.

22   ANAO, 'Management of Australian Defence Force Deployments to East Timor'.

23   S Jackson, 'Baghdad Blitz', *The Australian*, 6 March 2003.

24   Jackson, 'Baghdad Blitz'.

25   S Miskin, L Rayner and M Lalic, 'Media Under Fire: Reporting Conflict in Iraq',
     Current Issues Brief No 21, <www.aph.gov.au/About_Parliament/Parliamentary_
     Departments/Parliamentary_Library/Publications_Archive/CIB/cib0203/03CIB21>.

26   Z Hibbert and P Simmons, 'War Reporting and Australian Defence Public Relations:
     An Exchange', Open Source, 2005.

27   Department of Defence, 'The War in Iraq: ADF Operations in the Middle East 2003',
     <www.defence.gov.au/publications/lessons.pdf>.

28   M Harris, 'Military Public Affairs in Complex Environments', *Australian Army Journal*,
     vol. 3, no. 2, pp. 137–44.

29   T Allard, 'Theatre of War', *Sunday Age*, <www.theage.com.au/news/in-depth/theatre-
     of-war/2007/06/02/1180205574233.html>.

30   T Allard, 'Theatre of War'.

31   K Middleton, cited in Dennis and Grey (eds), *The Military, the Media and Information*

Warfare, pp. 147–57 <www.army.gov.au/~/media/Files/Our%20history/AAHU/Conference%20Papers%20and%20Images/2008/2008-Military_and_the_Media.pdf>.

32 I McPhedran, 'Letter to Senator J Faulkner', 2009.

33 Middleton, cited in Dennis and Grey (eds), *The Military, the Media and Information Warfare*.

34 K Foster, 'Looking for Failure? Why the ADF Hates the Australian media', *The Conversation*, 2013; see also K Foster and J Pallant, 'Familiarity Breeds Contempt? What the Australian Defence Force Thinks of Its Coverage in the Australian Media, and Why', *Media International Australia, Summer*, 2013, pp. 22–38.

35 Anderson and Trembath, *Witness to War*.

36 S Ludlam, 'Public Information on Wounded Soldiers', Question on Notice, No. 1466 <scott-ludlam.greensmps.org.au/content/questions-notice/public-information-wounded-soldiers>.

37 D Hurley, Foreign Affairs, Defence, and Trade Joint Committee, *Hansard*, 16 March 2012, p. 43, <parlinfo.aph.gov.au/parlInfo/download/committees/commjnt/2dbe833f-6e45-4a8a-b615-8745dd6f148e/toc_pdf/Parliamentary%20Joint%20Committee%20on%20Foreign%20Affairs,%20Defence%20and%20Trade_2012_03_16_898_Official.pdf;fileType=application%2Fpdf#search=%22committees/commjnt/2dbe833f-6e45-4a8a-b615-8745dd6f148e/0001%22>.

38 ANU–SRC Poll, 'Changing Views of Governance: Results from the ANUpoll, 2008 and 2014', Report no. 17, August 2014.

39 H Sullivan, 'What Can Government's and Leaders Do When Trust Evaporates?', Edelman Research Insight <www.edelmab.com/post/can-governments-leaders-trust-evaporates/>.

Intervention – a duty to protect?

1 See C Fernandes, *Reluctant Saviour*, Scribe, Melbourne, 2004.

2 KA Annan, *We the Peoples: The Role of the United Nations in the 21st Century*, United Nations, New York, 2000, p. 48.

3 United Nations General Assembly, '2005 World Summit Outcome, Sixtieth session', items 48 and 121 of the provisional agenda. A/60/L.1.

4 N Coleman, 'The Unlimited Liability Contract and its Effects on Serving Military Personnel' in GR Lucas (ed.), *Routledge Handbook of Military Ethics*, Routledge, New York, 2015, pp. 276–85.

5 GR Lucas, 'Ethical Issues in the Use of Military Force for Humanitarian Intervention' in GR Lucas and WR Rubel (eds), *Ethics and the Military Profession: The Moral Foundations of Leadership*, Pearson Custom, Boston, 2008, p. 342; ML Cook, *The Moral Warrior: Ethics and Service in the U.S. Military*, State University of New York, Albany, 2004, pp. 74–75.

6 Australian War Memorial, <www.awm.gov.au/atwar/peacekeeping.asp>.

7 See A Elner, P Robinson and D Whetham (eds), *When Soldiers Say No: Selective Conscientious Objection in the Modern Military*, Ashgate, London, 2013; for an Australian perspective, see S Coleman and N Coleman (with R Adams), 'Selective Conscientious Objection in Australia' in Elner et al., *When Soldiers Say No*.

8 For example, according to UN figures there have been 36 military fatalities during the 67-year operation of UNTSO, <www.un.org/en/peacekeeping/resources/statistics/fatalities.shtml>.

9 EY Shibuya, 'Australia-Papua New Guinea Relations: New Pacific Way or Neocolonialism?', Asia–Pacific Center for Security Studies, Special Assessment October 2004, Asia's Bilateral Relations.

The challenge of moral injury

1   J Bale, 'PTSD and Stigma in the Australian Army', Army Research Paper No.
     3, Directorate of Future Land Warfare, 2014, <www.army.gov.au/Our-future/
     Publications/Research-Papers/Army-research-papers/ARP3>.

2   F Reid, *Broken Men: Shell Shock, Treatment and Recovery in Britain 1914–30*,
     Bloomsbury, London, 2012; M Tyquin, *Madness and the Military: Australia's Experience
     of the Great War*, Australian Military History Publications, Sydney, 2006.

3   M Larsson, *Shattered Anzacs: Living with the Scars of War*, UNSW Press, Sydney,
     2009; J Damousi, *Living with the Aftermath: Trauma, Nostalgia and Grief in Post-war
     Australia*, Melbourne University Press, Melbourne, 2001.

4   J Shay, *Achilles in Vietnam: Combat Trauma and the Undoing of Character*, Scribner,
     New York, 1994.

5   B Litz et al., 'Moral Injury and Moral Repair in War Veterans: A Preliminary Model
     and Intervention Strategy', *Clinical Psychology Review*, vol. 29, no. 8, 2009.

6   E Tick, *War and the Soul: Healing our Nation's Veterans from Post-Traumatic Stress
     Disorder*, Quest Books, Wheaton, 2005; RN Brock and G Lettini, *Soul Repair:
     Recovering from Moral Injury after War*, Beacon Press, Boston, 2012; N Sherman,
     Afterwar: Healing the Moral Wounds of our Soldiers, Oxford University Press, New York,
     2015.

7   EA Dombo, C Gray and BP Early, 'The Trauma of Moral Injury: Beyond the
     Battlefield', *Journal of Religion and Spirituality in Social Work: Social Thought*, vol. 32,
     no. 1, 2013; WP Nash, 'Moral Injury and Moral Repair: Overview of Constructs
     and Early Data', 13th Annual Force Protection Conference, UCSD, 2010; D Wood,
     'Healing: Can We Treat Moral Injury?', *Huffington Post*, 20 March 2014.

The Army and government objectives

1   One of the most outspoken and often cited is Michael Evans, who wrote *The Tyranny
     of Dissonance*, Land Warfare Studies Centre Study Paper No 306, February 2005.

2   M Evans, 'From Deakin to Dibb: The Army and the Making of Australian Strategy in
     the 20th Century', Land Warfare Studies Centre, Working Paper No. 113, June 2001,
     pp. 36–38.

3   Evans, 'From Deakin to Dibb', pp. 36–38.

4   Cited in J Blaxland, *The Australian Army from Whitlam to Howard*, Cambridge
     University Press, Melbourne, 2013, p. 279.

5   The Australian Army, 'Complex Warfighting', Department of Defence, Canberra,
     2004.

6   P Leahy, 'Hardening and Networking the Army: Towards The Hardened and
     Networked Army', *Australian Army Journal*, vol. 2, no. 1, pp. 27–36, <www.
     army.gov.au/Our-future/Publications/Australian-Army-Journal/Past-editions/~/
     media/Files/Our%20future/LWSC%20Publications/AAJ/2004Winter/04-
     TowardsTheHardenedAndNe.pdf>.

7   Department of Defence, 'Adaptive Campaigning: The Land Force Response to
     Complex Warfighting', Canberra, Australian Army Headquarters, 2007.

8   See, for instance, <www.army.gov.au/~/media/Army/%20Our%20future/Publications/
     Key/ACFLOC_2012%20main.pdf>.

Postscript

1   Australian Army, 'Army Institutional Lessons Study', <www.army.gov.au/Our-future/
     Research/Institutional-Lessons-Study>.

2   Commonwealth of Australia, 'Land Warfare Doctrine 1: The Fundamentals of Land Power', Canberra, 2014, p. 5.

3   Commonwealth of Australia, 'Australian Army: Our Future, Army Modernisation Update', Canberra, 2014, p. 5.

4   For a few examples see LH Liew, 'As Asia's Quarry: Implications of Australia', <www.griffith.edu.au/__data/assets/pdf_file/0017/246113/Liew.pdf>; J Adonis, 'We Love Being Dumb and Dumber', *Sydney Morning Herald*, 8 January 2015, <www.smh.com.au/small-business/managing/work-in-progress/we-love-being-dumb-and-dumber-2015018-3nraf.html>; A Simmondis, 'Why Australia Hates Thinkers', *UNSW News*, <newsroom.unsw.edu.au/news/social-affairs/why-australia-hates-thinkers>.

5   R King, 'How Stupid Are We?', *Australian Army Journal*, vol. 6, no. 3, Summer 2009, pp. 181–96; J Bryant, 'Are we a Thinking Army', *Australian Army Journal*, vol. 3, no. 2, Winter 2006, pp. 191–200.

6   J Brown, *Anzac's Long Shadow: The Cost of Our National Obsession*, Redback, Collingwood, 2014.

7   A Palazzo, 'The Future of War Debate in Australia: Why Has There Not Been One? Has the Need for One Now Arrived', Land Warfare Studies Centre, Canberra, 2012.

8   Department of Defence, 'Pathway to Change', <www.defence.gov.au/pathwaytochange/>.

9   Australian Army, 'Army Research and Development Plan', 2015, <www.army.gov.au/Our-future/Reseach/Army-Research-and-Development-Plan>; J Dunn, 'In a Volatile World, Diversity is the Answer,' *Australian Financial Review*, 30 June 2015, <www.afr.com/news/special-reports/age-of-disruption/a-less-predictable-future-20150628-gi078u>.

10   For one example, see 'Army Research Scheme', <www.army.gov.au/Our-future/Reseach/Research-scheme>.